Praise for the first edition of *Platform Souls*

'An elegy: for the steam trains already vanishing when Whittaker's hobby began in 1964; for the short-lived diesel age which followed; for an era of near innocence. … Delightful and unexpected.'

Times Literary Supplement

'Whittaker writes with humour and considerable evocative power … For anyone who will admit to having a childhood brush with this now derided hobby, *Platform Souls* brings it all rushing back.'

Independent

'Destined to become the *Fever Pitch* of the sidings and embankments, required reading for all thirty- or forty-something – and possibly current – "gricers" … it is the aching nostalgia, hanging like the smoke from a Stanier engine on Shap Fell, that lingers most in the mind.'

Roger Tagholm, *Publishing News*

'Whittaker writes with great warmth and wit and his autobiographical style makes *Platform Souls* an engaging read, even for those who don't particularly share his love of railways.'

Shropshire Review

'[T]he author's words sing off the page'

Burton Mail

D0348954

PLATFORM SOULS

THE TRAINSPOTTER AS 20TH-CENTURY HERO

REVISED EDITION OF THE CULT CLASSIC
WITH A FOREWORD BY ANDREW MARTIN

NICHOLAS WHITTAKER

ICON

This edition published in the UK in 2016
by Icon Books Ltd, Omnibus Business Centre,
39–41 North Road, London N7 9DP
email: info@iconbooks.com
www.iconbooks.com

Originally published in 1995 by Victor Gollancz,
and in a revised and updated edition in 2015 by Icon Books Ltd

Sold in the UK, Europe and Asia
by Faber & Faber Ltd, Bloomsbury House,
74–77 Great Russell Street,
London WC1B 3DA or their agents

Distributed in the UK, Europe and Asia
by Grantham Book Services, Trent Road,
Grantham NG31 7XQ

Distributed in Australia and New Zealand
by Allen & Unwin Pty Ltd,
PO Box 8500, 83 Alexander Street,
Crows Nest, NSW 2065

Distributed in South Africa by
Jonathan Ball, Office B4, The District,
41 Sir Lowry Road, Woodstock 7925

Distributed in India by Penguin Books India,
7th Floor, Infinity Tower – C, DLF Cyber City,
Gurgaon 122002, Haryana

ISBN: 978-178578-105-6

Typeset in Dante by Marie Doherty
Printed and bound in the UK by Clays Ltd, St Ives plc

CONTENTS

THE EIGHTIES

THE NINETIES

THE NOUGHTIES

Nick's mum

You said this was a holiday! A young lad is set to work
polishing a steam loco at Butlin's, Pwllheli, summer 1965.

About the Author

Nicholas Whittaker is the author of well-received histories of confectionery (*Sweet Talk*) and toys (*Toys Were Us*), as well as an account of life in the offices of *Fiesta* and *Razzle* magazines in the 1980s (*Blue Period*). He has written for the *Telegraph*, *Guardian*, *Daily Mail* and *Sunday Times*. He lives in London.

ACKNOWLEDGEMENTS
(in no special order)

Bill Wright for all the wonderful photos. Apart from the splendid cover, the rest are reproduced here in black and white, but it is well worth checking out Flickr for the full colour versions: www.flickr.com/photos/barkingbill

Walter and Aidie Parker, and the collection of the late Alf Moss, for helping with the photos of Burton and Crewe.

Steve Burdett for the China Clay and Henley pics.

Philip Cotterell, Andrew Furlow, Leena Normington, Nira Begum and Tom Webber at Icon Books for their enthusiasm and support.

Duncan Heath, Icon's Editorial Director, for his guidance and saintly patience with the copy-editing.

Ian Preece, my mentor for the original 1995 book and still today the unstinting voice of common-sense editorial nous.

Marie Doherty, for her elegant typesetting.

Andrew Martin, for his wonderful introduction, which makes me sound a lot more intellectual than I really am!

Staff at the London Transport Museum.

Richard from Clapham Junction.

Gary Johnson at British Railways Books.

I take full responsibility for any errors, of course, which I blame on too many coffees and listening to *Who's Next* on full volume. Little wonder that I can hardly hear the station announcements these days …

FOREWORD
by Andrew Martin

The full title of this book is deliberately provocative. It was first published in 1995 when 'trainspotterish' had come to suggest any futile male pursuit with anal-retentive overtones.

A railway publicity officer called Ian Allan invented train-spotting in 1942, by publishing lists of locomotives that could then be ticked off when sighted or 'copped'. The satirists concentrated on the 'ticked off' part, but the important bit was the 'when sighted'. The need to actually see the engines (dispensed with, admittedly, by the wretched 'fudger', who ticked them off without troubling to leave his bedroom) required the true spotter to be a dynamic, mobile figure.

I first had an inkling of this in the late 1970s when I was in the same class – at a northern secondary modern – as a very keen spotter called Chris Smith. He was far from being the nerd of the emerging mythology. For a start, he was hard; you wouldn't mess with him. He also got about. My dad worked for BR, so I had free train travel, and I would see Chris Smith from trains, as he occupied a variety of lineside posts, some an impressively long way out of town. I was about to write that the young Nicholas Whittaker (author of the book you are about to read) was like the young Chris Smith, but since *Platform Souls* is one of the best books ever written about rail enthusiasm, there would be more propriety in saying that Chris Smith was like Nicholas Whittaker.

Whittaker and his fellow spotters didn't wait for the trains to come to them; they went to the trains. Engine sheds were 'bunked': that is, furtively invaded. A good deal of bravery was required, and *Platform Souls* takes us into a *Beano* comic world of scruffy boys inventing 'dodges', sneaking through holes in fences, being chased by red-faced adults in official uniforms. Even when not bunking, the spotter was at large, perhaps travelling – by train of course – to a bunk. 'We'd strike off early, with sandwiches and flasks of Heinz soup tucked into our tartan duffel bags.'

There's nothing especially virtuous about trespassing, but the point is that the trainspotter actually *left the house*; he made his own entertainment. This seems more of a virtue now than in 1995, but even then Whittaker seems to have foreseen our thraldom to the solipsistic world of a little glowing screen: 'As society becomes more TV-dependent and we enjoy everything by proxy – sport, crime, road accidents, even practical jokes – so we are encouraged to despise eccentricity. Once harmless hobbies are redefined as sad and definitely untrendy.'

It's true that, after the 'bunk', the spotter came home to make order out of chaos. 'Our disorderly lists of cops had to be processed, each one slotted into its appropriate place in the *ABC Combine* and marked with its red underline.' But in *Platform Souls* these quiet interludes are akin to scenes of a soldier cleaning his rifle after a battle; they do not betoken a passive existence.

Those who maligned the spotters, then, did so partly out of ignorance. Whittaker puts forward another reason. For most of the period covered by this book the car was king, and trains were seen as a second-class form of transport patronised by second-class people. But I think it is also true to say that the spotters began to seem to be infected with the boringness of the trains they spotted.

In the first part of *Platform Souls*, dealing with the Sixties, Whittaker introduces the reader to the Diesel Multiple Unit: 'the bog unit', he and his friends called it, since it offered 'no frills, bog-standard travel'. The DMU resembles a line of carriages; there is no locomotive. Whittaker mentions it almost in passing, as his means of getting from his home station of Burton to Wolverhampton, where he hoped to see some of the enchanting green locos of the former Great Western Railway, the kind with such quintessentially English names as *Witherslack Hall*, *Tudor Grange*, *Cadbury Castle*, *Hinton Manor*. ('To the bookish child that I was, it conjured up a weird and wonderful England populated by Agatha Christie colonels, Wodehouse aunts and Elizabethan plotters.')

That was in 1965 – one of 'the last years of the iron age' – when there were plenty of such aristocrats left, even if their brass nameplates had been prised off, or they'd been demoted to hauling filthy goods trains. Today, the entire network has been given over to worm-like trains that might as well be 'bog units'.

But *Platform Souls* resists the soft-centred nostalgia of so much railway writing. The spotters of the book are young men, after all, not a bunch of wet antiquarians. Even though Whittaker loved steam ('Diesels could never be as alive as steamers, they didn't work by the same dirty and elemental chemistry'), his account of its decline and disappearance is nuanced. He liked the Western class of diesels, for example, because their wide windows reminded him of Yves St Laurent's specs.

Here he is in 1966, a couple of years before steam's full-stop: 'Britain's railway workshops (still a dozen of them even then) were busy building the future and we trainspotters had the privilege of seeing many of these diesels spanking new, fresh out of Derby or Crewe.' Another virtue of trainspotting is thereby disclosed: its practitioners were in tune with something Britain could be proud of doing well: engineering. This virtue also seems magnified from today's perspective, when we have a shortage of engineers, and all politicians would like to 'rebalance' Britain away from the 'service economy' and the sedentary, demeaning and dead-end work it offers young people.

I like it when Whittaker does give way to nostalgia, however: '… the sepulchral gloom of the sheds, the clang of buffers in the goods yard, the ghostly whistle in the small hours, the night train throwing panicked shadows against the slummy houses.' This is a beautifully written book. Scenes are fixed in the reader's mind with a few apparently casual sentences. Here is the old Burton station, which was replaced in 1970 with a 'Lego kit': '… a grand Victorian building, proud with filigree and importance, coiled around with the thick brown aroma of history.' Or here is the Paris Metro, which Whittaker – like any right-minded person – loved on sight: 'It wasn't just the trains, but the whole ambience: the bready smell, the warning hooters, the sad Africans with their lazy brooms.'

The writing is such that *Platform Souls* will be enjoyed even by those with no particular interest in trains, should they be adventurous enough to pick it up. The book can be savoured as a classic memoir of growing up, as Whittaker's gang of spotters gradually disperse, encumbering themselves with jobs and long-term relationships, but periodically re-convening for railway jaunts. (These passages, full of bittersweet affection and recriminations, reminded me of the Seventies sitcom, *Whatever Happened to the Likely Lads?*)

I see no reason why *Platform Souls* shouldn't be enjoyed by that category of persons to whom trainspotting is supposedly anathema. I mean women, of whom there are plenty in this book. It is a testament to Whittaker's love of both trains and the opposite sex that he sometimes attempted the apparently impossible: to go trainspotting *with women*.

He brushes over the emotional details, but it's not so very surprising to the reader when he discloses that, in the late Eighties, he suddenly 'acquired' a twelve year-old son. He attempts to bond with the boy over what else but trains. So many of the railway places, and all the steam engines, having departed from the real world, he takes his son to the National

Rail Museum in York: 'The place was full of lovingly restored railway engines, every one as pretty as a carnival organ.' This visit to 'trainspotting's trophy room' falls flat, so the pair go to a preserved steam line, the Severn Valley Railway, but the '*trompe-l'oeil*' of a preserved line doesn't do it for Whittaker or the boy. The scale is too dinky; the set-up too ingratiating: 'No one bothers us … I wish we weren't welcome.' He longs for 'some old codger of a foreman to come out of his office and chase us off'.

But this introduction is slipping into the lachrymosity the book avoids, so let me conclude by mentioning that, in 2015, the motor car has been comprehensively dethroned. Traffic congestion and global warming have seen to that. Railway ridership is at its highest level since the 1920s, albeit over a much reduced network. We have one high-speed line, and it looks like we'll soon have another. Our trains might once again be fit to be spotted, and it could be that a new generation of enthusiasts will reject what Whittaker calls the 'emotional poverty' of atomistic car culture, in favour of 'the joyful communism of the trains'.

AUTHOR'S PREFACE
TO THE 2015 EDITION

It's a rare privilege for an author to get a second crack at one of his books – a 20th-anniversary edition, no less. Many would pay dearly for the chance, to correct stylistic *faux pas*, to shift paragraphs around, add afterthoughts and hindsight. But therein lie many dangers, along the lines of 'If it ain't broke, don't fix it'. Changing one small thing could lead to all sorts of mix-ups.

I have tried to steer a middle course, tweaking here and there, adding a few light touches. The picture I painted of our steam days stands the test of time, I think, as does the later diesel era. I have added a few small brush strokes here, a memory omitted from the original, but by and large I have tried to leave well alone.

It's only in the later periods that I saw much need for change, removing references to Eurostar at Waterloo, for instance, but even there I have trod carefully lest things start to unravel.

I could probably have added a postscript of some kind to every chapter, but I thought that a clumsy approach. As for style and simile, well, as we all know now, there are only fifty shades of grey, so if I have repeated some in my descriptions of the steam age, I beg your forgiveness. And to any readers who find that I have left some threads unpicked, or missed those that should have been removed, I offer my apologies.

Twenty years after the first edition of *Platform Souls*, I think the trainspotter has, so to speak, come in from the cold (though he still braves it often). Not only are people leaving the trainspotter unmolested, but many who used to berate him and his hobby now seem happy to cash in on Britain's love of railways. One night I turned on the TV and found railways on three channels at once – they seem to figure larger now than in the heyday of trainspotting! Michael Portillo, Chris Tarrant, Dan Snow, Pete Waterman, Fred Dibnah – all have fronted railway-themed programmes. Having a slot on BBC2 or BBC4 certainly seems proof of a discerning audience. Back in 1996 there was even talk of me doing a series on Sky TV. I was invited to Canary Wharf for discussions, but nothing ever came of it.

The demand for all things 'railway' shows no sign of slowing – books, DVDs, tickets and railwayana. If you've got the dosh you can even buy an old station to live in. 2015 will see over fifty steam trips on the old Settle and Carlisle alone. Britain's scores of preserved railways all continue to do well. If there's not enough steam here in the UK, then specialist railway holiday companies will gladly fly you off to Ecuador, Romania, Cuba, even North Korea, where you can snap away to your heart's content, albeit under the watchful eye of state security who are far less indulgent than old Alf the steam shed foreman.

Despite all this interest in railways, people who should know better still get their facts wrong. Only recently I read an otherwise well-researched history book, the first page of which had the protagonists taking a Great Central Railway train from King's Cross. While TV makes great efforts to achieve historical accuracy – heaven forbid that *Downton Abbey*'s Lord Grantham is seen with the wrong kind of fish knife! – such stern fact-checking never seems to extend to scenes involving railways. So long as it's some kind of steam loco and there's a porter with mutton-chop whiskers, then it will do. No matter that the so-called London express is being hauled by a dumpy 0-6-0 freight loco! Then again, it's nothing new. Alfred Hitchcock was making the same mistakes in *The 39 Steps*.

It's part of the trainspotter's job to put these people right!

One of the best things about this new edition is that it gives me a chance to re-dedicate the book. The original gratitude still stands, of course, to my late mum with thanks for all the well-packed sandwiches and the pocket money, and to my children, even if they never did become railway enthusiasts. But it's with a mixture of sadness and celebration that I dedicate it to two people who passed away too soon. That original edition contained a paragraph about the old trainspotters who were dying off, men born not long after the Great War, with names like Albert and George. I never thought for a moment that I would be adding any of my own friends to that list.

First, timewise, is Adrian 'Bolt' Brown, the junior school classmate who got me started back in 1964. As W.C. Fields might have put it, 'It was Bolt who turned me on to trainspotting and I never even had the decency to write and thank him.' Indeed, although I had a notion that Adrian still lived in Burton-on-Trent, I never bumped into him, or perhaps I did and simply failed to recognise him after the passing years. A few years after *Platform Souls* was first published, I saw his death announced in the *Burton Mail*. I don't even know if he ever read the book or knew about his small but important part in the plot.

Second place on my Roll of Honour must go to school friend and trainspotting mate Andy Parker, who passed away in 2011, a great shock to me and many others. We had shared many trainspotting adventures. We had been firm friends all the way through grammar school and well into our twenties, when I left Burton for London. When I returned in 1987 to have a family, it was Andy who spontaneously offered to sort me a job on the *Burton Mail* and our renewed friendship lasted from then right until the end. On my last visit (though neither of us knew it) we spent a whole afternoon talking about music, stamps (more serious ones than the gaudy communist bloc stuff he was collecting in 1964), books, birds (feathered) and railways.

We said our goodbyes and I got the bus back into Burton, never thinking that it would be the last time we would talk about steam days.

His funeral was attended by hundreds. If he had looked down on us that day, he would have known how loved he was, in Burton and beyond. Our old friend Kev came all the way from Australia to attend. I could probably fill another book with stories of our youthful adventures. All I can say is that no one could have wished for a better friend and even if we spent some of our lives in different parts of the country, our friendship was so enduring that picking up the threads again was always easy.

So, to my dear mum, to my children, and now to Andy and Adrian, I dedicate this 20th-anniversary edition of *Platform Souls*.

Nicholas Whittaker
London, March 2015

PROLOGUE TO
THE ORIGINAL EDITION, 1995

Author's note: *I firmly resisted making any changes to my original Prologue, though it was hard and much of it could have been commented on or rewritten with hindsight. But that would have been meddling with the past and I include it here unedited for historical accuracy, and to show you how it was back in those spotter-bashing Nineties.*

If there was an ugliest railway station competition, and I were one of the judges, I'd stick my neck out for Birmingham New Street. It's always been one of my least favourite places. I don't mind the dark cuttings with their tenacious ferns and furred sediment that's been trapped on the ledges since the steam age. Rather, it's the station itself that I hate. Low-ceilinged, harshly lit, square-cut, it's one of the real horrors of the Sixties. We have plenty of lovely stations – York, Bristol Temple Meads, St Pancras, Rugby – but Birmingham was built to be despised. Not only that, it's so drearily suburban. There are Class 90 electrics on the Euston shuttle trains and Flying Bananas on the Bristol–Newcastle route, but the rest is all local stuff, Sprinter units ferrying workers and shoppers to places like Aston and Walsall and Dudley.

Yet these are the moans of one man, obviously not shared by the scores of trainspotters who come here every weekend. Men like Alan Knowsley, amiable and balding, the left-hand pocket of his jacket so distorted by spotting books that it keeps its square shape even when he takes them out. As he looks around the gloomy concrete canyon at the top end of platform 8, his face is lit by the slightly crazed smile of a psychic. While shoppers and students wait for the 11.45 to York, Alan can see ghost trains and hear the crackle of ancient loudspeaker announcements.

'Imagine, Jason, the exhaust on a Coronation taking one of the big expresses out.' Alan gazes towards the top floors of the looming rotunda, imagining a billowing column of engine smoke.

Jason, his son, looks puzzled. 'Big express' has a quaint ring to it now. He's heard of InterCity and Cross-Country, smart marketing concepts invented by men in red specs and fancy braces, but big express? It sounds like something off kiddies' TV. He folds another Juicy Fruit between his teeth and tries to take it seriously for his dad's sake. But Alan's on to a loser. No matter how many tales he thinks up, he'll never convince Jason there was a time when all a lad needed to be happy was a biro and notebook and a duffel bag with some Marmite sandwiches.

Trainspotting carries a heavy cargo of nostalgia, and there's nothing wrong with that. If it's good crack now, it was even better three decades ago. There were more trains, livelier stations, busier engine sheds. The country was a different place then.

In the Fifties, Alan's army was a hundred thousand strong: *Just William* kids standing at the trackside to salute the trains and their drivers. This was England at its monochrome best: smoky and proud, sadly oblivious to the political skulduggery that was going to change it for ever. But those kids have long gone. Today's trainspotter – he'd prefer 'railfan' – is a grown-up with a credit card. He has made a Faustian pact with Dixons and comes fully equipped with camcorder, Pentax with auto-wind and telephoto, and a personal stereo on which to listen to Fleetwood Mac between trains.

Progress is inevitable, but there's been a more drastic change. The trainspotter has become everyone's favourite wally. With blacks, gays and big-boobed women all off the right-on comic's agenda, here's a man you can titter at in safety, political integrity unblemished. The Identikit is hideous: a gormless loner with dandruff and halitosis, a sad case obsessed by numbers, timetables and signalling procedures. He has no interest in girls, and girls have even less interest in him.

What on earth happened? No one used to take the piss. Trainspotting was our national hobby, as English as morris dancing and looked on with indulgence. We had the best trains in the world, it was only natural that kids took an interest.

Those comics have a lot to answer for. They've made a pariah out of a harmless eccentric and totally destroyed the market in anoraks — all for a cheap laugh. Yet no one has ever specified exactly what the problem is, or explained why trainspotting is any more futile than, say, golf, stamp-collecting or keeping tropical fish. The character assassination has been so complete that to protest innocence is only to dig a deeper hole.

As society becomes more TV-dependent and we enjoy everything by proxy – sport, crime, road accidents, even practical jokes – so we are encouraged to despise eccentricity. Daftness is for TV personalities, not for the likes of you and me. Once harmless hobbies are redefined as sad and definitely untrendy. And unselfconscious trainspotters, unaware they need an excuse for their interest, are sitting targets. I suspect that further scorn lavished on trainspotting is an inevitable side-effect of a culture obsessed by cars. Interest in any other form of transport is regarded as eccentric. Fast cars and posh cars are aspirational, but railways (and buses) are seen as a second-class form of travel, ergo any interest in them must be suspect and pitiable.

But how far will it go? In December 1994, a man found guilty of stealing rare bird eggs was described by the prosecution as a kind of 'railway spotter' – one more step in the demonisation process, and a rather sinister one. It's one thing to make fun of a man for liking trains, but to use him as a stereotype for a criminal is surely dangerous. The trouble is, people have never forgotten that Michael Sams, the infamous kidnapper-murderer, was a quiet man whose hobby was trainspotting. He was even wearing his enamelled loco badges when he carried out his crimes. Such things sink into the collective subconscious, and stay there.

Years ago Birmingham had another big station: Snow Hill. With its Great Western colours and holiday posters, it whispered rumours to small trainspotters of places beyond their ken; places like Oxford and Paddington, Torquay and Weymouth. I first went there in the spring of 1965. My mum and nanna were off shopping in Birmingham, and instead of me whingeing all afternoon I suggested they dropped me off at Snow Hill and came back for me later. I'd heard about Snow Hill and was prepared to love it straight away; there was even a red carpet on the stairs down to the platform! What a welcome. The trainspotters' view was limited by a black tunnel mouth at either end, yet instead of being irritated, I was fascinated. The tunnels tightened the station's perspective and reminded me of the little doorway in *Alice in Wonderland*; when the train emerged on the far side there would be sunshine and open skies and a great sense of adventure.

But I find myself talking of the past too often. It's the present I'm seeking to understand.

'Look, Dad!' yells Jason, suddenly galvanised. 'There's *The Clothes Show*.' As the Class 90 electric slips out of the station with its Euston-bound train, Jason takes an interest. He's finally found something he can identify with.

Alan smiles bravely. The engines he remembers from the Golden Age had names like *Princess Elizabeth*, *Gold Coast*, *Pendennis Castle*, names which reflected the glories of royalty and Empire. Hardly PC, of course, but better than today's tributes to important customers: *Rugeley Power Station*, *Blue Circle Cement*, *The CBI*. *Britannia* and *Royal Scot* were names revered by all boys, majestic steamers that thundered past on north–south expresses. Still, electrics are better than nothing. Alan swings his camcorder towards the Class 90. Its driver gives a cheesy grin. With the number of home videos being made these days, it won't be long before someone sets up a make-up department for image-conscious ASLEF men.

But I can understand Alan's predicament: it's not just the engines that fascinate the trainspotter. He clings, like a burr to a tapestry, hooked and entangled in the whole fabric of the railways. He loves the addictive smell of diesel fuel, the signals that blink from red to green, the rattle of station announcements, the driver with his pipe, and the tortured squeak on the rails as a 'Brush' pulls 500 tons of carriages out of the station.

And then there's silence, one of those odd moments you get, even on the busiest station, when nothing moves and all the signals are at red. Jason chews gum and kicks a fag packet up and down the platform. Alan has time to think, and I can imagine him worrying about the future. The trainspotter is an endangered species; the railway magazines are full of obituaries these days, tributes to pals from the golden years at Paddington, Crewe and York:

> … the stained glass window in his local church, paid for by friends and incorporating Ted on the footplate of *Pixie*, will ensure that his memory lives on …

Dads try their best to pass on the eccentric gene, but today's youngsters are more interested in trainers than trains. Trainspotting promises no excitement now. When a country despises its railways like we do, it's no surprise that our youngsters don't carry a torch for them. But it's not just the jokes that keep the kids away – there are no role models any more. Railwaymen used to be our heroes, gritty working-class men with denim overalls and jaunty caps. We couldn't wait to grow up and work alongside them. Who could aspire to be a railwayman today, squeaky clean in corporate uniform and parroting phrases from the *Customer Care Manual*?

EARLY YEARS

Steamer Gates: 1964

It was Adrian 'Bolt' Brown who introduced me to trainspotting in those first summer holidays after leaving Christ Church Junior School. Considering I'd not long been accused of breaking his arm during a boisterous game of Wagon Train in the playground, I thought it generous of him.

His offer came at just the right time and I was grateful for the distraction. I had already guessed that our lives would never again be as easy as they had been for the last six years. Junior school had been full of joy. At secondary school there would be no playing marbles in drain covers, no belting out 'Go And Tell Aunt Nancy' to Miss Jones' plodding piano, no squabbling for the privilege of fetching Sir's mid-morning tea – no ringing of an old-fashioned hand bell to signal home-time.

I had other reasons for sadness. My heart was as broken as Bolt's arm. The object of my affections was Olga Jaworski, a brown-eyed girl in a pink cardigan. I had happily ignored her for the past four years, but now, in our last year, I had become besotted, though far too shy to tell her so. Now we were going our separate ways, me to the grammar school, Olga to the technical high. My junior heart was all churned up.

Little did Olga or I know how quickly she would be brushed aside for the smoky charms of British Railways …

Trainspotting was as simple as it was brilliant, Bolt reckoned. A biro and a sixpenny notebook were the only kit you needed – any kid could afford it. Then you went along to 'Steamer Gates' and just sat there, watching trains. There were plenty of them then, with enough variety to keep any

3

curious child happy: thundering expresses with passengers' faces pressed to steamy windows; rattling freights packed with boxes, bottles and barrels; and long, slow, seemingly endless coal trains that left us choking in clouds of black dust. Four lines ran in parallel through Steamer Gates and it seemed that none was unoccupied for more than a few minutes.

I'd always been aware of the railways. Burton-on-Trent was criss-crossed with lines that ran between its numerous breweries, maltings, hophouses, cooperages and loading bays. Dawdling home from school I was often stopped in my tracks as level-crossing gates swung out across the street and a clanging iron bell heralded another train. With no more urgent worries than nibbling the diddies off a liquorice pipe or preventing my ice lolly dropping off its stick, I was happy to stop and watch.

From a mysterious hinterland of brewery buildings, a red Toytown tank engine would emerge, chugging through the gates with half a dozen wagons. Motorists huffed and glanced at their watches, but I was fascinated by what I saw. And then the train was gone, the sight and sound of it swallowed up between high brick walls and shadowy wharves. The car drivers gave a collective sigh of relief, the crossing gates swung open and we all went on our way, the motorists about their grown-up business, me home for my tea – milky tea and sandwiches of Stork and honey.

Yet the idea of trainspotting had never crossed my mind until Bolt suggested it. I liked Bass's tank engines, I told him, but he just laughed. That was kid's stuff, cutesy little puffer trains on an overgrown model railway. The serious business took place on the main Newcastle–Bristol line which ran through the town just a few hundred yards from Christ Church school.

Trainspotting was second nature to the boys who lived in the back streets around there. They went to bed with the clangety-clangety-clang sounds of shunting for a lullaby, and the railways must have burrowed deep into their subconscious.

I'd been through a few hobbies of late – car-spotting, fossil collecting, magnetism – but they were all lonely hobbies, show-off hobbies, the eccentric pursuits of an only child. In any case, there were no fossils in Burton; the Jurassic Period seemed to have missed the town altogether. So I thought I may as well give trainspotting a go.

It must have been one day soon after school broke up, the last week of July. Bolt probably expected me to get bored and slope off after half an hour, but I was quickly hooked, drawn into a boys-only world. Perched precariously atop the level-crossing gates, and later sprawled on a scruffy embankment with grass seeds in our jumpers and a shared bottle of cherryade, I knew straight away this would be the perfect way to while away the days of a significant summer ...

I had the pen and the notebook, but there was more to it than that – rules to be learned and lore to absorb. For the first time I'd started on a hobby that couldn't be swotted up from books. The only way to learn was to watch, listen and remember. The difference between a steam engine and a diesel was easy enough, but I soon learned to distinguish between a Duck Six (Bolt: 'It's got an 0–6–0 wheel arrangement, see?') and a Jubilee ('It's a 4–6–0 and it's a namer'). The Jubilees sounded like fun and I loved their exotic names – *Sierra Leone*, *Bechuanaland*, *Punjab*, *Trafalgar* – but this was years before I grew up to despise the glorification of Empire.

There were bound to be mistakes, but a chorus of mockery from the others ensured that I'd never again jot down a destination head code ('That's not a number, you clot!') or feverishly try to record the numbers of the carriages as they rushed by. Before the end of the day I would even join in the loud jeers of 'Scrap it!' directed at any loco we'd already seen. Bolt was more daring: instead of the childish 'Scrap it!' he had an arsenal of swear words. 'You old bleeder!' he shouted at the over-familiar 8-Freights and Ozzies.* The enginemen could only glare back at him – if they'd been motorists they'd probably have stopped to box his ears. I was too well brought-up to use such language, but I thought it was wonderfully daring.

I certainly wasn't prepared for the ecstasy that greeted one steam loco as it came upon us. Yes, it was green and clean, with well-polished copper piping, but why the fuss? 'Brit!' they yelled as I jotted down the number, 70004. I noticed it had a nameplate too – *William Shakespeare*. 'Brit!' they shrieked, tossing each other's caps and jerseys into the air and whooping like Apaches. Didn't I realise how lucky I was? they demanded. To see a Britannia on your first-ever day – complete jam! I was a 'soddin' lucky bleeder!' agreed Bolt, obviously pleased that I had seen such a prize. All the best passenger locos had a 'Pacific' 4–6–2 wheel arrangement and smoke deflectors, he told me. I understood the 4–6–2 bit easily enough, but why was that a 'Pacific'? Bolt didn't know – it just was, that's all. My questions irritated him. Me seeing a Britannia wasn't enough for him – he had to make me understand how important it was too.

They called it Steamer Gates, but by the time I arrived the golden years of steam had already passed. It was a form of transport and a way of life already fingered for destruction on an immense scale. Falling in love with Jubilees and Duck Sixes was pointless: they were has-beens, clanking un-oiled leftovers of once-vast classes. Like the Scots and the Coronations, they had now surrendered their duties to diesels, to the shiny green Bo-Bos, Brushes and Peaks. With our warm pop and Smith's crisps, our notebooks and pens, even a secret cigarette or two, we'd been set up as witnesses to a swan song. Children of the interregnum, caught in the

---

* There is a Glossary of Railway Nicknames at the back of the book.

6

uneasy period between the glories of the steam age and the cleaned-up InterCity-branded future.

Railwaymen were different in those days, working-class blokes in faded denim overalls. They strolled past us at Steamer Gates, swinging their billy-cans full of tea (to be heated up later on the loco firebox), puffing on Woodbines, grumbling about their bosses, wives and neighbours. In a good mood they might greet us with a nod and a wink. Being acknowledged like this made us feel great. All of us wanted to grow up and work with men like these, as a driver preferably, or a stoker, or, for those who didn't want to get dirty, maybe even a signalman, like the one who worked the box by Steamer Gates.

Signalling was another job that needed muscle. In those days it was all done by wires, long, long steel cables that ran through a complex system of levers and pulleys to raise the red and yellow signal arms that might well be hundreds of yards down the line. The Steamer Gates signalman certainly had his work cut out, controlling this busy stretch of main line and keeping his eye on a rabble of hot-headed kids.

One of our favourite tricks, when he wasn't watching, was to jump down to the track nearest to us, the slow freight line, and carefully place a penny on the rail. We never had to wait long before one of the lumbering coal trains turned that coin into a misshapen burnished medallion double its original size.

At Steamer Gates, the road sloped down to pass under the railway and part of the signalman's job was to open the crossing gates for any vehicles too high to pass under the bridge. When there were no engines to look at, we would amuse ourselves by throwing a pullover up into the photo-electric beam which set off the klaxons and the flashing message: DANGER – VEHICLE TOO HIGH. Cyclists and milk float drivers knew damn well they were okay to get through, but still they would stop and scratch their heads and look guilty – until they caught sight of us chortling.

Down the line from Steamer Gates was Anglesey Rec, a field of worn-out grass enclosed on three sides by railway lines. Beyond the mesh fences, trains provided a constant background to the kickabouts and messing about on swings and it was only natural for the local kids to take an interest.

Alongside the Rec was a car dump and when train activity tailed off we sat in the knackered Rileys and Morrises, making engine noises and wrenching at the steering wheels, jerking the gear sticks and furiously winding windows up and down (regardless of whether or not there was any glass in them). A long time before we had Mad Max there was Barmy Bolt, cruising the ruins of Sixties England in his green Morris Minor.

In 1964 we were living the last years of the iron age. Sometimes, clanking shamefacedly past the Rec, came a sad procession: a Jubilee on its last-ever job, steaming its own way to the scrapyard, towing a couple of redundant Duck Sixes and a defenceless Jinty. Yet we weren't so sad. They were numbers to be recorded, after all, and we were privileged to be among the last boys to ever see them. Death meant little to us then. Anyway, these locos wouldn't really die. The molecules of iron, brass and copper would be recycled. The old steamers would be buckled, crushed and sliced with oxy-acetylene torches on their way to reincarnation. Pressed, stamped, melted and extruded, they'd live again in teapots, fridge doors and bicycle wheels, even in the staples that held our school exercise books together. We had yet to learn the maxim, 'Matter can neither be created nor destroyed' – but we already knew that.

Across the line from the Rec, permanently veiled in smoke and floating ash, were 'the sheds'. Officially known as Motive Power Depots, railway sheds were tantalising but forbidden places. Burton had a huge MPD (code 16F) comprising two roundhouses side by side and a yard forever busy with locos coaling up or being cleaned. Apart from the few Jubilees that lingered on, Burton's allocation consisted mostly of commonplace 8-Freights and Blackies. Mixed in among them were four diesel shunters and the odd Bo-Bo diesel. Occasionally, in the shed yard, would be a visiting 92-er, an impressive giant with smoke deflectors and ten huge driving wheels.

With Bolt as my guide, I did my basic training in 'bunking sheds'. First came the long walk along an ash-path from Steamer Gates, past a fragrant wood yard and over a dirty brook. Taking stock of any dangers, you then had to duck past the railwaymen's canteen and slip through a tiny brick doorway into one of the two roundhouses. It was such a small gap in the wall, but in that moment you passed from the fresh open-air world into a sulphurous gloom, illuminated only by shafts of light from the soot-blackened skylights. We stood there on the threshold, like mischievous elves in a giant's lair. Leaning against the wall were huge spanners, as long as our legs. I had never trespassed like this before. Thrilled yet wary, our ears were cocked to a corrupted silence punctuated by the hiss of steam, pigeons in the rafters, and somewhere, far off, the sound of someone banging a hammer on metal.

And all around us stood the engines. I'd never been so close to one before, and without a platform I only came up to the tops of the wheels, feeling the true frightening scale of things. Still, how thoughtful it was for British Railways to arrange all these locos for the convenience of us spotters: one quick circuit of the turntable and we had another twenty numbers jotted down.

Not that kids were welcome in the sheds. We slipped through another brick doorway into the second roundhouse to get more numbers, but Bolt decided against venturing into the yard – there were too many railwaymen around. We went back the way we'd come, and as we passed the canteen a man in overalls shouted something along the lines of 'Cheerio, lads, see you again' – although on reflection I think I may have misheard and what he actually said was, 'Bugger off, you little sods! If I catch you round here again …'

Despite these warnings, we carried on regardless. On future visits we even dared to 'cab' some of the locos. Setting foot on board the cindery footplate of an engine entitled you to put a 'c' (for 'cabbed') next to that number in your *ABC* spotting book. It didn't take me long to get addicted to these guerrilla raids into the heart of railway territory. We regarded the shed foreman and the loco crews as spoilsports, but they must have had many a heart-stopping moment as they watched lads wandering around between the moving railway engines.

My friendship with Bolt was cut short in an unpleasant way. We'd been in a phone box one day – mere curiosity probably – when the man from the Post Office came charging out and accused us of ringing 999. We may have been larking about, but we definitely didn't do that. After taking our names and addresses, he sent us away with a flea in our ear and that evening the police visited each of us at home and gave us a severe ticking off. My mum was aghast and I denied it tearfully, but no one would believe either Bolt or me.

How could two harmless lads get treated so badly? The only explanation I can think of (in retrospect) is that Bolt often wore a leather jacket with ROLLING STONES painted on the back. The Stones were bad news just then (they'd just pissed on a garage wall) so fans of theirs were hooligans by default. From then on, Bolt and I were forbidden to knock about together. Protests were useless and anyway Bolt was destined for Anglesey Secondary Modern, so it was unlikely we'd see much of each other now.

The summer holidays were over and in those six weeks I'd had my basic training as a trainspotter. From then on I'd have to find my own feet. Bolt had turned me on to trainspotting (and to the Rolling Stones) and it seemed like I owed him something. But even if I had been allowed to say goodbye I would have struggled to express my feelings. In any case, how could I have guessed that a junior school fad would change the whole course of my life?

POSTSCRIPT. Twenty years later, browsing the railway section in a second-hand bookshop, I was astounded to find a photo of us both. The book was a history of Derby Loco Works and the photo a scene from the 1964 open day and flower show, where we had been unwittingly snapped while clambering up onto the buffer beam of the day's star exhibit, Coronation 46245 *City of London*.

It was a queer happenstance and I felt overwhelmed by nostalgia for that long ago summer of coal and smoke, the fragrances of wormwood and diesel and the taste of lukewarm cherryade. Normally, I might have bought the book, but some superstitious fear warned me off. I felt spooked by these two smudged ghosts from the Sixties, especially the skinny eleven year-old who looked a bit like me but stared back as distantly as any stranger.

The (Not-So-Great) Great Western

As a Burton kid, I'd got used to the Midland Region's Duck Sixes, 8Fs and Blackies, so my first sighting of a Great Western loco came as a thrill. Ironically, it wasn't at Bristol, Swindon or Paddington, nor any of those famous GWR locations. I wasn't even out trainspotting at the time, but on a coach trip to Dudley Zoo with my mum.

Alongside the zoo, under a road bridge, was a disused station, still in use as a parcels depot. It held no interest to me ... until I caught sight of a thin pillar of smoke rising over the wooden roof and insisted we go down for a look.

And there was 7813 *Freshford Manor*, green and brassy in the latticed shadows, simmering quietly and looking in no great hurry to go anywhere. I stared, somewhat mesmerised. Not only did this loco have a four-digit number (in 1948 every company except the GWR had been forced to add an extra digit to their loco numbers) but the numberplate and nameplate were cast in solid gleaming brass. There seemed to be no one else about, no activity on the platform, no sound at all except for the whisper of escaping steam and the distant sounds of the zoo. It was an enchanted moment, one which stayed with me in perfect detail for the next fifty years, so impressed on me that when I took my own children to Dudley Zoo a quarter of a century later I could hardly bear the memories.

Lions, chimps and zebra held no interest now. I trailed around the zoo with Mum but all I could think of was *Freshford Manor*. As soon as we got home I rushed for my *ABC Combine* and underlined it. For weeks it was my proudest exhibit and

I would sit poring over it for ages. And the more I looked the more irritated I became by the solitary red line in an otherwise virgin section of the book.

The more I looked at the other GWR locos, the more fascinated I became. They had such quintessential English names – *Witherslack Hall*, *Tudor Grange*, *Cadbury Castle*, *Hinton Manor*. To the bookish child that I was, it conjured up a weird and wonderful England populated by Agatha Christie colonels, Wodehouse aunts and Elizabethan plotters. I'd got a taste for the Great Western and wanted to see more.

My first chance came when Mum and Grandma announced they were going on a shopping trip, to 'the big shops' as they called them, in Birmingham – and I was to accompany them. It sounded utterly boring, but I had no choice. From past experience I knew Grandma would be wanting to measure me up for socks and Y-fronts and any request for sweets would be met by a lecture on tooth decay. But then I remembered spotters talking of the city's old GWR station, Snow Hill. I had to go. I begged my mum, saying she could drop me off there, then she and Grandma could come back for me after their shopping. Mum agreed to it, though Grandma seemed peeved at losing a chance to torment me with string vests and garters.

Snow Hill – I loved the name of it – had several platforms and the stairs leading down to them were carpeted. Carpet – in a railway station! I didn't know that it was a marketing gimmick from Cyril Lord, and assumed the carpet was a leftover from the Great Western's luxury attitude. I bought a platform ticket and went down. Mum had given me sixpence for the chocolate machine, and so I passed a couple of happy hours before they came to collect me. Grandma had bought me a new pair of gloves but I couldn't give a shit ...

In 1965, a couple of years after Beeching, Burton still fancied itself as important, boasting a buffet, a bookstall and a waiting room kept cosy by a crackling coal fire. As well as the north–south expresses that passed through, we had local services to Leicester and to Wolverhampton, the latter one offering a direct line into GWR territory.

On a freezing Saturday in January, I set off there on the 10.28, a rattling DMU, determined to add some Castles, Halls and Granges to that one solitary Manor in my book. DMU, by the way, stood for diesel multiple unit, better known to us kids as 'bog units'. A despised hybrid, these trains were neither carriage nor loco and many trainspotters did not even bother to take down the numbers. DMUs offered no-frills, bog-standard travel – hence the name. They had dirty windows which rattled in their frames, seats that vibrated obscenely if not weighed down, and engine fumes that often seeped inside the carriage to give you a thick head. The only plus was being able to sit behind the driver and see the way ahead just as he did, watch his practised hand on the controls. As we slipped past the spires of Lichfield cathedral towards the drabness of the Black Country, I felt as intrepid as any of those explorers I'd read about.

At Wolverhampton I hurried down the road from the High Level station to the Low Level one, a surviving example of GWR style with chocolate-and-cream paintwork and the dusty smell of history. At the far end of platform 1, I caught sight of my next four-figure cop – 7022 *Hereford Castle* – the first of two Castles seen that frosty day. It wasn't as pristine as *Freshford Manor* had been, but even under the grime you could see it had pedigree. In the loco hierarchy a Castle had to be worth at least two Manors. I watched as 7022 was coupled up to a Paddington-bound express and yearned to be one of the lucky passengers.

Fortified by cups of British Railways tea and bridging the gap with Cadbury's Snacks (the finger ones, seven to a pack), I sat down on a luggage trolley and watched a sporadic parade of Granges and Halls which chugged in and out of the station. In between these smoke-shrouded entrances and exits, a cheerful little pannier tank busied itself shunting parcel wagons.

My second Castle arrived early in the afternoon. But this was no star turn. Pulling half a dozen goods wagons, it limped through the station, leaking steam from its old machinery, shame-faced at performing such lowly duties. The grime was caked on so thickly I couldn't even tell what colour it was – certainly not Great Western green. This one, 5014, should have been *Goodrich Castle* according to my book, but where the nameplate had once been there were three bare metal brackets, a sight with which I was to become all too familiar.

At tea time I reluctantly headed back to the High Level station and got the boring DMU back to boring old Burton. Still, I'd definitely got the Great Western bug and couldn't wait to spread the gospel …

If I hadn't made friends with him, Andy Parker might have been quite happy collecting stamps. Not even serious stuff, but those gaudy stickers from Romania and Turkey. It was a good hobby, he said, and he even claimed to have learned Russian from it: 'Noyta CCCP, da?' I wasn't impressed – it sounded gibberish to me.

Andy had been thinking of joining the school stamp club, but I knew he'd be unhappy there. The club was for bespectacled swots who specialised in Victorian definitives and South African triangulars. No, he would have much more fun trainspotting with me. At least you didn't need your own tweezers to be taken seriously, and since his mum had just bought him a splendid duffel coat he might as well take up an outdoor hobby to go with it.

He thought it over for a while, but still needed convincing. So I worked on him all the way home from school and treated him to a Jamboree Bag. The deal was sealed. I had my first convert. 'Wait till you see Snow Hill,' I said. 'They've got red carpet on the stairs …'

But when we got there the carpet had gone – and so had his faith in me. Hoping for a better show, I herded him aboard one of the 'cat's whiskers' DMUs to nearby Tyseley. Breaking daylight and rattling past Moor Street station, still within sight of the city's office blocks, we seemed to enter a looking-glass world where trains ran the wrong way, signals pointed downwards for go, and the tracks had huge gaps in between (a legacy of the GWR's broad-gauge days). Bordesley Green, Small Heath & Sparkbrook, the long platforms passed the window – and then came Tyseley sheds, packed with GWR locos. Our rush to the window was followed by wails of protest as the locos were blocked from view behind an embankment.

Not to worry, though … the sheds were barely a minute's walk from the station and it looked like an easy bunk – no gaffer's office to dodge past, no staff canteen – just a wide open gateway without a gate. Trying to keep as quiet as is possible while crunching across cinders, we slipped into the sidings alongside the shed buildings. Even if we never made it inside, there were plenty of locos here, and with only four-figure numbers to jot down we would knock a useful 20 per cent off the bunking time!

Missing nameplates I'd got used to, but many of these locos were missing number plates too, their identities signed by slapdash chalk marks on the cabsides. I could tell Andy wasn't sold on my GWR tales and I had to admit it looked a pretty poor show. But then, here was a beauty, all shining green with painted red buffer beam and polished brass numberplates. Prairie 4555 wasn't a namer, true, but it would show Andy that the GWR still had claims to glory. I didn't know it at the time, but this tarted-up loco was a lovingly restored showpiece, destined for private ownership.

Still, it had been a successful bunk and having a book full of cops soon vanquished our doubts. We returned to Snow Hill, from where we caught another bog unit to Wolverhampton Low Level. According to the bunkers' bible, the *ABC Locoshed Directory*, the sheds at Oxley were a sixty-minute walk. We were just wondering whether it was worth the risk – we go all that way only to get chucked out! – when another spotter put us right: the best way to get there, he told us, was to catch a local train to Dunstall Park, one stop along the line.

The station at which the two of us (and only the two of us) alighted was small and little used, clinging on in the aftermath of Beeching. Over the wall were Stafford Road sheds, already closed and derelict by that time, as were the loco works across the road. We clambered over the gates for a look around and found the place littered with bits and bobs, worksplates certainly, numberplates perhaps, great piles of documents and dockets – all valuable records of the place in its heyday. But no locos (not even an emasculated King doing duty as a stationary boiler, as some fibber had it) so we turned our noses up at the dereliction and went off in search of Oxley sheds.

An odd thing about Oxley, one of the great cathedrals of steam, is that you approached it from below. Walking alongside a mucky canal and through the arch of a viaduct you would see the sheds, quietly smouldering at the top of a steep cinder path. And we were just setting off up this slope when a pair of crazed Alsatians came lolloping towards us, barking and snapping viciously.

'Come on,' said Andy, skipping out of their range, 'let's not bother with Oxley.'

They weren't spotter-munching British Railways guard dogs, as we'd first thought, but from the adjacent allotments, less concerned with railway trespassers than guarding their master's cauliflowers.

Oxley had plenty of Blackies and 9Fs on shed, but I was more interested in the Granges and Halls and it only took us a few minutes to bag several more. At the back of the depot there was a scrap line, a sad collection of derelict carriages and rusting engines – tanks and 8Fs, a couple of Jubilees, even a Gresley V2 Eastern Region. One-time rivals from different companies, here they stood in railway purgatory, rusting and ignored, coupled together in a last handshake …

Back at Dunstall Park, waiting for our train to Wolverhampton, I breathed in the damp nostalgia, the tiny waiting room, the hiss of gas lamps – a quaintness that signed the station's death warrant. The place was as out of time as Adlestrop or Buggleskelly. A couple of teenagers joined us on the platform and the girl bullied her younger brother into handing round his Nuttall's Mintoes. Andy and I were at an age when we fancied anyone in a skirt, but soon forgot the girl when we heard our train coming and looked up to see a dinky pannier tank at the head of two coaches.

It had been great day all round, I thought, but not good enough to convince Andy. The argument started over which one of us the girl with the Mintoes had fancied, but quickly degenerated into a slanging match. The Great Western was rubbish, he said. It didn't surprise me: I'd known all along that his loyalties lay elsewhere.

Inevitably the rest of my Western jaunts were solo ones, to Tyseley and Oxley again, but also further afield to Banbury and Oxford. The underlinings in my *Combine* were looking less sparse now, no longer isolated red lines here and there, but unbroken chunks of them, the mark of a seasoned spotter. At Oxford, sitting with my back to the dreaming spires, I caught the last of the Halls and Granges, and had my first glimpse of Southern steamers which came up from Dorset with the Pines Express and swapped engines at Oxford.

The Birmingham–Oxford line still had some steam-hauled services and on several of my trips I was lucky enough to have those same Halls and Granges for haulage. Would it always be like this – that the best trips were the ones where I had no witnesses?

A few months later the 'Great', which had stuck to the Western Region long past nationalisation, seemed well and truly vanquished. The fires were dying down and at Oxford, Banbury and Tyseley they raked out the fires one last time. The pride had gone from the railwaymen's hearts years ago and their fight to keep the GWR spirit alive was finally over.

I'd been allowed a tantalising glimpse of the uniqueness of the Western Region and I suppose I should be grateful for that.

Five years later, well after the end of all the steam on British Railways, I went back to Snow Hill with some schoolmates. It had fallen into dereliction then, full of nothing but echoes and bird droppings. I was supposed to be on a shopping trip with my girlfriend Sue (sister of a fellow trainspotter of course), but I couldn't resist one last look at the station. Sue wasn't happy.

'It stinks,' she said, stepping gingerly through the litter and broken glass.

'I just want to look,' I said.

Judging by her scowls and mutterings I was winding her up no end. How could I explain my need to linger, to sniff out vanished memories? Relics lay all around – the Waiting Room and Way Out signs, the stained timetables in the wrecked offices, the broken cups in the stale-smelling buffet – and I could hardly bear to leave them behind. Souvenir collecting was an integral part of trainspotting. But how could I have gone to Rackhams carrying a 'Gentlemen' toilet sign? If only one of us could drive, we could have come in a van and I could have loaded up with souvenirs …

'Come on …' Sue urged, pacing the empty platform and cursing her brother for getting her fixed up with a weirdo train-spotter. Would Jason King have treated a woman like this? No! He was a real man with manly pursuits and knew how to woo a woman with roses and champagne, he didn't go round picking up soiled luggage labels and talking rubbish about panniers and castles.

'I won't be long,' I assured her. At the age of seventeen I knew lots about railway timetables, but nothing about the timetables of romance, oblivious of that crucial point where a girl's patience finally runs out.

'For flip's sake …'

Then she found a diversion – a dead pigeon on the platform. It had fallen from the roof girders and was now just a skeleton with feathers on. It would have looked great on the cover of an Agatha Christie paperback. The sight of it seemed to disgust her and fascinate her at the same time, and then I could only watch in horror as she brought her boot heel down and crushed the poor tiny skull.

It had to be an omen. Sue was the first girl who had allowed any heavy petting, but how could there be a chance of lasting happiness with someone who got so bored by derelict railway buildings?

Crewe: The Trainspotter's Mecca

For trainspotters, Crewe was Mecca, Lourdes and Santiago de Compostela rolled into one. A place of pilgrimage. I'd had my first glimpse of it in late summer 1964, passing through on a day trip to Rhyl with Mum. I had heard so many tales of it and the excitement had started to build as soon as we left Burton. Expectations were high. Now though, as we got near, I began to fear being overwhelmed, unable to handle the reality.

And then we were there, and it took my breath away …

As we ambled in from the Derby line, the tracks seemed to swerve in on us from all sides, switching, meshing, taking the simple geometry of a single track and weaving it into a magical metallic tapestry. Here was absolute 'railwayness' on all sides – rails below us, electric wires above. To our left was a sprawling smoke-veiled depot with scores of locos, but it had slipped away, out of my vision, before I even had chance to gasp.

Our train wasn't stopping, or even slowing down. The sight of so much 'railwayness' made me laugh with joy, but it quickly turned to panic. Dashing from window to window, treading on everyone's toes, I couldn't take it all in – black steamers with glinting nameplates, green diesels with big important noses, blue electrics which kissed overhead wires with a crackle and a flash. Numbers danced in front of me and quickly slipped away. My hand juddered wildly as I jotted them down. I'd seen twenty, thirty, forty locos in as many seconds, but as we curved away on the line to North Wales and

I looked at my notebook all I saw were the wild scribbles of a child, from which I could decipher only half of the numbers.

Back at school I told Andy all about it, proclaiming the vision like some wild-eyed evangelist. I had to go again – and he had to come with me. His parents told him no, at first, but he must have worn them down because not long afterwards his dad volunteered to take us there in the car, a fat black Wolseley. The idea of being chaperoned didn't appeal to me, but at least, as Andy pointed out, it wouldn't cost us anything.

And so, one Saturday, we made the sixty-mile trip. It seemed rather formal – putting the car in the station car park, dutifully buying a platform ticket, Andy's dad weighing up the pros and cons of each vantage point. Once we got down on the platforms it was just like I'd remembered it. Mr Parker intended to keep us on a tight leash, though: we could join the well-behaved groups of spotters at the far end of the plat-form, but he would certainly not allow any shed-bunking. If he'd been my dad I would probably have begged and begged, or thcreamed and thcreamed like the railway's own Violet Elizabeth Bott, but I could only suffer in tense but polite silence.

Across from the station – so near and yet so far – was Crewe North sheds, its yard packed with Britannias, Jubilees and Scots, simmering quietly or belching smoke, a railway pageant in a dozen shades of monochrome. Oh, if only we'd had a pair of binoculars! One or two of the older spotters did, and generously passed the loco numbers to less fortunate kids. But even they couldn't see everything. Only bunking would achieve that, and it was never going to happen. Looking back, I know it would have been unthinkable for any responsible parent to sanction such trespass.

So, despite the build-up, our trip didn't yield much in the way of boast-worthy cops. There were plenty of Blackies and Jinties knocking about the station, but we had enough of those back home. 'Namers' were what everyone came to Crewe for – it wasn't just the numbers of the locos we wanted, but the royalty and glory of them. I'd been lucky to see Britannia 70004 *William Shakespeare* on my very first day – but I wanted more. Confined to the platforms as we were, we only copped two Brits – 70048 and 70051 – taking my total to three. Recompense came when we saw one of the last of the Royal Scots, 46128 *The Lovat Scouts*, taking over a northbound express from the diesel that had brought it up from Euston. From where we were standing we had a glorious wide-angle view as it departed, roaring like a lion, wetting us with steam vapour – as if we were being baptised in railway glory.

I had to go again, and four weeks later I did, on my own this time, as I had to be if I was going to bunk the sheds and get more Britannias. Free of adult supervision, I crossed the footbridge to Crewe North and sneaked inside to make a successful bunk. I didn't realise it at the time, but I'd been very lucky – a textbook case of 'fools rush in'.

Flushed with success, I left the station and walked down the road to bunk Crewe South *and* the diesel depot. In that busy hour I copped not just two Britannias but a dozen, nearly a quarter of the class. There were only 55 of them, so I thought I stood a good chance of getting the whole set. Since they were barely fifteen years old, they were hardly likely to be heading for the scrapyard yet a while …

Before long Crewe had become a regular jaunt for us. In parties of two, three or four we joined the dozens – scores even – who roamed the platforms every weekend.

Derby to Crewe was a tedious journey on a rattling DMU that stopped at every titchy station, but there were always the sheds at Stoke to look out for. One Saturday, the day after the Aberfan disaster, Darb sat with his feet up reading the *Daily*

Mirror and tutting: 'Poor little bastards,' he said. A well-meant sentiment, but I couldn't understand why the children who had just died should be described as bastards.

If there was a trainspotting 'A-team', a scruffy Fab Four, it would have been Andy, Darb, Pipsqueak and me. Now and then we took a half-hearted 'guest' with us – classmates like Fat Harry, dandruffed and bad-tempered – so desperate to be included that they would suffer any boredom. But we didn't carry passengers; their ignorance of railways and unwillingness to even learn just made us despise them more.

As for the A-team, we all came from quite different homes: Andy Parker's parents had a stereogram in a polished walnut cabinet; Pipsqueak lived in a terraced house jam-packed with brothers and cooking smells; Darb lived in a flat above the cafe on Shobnall playing fields; and I lived in a council flat with my mum. Despite these differences, we were a cheerful bunch and if there were any gulfs between the wealth and status of our families then we never talked of it.

There was a kind of class divide, though. None of the boys from the grammar school's A-stream were into trainspotting – it wasn't a suitable hobby for the sons of doctors and solicitors. Nor for earnest pupils like Melvin Bugg, whose mother had once written to warn the headmaster that Melvin was 'hypersensitive' and should be treated kindly. I liked Bugg, but I knew that Crewe was no place for mummy's boys. One rollicking from a shedmaster and the poor lad would probably need therapy.

Yet when I look at train magazines now, I can't help but notice how many of the correspondents and photographers are doctors, clergymen and academics. Are they working-class kids who went upwardly mobile, or posh lads who repressed their train enthusiasm to please their parents and had to wait until adulthood to give full rein to it? If that's the case, do they feel any twinges of guilt? Probably not. Enthusiasm for steam trains, now devoid of its old associations, is a genteel, slightly eccentric pursuit, and quite in keeping with the English middle classes.

Crewe didn't really didn't exist before the railways. A halt was built here to serve the estate of Lord Crewe and it seemed like it might also be a good place for a junction, for lines to Liverpool and Manchester, North Wales and the Midlands. The place grew by industrial symbiosis, a multi-tentacled natural organism. One shed, two sheds, a loco works, diesel and electric depots, sidings …

Without adults to hold us back, we had no qualms about bunking the sheds. But Crewe North (5A) was virtually impregnable. Arguably the most important depot in the country, no self-respecting shedmaster would put up with a bunch of snotty-nosed kids running around among his polished fleet of Britannias and Jubilees. Which were the very same locos that attracted us in the first place. But there were safety reasons too: Crewe North was on the go all the time, with a constant parade of engines moving in and out of the sheds, coaling up, dropping their fires, being cleaned. Even for railwaymen it could be a hazardous place; for careless kids it could prove lethal. Hence the tight security. Here, it wasn't just a matter of being yelled at and thrown out – the importance of Crewe North meant that patrolling it was down to the Railway Police. One nabbed Andy and me as we crossed the footbridge from the station. We denied any intention of bunking, and said we were just standing on the bridge to get a better view. The policeman snorted in disbelief.

'Come on, lads, don't think you can pull the wool over my eyes.'

'Why – you got a wool-lined helmet then?' asked Andy.

He got a clip round the ear for his cheek. Stake-outs and evasion were all part of the sport, as was capture – and we'd have never dreamt of getting nasty about it. You got caught, you got your ear clipped, and that's how it was.

All the more surprising that I had managed to bunk Crewe North on that first solo visit. Bunking stories are still a regular theme in the letters pages of *Steam Railway* and *Steam World*, and most say how they got kicked out of Crewe North. I put down my success to beginner's luck, never to be repeated. It's a badge I still wear with pride. Of course, it had to be the one time I went on my own, so not everyone believed me anyway.

Crewe South (5B) and the diesel depot were much easier and security was lax. Crewe South was bigger than Crewe North, a great sprawling yard of steam activity, but slightly less glamorous, with more freight engines and only occasional Britannias. Without any obvious design to the place, security was virtually impossible and the parallel lines of locos were so long they made the place a smoky maze in which it was easy to avoid detection.

Sitting on Crewe station could never get boring. Dull moments were rare. But there was no single spot from which you could catch all the action. If you were at the northern end you missed the locals for Derby and Shrewsbury; if you were on the eastern side you missed trains on the far side. Hardest to keep tabs on was the freight line that sped through a cutting and into a tunnel to avoid the station altogether. The only way to get those numbers was to get across the footbridge to Crewe North, then stand at the side of the cutting to peer perilously down. The only way of seeing everything was by constant patrol, walking from one end of the station to the other, going up and down stairs to cross the platforms – an exhausting drill when repeated fifty times in one day.

Sometimes we took sandwiches and flasks with us, but we would also visit the buffet for extras: packets of crisps or a slice of Dundee cake in cellophane. There were machines for chocolate bars and Paynes Poppets, and a variety of drinks. It's a truism that machine drinks are dubious, but I rather liked the chicken soup. It looked like steaming urine with specks of green tinsel floating on top – my friends groaned whenever I drank it – but I'd been weaned on Oxo drinks made with cabbage water, so I loved it.

At the end of every trip we returned to Burton, tired but happy, with notebooks full of numbers, the pages curled and stained with fingerprints of diesel and smudges of soot. Back home, sitting at the table, we started on what was for many the best bit – the creation of order out of chaos. Our disorderly lists of cops had to be processed, each one slotted into its appropriate place in the *ABC Combine* and marked with its red underline. In this way, each number became a memory, encrypted, filed away in numerical order. I tried to do mine as soon as I got back, if I wasn't tired; or else I'd leave it until Sunday morning, lying full length on the carpet with ruler and pen, while I listened to *Two-Way Family Favourites* and waited for Sunday dinner. I prided myself on neatness. While some kids messed up their books with the first pen that came to hand – blue, green, red, even pencil – I stuck firmly to red and took great care to make sure each line was the same length.

Crewe doesn't have so much magic today. To me, it's as if that mysterious sprawling bazaar has been turned into a neat and well-behaved shopping mall, like so many of Britain's stations. It's hardly the railway Mecca it once was. A better analogy would be a small wayside chapel, holy to the faithful, a place to worship, but no longer demanding obligatory pilgrimage. It's still an important place on the railway map, but not half as much as it used to be, for travellers or trainspotters. There's no longer a need for all the changeovers – diesels handing over to steam, steam to electric, electric to diesel – or the constant streams of passengers scurrying from one platform to another to make their connections. Today's twelve year-olds might still be awed by the size of it, but they wouldn't get dizzy on its cocktail of railway fumes.

Maybe that's all it was, in the end, a kind of chemical addiction. We thought we'd gone to pay tribute to our history, but we were just unwitting guinea pigs for solvent abuse.

Trainspotting doesn't normally offer much opportunity for star-spotting, but it did have an establishment, a score of men who had been around since before Nationalisation and were still held in awe by their juniors. Chaps with double-barrelled names and anonymous initials – Pat Ransome-Wallis, G. Freeman Allen, Cecil J. Allen, L.T.C. Rolt, C. Hamilton Ellis, W.J.V. Anderson, H.C. Casserley – and a bespectacled and avuncular appearance, wise railway owls who seemed to know everything. Yet there was no snobbery. Trainspotting has always been a democracy, embracing all men, from right scruffs to Right Honourables. No names, no pack-drill. Unlike the golf club or the Chamber of Trade, no one cares about your income or your profession or who you know. Your knowledge of railways is what counts. It's one of the few areas where you'll see professors comparing notes with latch-key kids.

The one we all wanted to meet was the late Eric Treacy, Bishop of Wakefield. We knew that railways attracted clergymen for some reason, but a bishop was something special. Would he be wearing his mitre and carrying his crook, or would he be in plain clothes, the only clue being a slightly-too-purple shirt?

Many of the old guard have passed on now and the genteel establishment has dwindled. Of the few that remain, they all seem to be comfortably well off and own engines all over the place. The nearest thing trainspotting now has to a benevolent uncle is Pete Waterman, the millionaire record producer, a man so loaded that he seems to be buying a loco or a set of carriages every other week.

004

Sir Nigel Grizzly's Spearmint Seagull

Since I'd dragged Andy around the Black Country on a Great Western goose chase, it seemed only fair I should return the favour by joining him on a trip to the East Coast main line at Grantham, a town famous with trainspotters a long time before Mrs Thatcher.

Andy was a fierce champion of the old LNER, though he had never known it. He'd heard about it though, fed the propaganda with his Weetabix. His granddad had filled him with tales of his own boyhood alongside the King's Cross–Edinburgh line – eye-witness accounts of Gresley A4s and V2s, *Mallard* on its record-breaking run, the *Flying Scotsman* whistling its way towards the Borders. Loyalty was a family duty: at least one of the male children had to be programmed to carry the company crest and legends into the Seventies and beyond. Even if future generations of Parkers lived in a bubble on the moon, the LNER would not be forgotten. The space toddlers would still need some bedtime stories, wouldn't they?

So off we set one Saturday, just the two of us, with Andy taking over the role as guide. At Nottingham we had to walk around to the Victoria station, a cavernous place with a broken glass roof stained by decades of black loco breath. It had been an important stop on the Great Central, but Beeching had put the kibosh on that. Express trains no longer stopped here, replaced by sporadic 'semi-fasts' – a clumsy euphemism for semi-slow and rather annoying. It was a spooky place with little to charm a trainspotter. The long platforms were empty and the place had a miasma of doom. We had no wish to linger.

Our jerky DMU burrowed into the mouth of a tunnel at the end of the station. Somewhere inside that darkness, we crossed one of those invisible thresholds in the space-time-railways continuum, slipping away from the familiar sights of the Midlands, into something easterly and unsettling. A couple of miles on we passed Colwick, a smoky depot on the city outskirts, and headed for the flat fields of Lincolnshire.

There were no steamers left at Grantham – Gresley's Streaks and Peppercorn's A1s were long gone. BR's Eastern Region had embraced the diesel age wholeheartedly and the only steam to come out of King's Cross now was what escaped from the tea urn in the buffet. A handful of those legendary Gresley express locos had survived, banished to Aberdeen, to be used on fish trains and local passengers – too far away for us to visit. Even if we could have afforded it, would Andy have wanted the humiliation? *Mallard* held the world speed record for a steam loco, but if it had still been in service, it would have been lucky to get a job taking half a dozen milk tankers from Arbroath to Dundee. One of the survivors was *Kingfisher*, so it seemed appropriate that it was often now hauling a train full of fish. I couldn't resist teasing Andy about it. Those one-time supremoes of the LNER – I called them Sir Nigel Grizzly and Arthur Pepperpot – if they weren't already dead then they would certainly have wanted to die when they saw their wonderful locos now.

Andy would have liked me to witness *Golden Plover* at the head of the *Flying Scotsman*, just to see my jaw drop – but I'd have had my teeth wired rather than give him the satisfaction.

The golden days of the LNER had gone, we both knew it, but I had to admit that today's Deltics were a hell of a sight. You should have seen them! Roaring through the narrow confines of Grantham station, they rattled teacups in the buffet and pushed along a tumbleweed of wind that fluttered all the newspapers on the bookstall. This was 'shock and awe' long before Bush. No schoolboy could resist, even those who claimed to be diehard steam fans. We never saw anything like this go through Burton. Steamer Gates overlooked the railway equivalent of a road-hump, which would have sent any speeding trains into orbit. At Grantham, though, they came through like beasts from hell – 106 tons of green and yellow diesel.

'Passengers are advised to stand well back from the edge of the platform', warned the loudspeakers, and everyone could see that it was, indeed, advisable. The slipstream of a Deltic-hauled express was capable of whipping off a hat or two and a doddering pensioner or unwary child would have been tossed around like a rag doll.

But who was the diesel-lover now? It had never really crossed my mind before, but that was the accusation levelled at us by some of the diehards back at school. Pipsqueak, who came from a family of loyal steam fans, was most disappointed in me. He refused point-blank to come with us to Grantham – it would have been anathema to him, and a waste of precious pocket money. It was getting harder and harder to avoid diesels altogether now, he admitted that, but why go to a place where there was nothing but?

Diesels could never be as alive as steamers, they didn't work by the same dirty and elemental chemistry, but I couldn't hate them completely. Britain's railway workshops (still a dozen of them even then) were busy building the future and we trainspotters had the privilege of seeing many of these diesels spanking new, fresh out of Derby or Crewe. With diesels at least we stood a chance of collecting full sets of Peaks, Deltics or Bo-Bos. Unlike those lucky northern kids, none of us would ever get all our Jubilees, Scots or Coronations: I'd started too late and lived in the wrong area. Even when I eventually got close to 'classing' the Britannias (I only needed six) they scrapped the ones I needed. Didn't they realise the heartache it caused!

Like it or not, Andy and I were children of the diesel age. Neither of us had known the real GWR or LNER, but still worked as tireless cheerleaders for our 'teams'. We couldn't race Castles against A4s, so we argued constantly about Westerns versus Deltics. I hated to admit it, but for power and thrills the Deltics won hands down.

But Grantham wasn't just about Deltics. Halfway through the afternoon came the Yorkshire Pullman, a train of brown and cream coaches with flickering glimpses of brass light fittings, white tablecloths and silver cutlery. It was a train from another age, slipped through a loophole in time. The carriages had all sorts of fancy names – *Amethyst* and *Topaz*, *Medusa* and *Pegasus* – and as they were listed in the *ABC* books, it was permissible to collect them. Permissible but almost impossible. Knowing that it would come through at 70–80mph, we tried to be methodical, agreeing beforehand that each of us should jot down every other carriage. But we always got it wrong somehow – 'I thought I was getting the odd ones and you were getting the evens!' – and ended up with maybe three out of the ten.

Occasionally one of the Deltics deigned to stop at Grantham and we sprinted to the end of the platform for a closer look. Too close a look sometimes. The yuckiest thing were the yellow warning panels at the front, which would be sticky with splatted flies and assorted gnats, some still buzzing in insect agony. These diesels were like giant swatters sweeping through the countryside, so fast that even a fly wasn't smart enough to dodge.

We felt small and slightly fearful alongside those green monsters. Even at rest they commanded respect, but when they revved up for the off, we hooted with delight. The platform trembled and we could feel the vibrations through our shoes, groping up our hairless legs, filling our guts with something approaching orgasm.

There were plenty of other diesels passing through – Brushes, English Electric Type 4s, even the North-Eastern Peaks – and, most afternoons, two Southern Region Bo-Bo diesels which had come all the way from the London suburbs with a Blue Circle cement train. Rarities like this were always a delight, giving us a chance to cop engines from exotic parts without having to actually go there. It seemed to work in our favour: spotters in Woking or Southampton would have to wait until hell froze over before they had a visit from a Deltic or Peak.

What Grantham didn't have, though, were any railway sheds. We couldn't go slipping through gaps in fences or clambering over gates. At Wolverhampton, Burton and Crewe we had the sport of bunking, but at Grantham we could only be well-behaved spectators – loving the locos, but unable to feel total involvement. If we'd had any money we might have hopped on one of the Deltic-hauled trains and taken a ride to Peterborough or Doncaster and chanced a visit to the depots there.

Another thing I liked about the old LNER – though I never admitted as much to Andy – was a refreshing absence of toadying. The GWR and LMS had named their locos after castles and kings, colonies and regiments, stately homes and old men like Tennyson and Kitchener. Railways were, at the end of the day, part of the establishment, and so trainspotting was inevitably tied in with patriotism and British values.

But the LNER bosses – and I only had the old spotting books to go by – had had a wilder imagination. They named their locos after birds (*Wild Swan*, *Kingfisher*, *Mallard*) or Walter Scott characters (*Madge Wildfire*, *Guy Mannering*); A3's even had the names of famous racehorses like *Captain Cuttle*, *Spearmint* and *Blink Bonny*.

Trainspotting had really opened up my world. As a bookish child I had travelled the Silk Route with Marco Polo and sailed round the Horn with Magellan – and yet I had scarcely known my own country. Now, in between the spotting, I slowly put the jigsaw together – the ramshackle workshops of the Black Country, the pottery kilns of Stoke, the foggy cabbage fields of Lincolnshire. But with each trip we were faced, more and more, with the railways' twilight, the evidence plentiful and undeniable. Lines were being closed, stations lay derelict, and steam engines were filthy and neglected. And yet we clung to the myths and legends, loyally defending our adopted companies as if they were rival football teams.

Even today, old spotters gather in pubs and clubs, still arguing the odds over halves of bitter and clacking dominoes – whether Gresley was a better railway chief than Stanier, whether A4s were smoother runners than Coronations, whether LNER drivers were friendlier to young spotters than those of the LMS.

005

My Brilliant Backyard: Burton, 1966

Burton Grammar School had clubs for stamp-collectors, chess buffs, radio hams, even a French Society for bilingual swots. Nothing for trainspotters, though – it wasn't the kind of activity a grammar school wanted to encourage. Even if such a club had existed I'm not sure anyone would have joined it: the last thing we wanted was to be officially approved, to go on club outings, packed into a minibus and chaperoned by an off-duty geography teacher with a *Flying Scotsman* biro.

The old grammar schools were often built on hills, a symbolic challenge, so they said – the idea being that you had to work hard to get to the top. That may be true, but the best thing about the lofty position of our school was that, in the right classroom, you had a view over the whole town, with the main line running along like a silver wire glinting in the sun. We were too far away to see any numbers, but you could make out the green of a diesel or the black of a steamer. When lessons got boring, I stared dreamily out of the window and made railway doodles on my exercise books.

Maths teachers aren't known for kindliness and they went mad when I handed in my homework: not only was it half-baked, the doodles on the cover were totally irrelevant. If I'd drawn protractors and stylised formulae I might have got away with it, but a crude steamer with three childish coaches was too much and I was ordered to make a neat cover out of brown paper.

We often moaned about the predictability of Burton's rail traffic, but in reality we were lucky. In other towns kids just stood by the line and watched trains go past, left to right or right to left. Burton's brewing industry had spawned an extensive maze of lines and shunting yards and although Steamer Gates was our main meeting place, there were plenty of other good spotting spots …

Little Burton Bridge

Andy and I walked to school and back most days, a good two miles, but we thought nothing of it. Mornings always seemed to be a rush, owing to Andy's slow habit with Shredded Wheat, but after school we took a glorious dawdle. Every day brought a laugh of some sort, and there were plenty of corner shops to call in at for sweets, ice lollies or ciggies. Most days we'd stop off at Little Burton Bridge, a pocket community of about a dozen tiny houses jam-packed together under the railway arches. Some of the bedrooms were just feet from the shunting yards. How the hell did anyone sleep! Yet we couldn't help feeling envious of the kids who lived there, so close to the action.

During our stop-offs there'd always be at least one train passing through, as often as not just an 8F or an Ozzie on a coal train. Built by the War Department to an Austerity design (hence the name), Ozzies were drab and clumsy, unloved by spotters and railwaymen alike. We made a note of the numbers, but felt no affection for them. How guilty I feel now for my indifference; I'd love to see one again but none were ever preserved so I can't even go and pay penance.

One teatime we were kicking our heels waiting for something interesting to come along. Actually, Andy was kicking his heels; I was kicking idly at the derelict fence, knocking off large bits of wood with glee. An old gent stopped to watch us.

'All right, lads? Any expresses?' he asked.

We shook our heads, wondering what he was up to. He came nearer and I could smell his breath, a sickly hum of damp bread and Marmite.

'No? Shame. Any railway hooligan specials?' he demanded nastily. 'Any cattle trucks for teenage shit?'

With that he began to swing his shopping bag round over his head, bringing it in sharp contact with my head.

'That's for defiling British Railways property,' he snarled, making a grab for my sweaty collar and hurling curses as we fled.

Steamer Gates

Within the general Steamer Gates crowd there were all kinds of rivalries. As well as the usual school or football rivalries, there was an ongoing feud between steam fans and diesel lovers. Andy and I may have disagreed about the merits of Castles vs. Streaks, but in our contempt for diesel-lovers we were united. It wasn't the engines themselves that we despised – we collected them, after all, though we could never actually *love* them. But we could not tolerate the company of kids gleeful about the demise of steam. Diesel-lovers were lepers – but worse, lepers with clairvoyance. We knew full well that steam was doomed, we needed no reminding. Even if steam engines were on their last legs, we would defend them until the end. We couldn't just cast them aside for the sleek green diesels. We gave diesel-lovers names – the Scottish Brush Kid, the Bo-Bo Bleeder and the Shunter Bloke – and put them on a blacklist, outcasts who should carry on their evil spotting ways at a distance.

Equally despised were the fudgers, kids so desperate for glory that they filled their books with fraudulent cops. They claimed – at the age of twelve or thirteen – that they had been on unaccompanied trips to the north of Scotland to see engines that we could only dream of. They would make out that they had an understanding with the shedmaster at Dundee: that he used to drink with their dad, and so the son was welcome to visit whenever he felt like it and would even be allowed to fire an A4 to Aberdeen.

Sometimes we half-believed them – there were parents who let their children roam the country like gypsies – but when those same kids told us they had to be in for six or they'd get in trouble, we just fell about laughing.

Most classes of steam loco had unofficial names. Those not grand enough to be recognised as a Hall, a Jubilee or a Britannia would be nicknamed by the drivers or the spotting fraternity. And so there were 8-Freights, Ozzies, Blackies, Duck Sixes and Crabs among others. Nicknames varied from region to region: to the kids on Merseyside, for instance, Blackies were known as Mickeys. Diesels also had names: approved ones such as Peaks, Warships and Deltics, and nicknames such as Tats, Bo-Bos and Baby Deltics, or Whistlers, Hoovers and Growlers – names which were derogatory reflections on performance.

Nicknaming goes on today, though its range seems diminished. It asserts the trainspotter's right to be judgemental, but also his need to feel involved in the overall culture of the railways.

We were not oblivious to the times we were living in. Style was important: Levi's, Chelsea boots, polo necks. (The spotter in school cap, short trousers and gabardine mac was already a thing of the past.) Music played a big part in our lives. Bolt had turned me on to the Stones and I'd become a bigger fan than he was. In the evenings someone would turn up at Steamer Gates with a transistor radio and we'd listen to Radio Luxembourg. One evening Jimmy Savile played the whole of the Stones' new LP *Aftermath*, and the steamers clanked by with their coal trains to the poignant refrain of 'Baby, baby, baby you're out of time ...'

Wetmore Sidings
Some of us trainspotters needed a secret place. Steamer Gates, Little Burton and the Iron Bridges were all on my social circuit,

but Wetmore Sidings was nearer home and I spent half of my evenings there. Sidings branched off from both sides of the track, so when nothing much was happening on the main line I sat and watched the wagons being shunted by an old Jinty or one of the dumpy diesel shunters. Shunting must have been repetitive for the men whose job it was, but I found it fascinating. No matter how many times the Jinty or diesel-shunter went through the same procedure, it was always fun to watch. These men knew what they were doing and had it down to an art: each loose wagon gliding along with the grace of a ballet dancer until it connected with the others, just hard enough to set up a relay of clanging buffers, an evocative sound so rarely heard nowadays.

The old steamers truly were living things, with foibles and character … but their health was causing us great concern. They could still put on a show of bravado, barking like beasts from the gates of hell, but it was often a fierceness born of pain: close up you could hear the loose bits clanking and see steam leaking from places it shouldn't have. But the railwaymen did their best: cleaning them up, lovingly oiling them, tenderly feeding them coal; and then they could purr along so softly that you would be quite unaware until they were right beneath your feet, blasting smoke and steam through the loose planking of the footbridge.

Few other spotters troubled me at Wetmore. There'd been plenty in the past: the sides of the footbridge were etched with engine numbers and names with a threatening ring – Gaz, Kev, Duggy – but whoever they were, they were long gone. I was king of the castle now. As well as standing guard on the footbridge itself, I'd built a simple eyrie by wedging an old sleeper across the joists supporting the wooden stairway.

I usually had the place to myself, but there were occasional visitors, like Trevor, a slightly subnormal chap who turned up one day with a packet of Refreshers. He offered me one as we watched the Jinty on shunting duties.

'You don't have to crunch 'em,' he said, irritated by my failure to suck. I tried to ignore him – my Refresher, my rules.

'I know a bloody good trick, though,' he rambled. 'Get a cup off your mum, bash up half a dozen of them with the handle of a knife, then fill it up with water.'

He looked at me, as if expecting applause.

'See! You get can get a big drink of pop from a thruppenny packet of tuffies!'

Trevor was harmless enough really; he just liked watching trains, like me, but I was jealous of my territory and bristled whenever anyone appeared on the footbridge. It was a public right of way, after all, but with the narrowness of the walkway I had a Little John complex about defending against interlopers.

Curfew, for me, was about 8.20, time of the mail train for Bristol. It rushed through with a blur of red Royal Mail livery and as it clattered into the distance I'd head off home to watch *The Avengers* or *The Saint*.

Burton's rail traffic was fairly predictable, but there were surprises. One evening, when the mail train had passed and I was about to leave, the rattle of signal wires and the clang of signals going up tempted me to stay. It was getting dark, but I didn't have to wait long: I could see smoke in the distance and whatever it was came towards us pretty damn fast. The plume of white and grey got nearer, squashed itself under the road bridge – and a thrill shot through me as a Royal Scot hurtled through on a fast goods. But it was too dark to make out its number!

Not surprisingly, when I told them at school next day, everyone refused to believe me. I even heard the dreaded word 'fudger' whispered. Doubts started to plague me then: had I really seen a Scot, or had it been a trick of the twilight?

Stretton Junction

I could see trains from the front window of our first-floor flat, on a freight branch that went from Wetmore Sidings and took the long way round to Derby. It was never very busy, but a few trains passed that way in the early evenings, not long after I'd got home from school.

The line was on a curved gradient out of the sidings, so the engines struggled, sending clouds of smoke up over the roof-tops, so you knew of their approach long before they actually came in sight. Many a time, having just sat down for tea, I'd see the tell-tale smoke, fling down my knife and fork and dash out in the hope of catching a B1 on its way to Eggington Junction.

The B1s were fairly ordinary freight engines, but their origins in the Eastern Region made them an exotic cop. Kids in Nottingham and Doncaster probably despised them, but we welcomed the few that strayed our way each month. Many were named after antelopes: *Springbok*, *Chamois*, *Wildebeest* and *Klipspringer*. A novel enough idea – until they ran out of antelopes. They should have stopped there, but instead they went on to use the drab names of railway bigwigs: *Geoffrey Gibbs*, *Leslie Runciman* and the ridiculously improbable *A. Harold Bibby*. As for *Fitzherbert Wright*, he sounded like one of the toffs out of *The Magnet*.

Gnu was the B1 I yearned to see. It had the shortest name-plate attached to any loco and I was told they'd had to put extra spaces between the letters, just to make it long enough to put two bolt holes in!

Panicked by the idea of missing a cop, the race was on. 'Get stuffed!' I yelled at the kids who wanted me to stop and play tick. Then it was a hop, skip and a jump across the allot-ments to the abandoned trackbed behind our house. From there I had a clear run up to meet the freight branch at Stretton Junction.

A clear run? Abandoned railways do not make good

running tracks. There are dents every yard where the sleepers once lay, odd bits of cast-iron to stub your feet on, and ground-trailing brambles to send you sprawling headlong in the gravel and cinders.

It never was *Gnu*, of course. I'd sit there, panting and croaking, proud to have got there in one minute flat – only to find myself staring at some crummy 8-Freight I'd seen ten times already. I didn't even have the breath to shout 'Scrap it!' Looking across the line I could see the signalman laughing at me. There's something to be done about that lad, he'd think, reaching for his tea and reflecting on the madness of trainspotters.

Drained of adrenalin, I felt nervous now. A tramp nicknamed Barabas was rumoured to live in an abandoned air-raid shelter just down from the junction. What if my running past had disturbed his kip? What if he appeared now – a dirty and menacing shadow, blocking the path between me and the safety of home.

A telescope would have saved me an awful lot of trouble …

The Iron Bridges

I never did understand why they called it the Iron Bridges, since there was only one bridge. Pedantry apart, the latticed crossing commanded a good overview of Burton's railway action, from the station to the south to Wetmore Sidings in the north.

Girls had begun to edge onto the scene now. We were still spotting, but we'd all hit puberty and our hormones were playing up like a Last Night of the Proms crowd. Anything in a skirt or shapely denims got our attention and much of our chatter was obscene. Everyone claimed to have done 'it' already, but despite trying to act cool it didn't take much to distract us from our trainspotting.

Violence rarely figured in our lives. If you were a spotter you were more or less okay, at least with anyone else who shared a love of trains. Steamer Gates was certainly safe enough, but away from safety in numbers there was always a chance of being picked on by lads with other interests, random gangs looking for a patch to claim as their own territory. Being a grammar school boy was provocation enough to some – enough to get you a smack in the gob any day. They might try to parley by discussing football, but knowing nothing about football was to double your sins. Fortunately Andy was also a football fan (Leeds United) and his ability to swap chit-chat about Billy Bremner with local bully boys often won us a reprieve from a bashing.

I didn't have any friends who weren't spotters – not best friends anyway. But it was surprising how many kids would take up spotting in order to become your friend. Declan Mulroney, for instance, a grammar school new boy from outside of Burton. Stigmatised by an Irish name and sticky-out ears, he was desperate to fit in. To this end I blackmailed him into ditching his stupid bus-spotting hobby and accompanying me on a trip to Manchester. But he was a good-natured kid and didn't resent these conditions. I could never be sure, though, if he really liked trainspotting or whether I had forced it on him. Whatever the case, we soon became good friends and it was my turn to be sad when he moved on to another school just a few months later.

Horninglow Station

After closure in 1949, the dinky station at Horninglow became a transport cafe. The platforms were chipped at the edges, overgrown by grass, but inside the old booking hall lorry drivers could tuck into eggs 'n' bacon. The line itself remained open and passing freights would set the diners' forks jangling against their tea mugs.

The 2nd of April 1966 brought an end for the line itself. Andy Parker and I went along with a banner we'd made: 'Up

With Steam' it proclaimed, on a piece of white sheet nailed between two sticks. With the goofy optimism of youth we held it high and proud, but no one took much notice. The signalman leaned out at the window rail, cupping his cigarette to protect it from the steady drizzle.

Eventually he received the bell and set to on his cranking wheel, swinging the gates across the road – what was then the main A38 road to Derby. We waited. And waited. Then we saw the yellow zebra stripes of a diesel shunter approaching, and it limped by us with a trail of empty coal wagons. The *Burton Mail* photographer took a snap – and that was it. The signal-man – depressed, redundant, nostalgic, who knows – locked the box and walked off towards the pub.

Even in 1966 we were always on the lookout for souvenirs, anything that could be unscrewed or jemmied from its moorings and put away for posterity. There were plenty of derelict stations and plenty of signs: Refreshment Room, Gentlemen, Tickets, as well as countless Trespassers Will Be Prosecuted signs. Some didn't just have the warning, but included sections from the relevant Acts, all cast in tiny ¼-in high letters. Such craftsmanship, such pedantry! Horninglow still had a cast-iron station nameplate, but how it had survived so long I couldn't guess. Surely one of the lorry drivers with an eye for a quick buck would have prised it away from its mount and sold it by now. But no one had, and there it was – a fabulous prize.

When the rest of the bystanders drifted away, and with no one left to watch us, Andy and I set to work with a screw-driver – prising and levering, pulling and jiggling, splintering the wood – until eventually the nameplate loosened and came off. Jubilant and breathless, we took one end each and headed off before anyone saw us. There would be no argument about custody of the sign: Andy's parents would have had a fit if they'd found it in their garage, so it was agreed I should keep it in my bedroom.

'Hey, you!'

The shout froze us in our tracks. Striding towards us from across the road came a burly middle-aged man.

'I'll take that,' he said sourly. 'That's stolen property, that is. You're lucky I don't call the police …'

And we gave it away. Just like that, as Tommy Cooper might have said – except that it wasn't at all funny.

Now, to complete the anecdote, I must digress. This is what I wrote in the first edition of this book:

And for all I know the bastard still has it. It probably graces the wall of his tool shed, admired by visitors. No doubt he notes the prices that such relics fetch nowadays and prides himself on his 'investment'. Even now, thirty years later, I'm still sore about it. This is my own personal Elgin Marbles. That sign should be up on my wall, I should be glancing up at it even as I write, filled with nostalgia for a damp spring day in my childhood. It was stolen, wasn't it? By him, that is, not us. How could we have stolen it from people who neither knew nor cared about its existence? How could it belong to the North Staffs Railway when it had gone out of business in 1923? Such souvenirs were surely treasure trove, finders keepers.

In 2004 I was in the library in Burton, taking out a couple of books. The lady librarian paused midway through swiping my bar code. 'Ah, you're that chap who wrote *Platform Souls*, aren't you?' I nodded, wondering if she was going to ask for an autograph. 'My uncle was in that,' she continued. I was puzzled. Did she mean one of my trainspotting mates? 'He lived opposite Horninglow station. He was the one who saw you stealing that nameplate.'

'It wasn't exactly stealing,' I argued. My irritation was tempered by a need to know.

'What happened to it, then? I suppose he sold it for a fat profit?'

'Oh no,' she said. 'Nothing like that. He said it was a nice rigid piece, so he used it as a shelf in his shed.'

I could barely speak. He had used it as a shelf?

'Yeah, well, what happened, has he still got it?'

'Oh no, that was years ago. It got all bent and had oil and paint drips on it, so he chucked it away.'

She laughed at the thought as she date-stamped my books. Readers, she laughed. I thought it must have been the cruellest postscript ever.

Between 1966 and 1970 the railways were virtually stripped bare by trainspotters. Anything that could be unscrewed, pulled down or hacksawed off could be taken away and hidden. There was a nationwide panic to save all those familiar items that had been in place for fifty or a hundred years: signal arms, clocks, benches, tea urns, railwaymen's hats, guards' whistles, luggage trolleys.

The better-off can afford £5,000 for a distinctive nameplate or £700 for the smokebox numberplate from a Scot, but the rest of us make do with a few buttons, a shed-plate or an old timetable. The functional station nameplates of the 1970s are now regarded as antiques and find ready buyers.

All this I can understand, but a lot of it shades into nutcase territory. Just like those fans who would save a tissue a Beatle had wiped his nose with, there are people who collect odd bits of metal which have the most obscure claims to a heritage – a sawn-off piece of a handrail from Carnforth signal box, a tinny seat from the driver's canteen at Crewe, a teacup once used in the dining car of the Cheltenham Flyer.

Collecting relics throws up some ethical dilemmas too. For instance, can you count an engine as 'copped' if you own its numberplate, but have never seen the complete loco in action?

I'd say no. Yet on trips round Crewe Works we would often count bits of locos, if they were big enough – a whole boiler from a Britannia, for instance, or the detached cabside from a diesel. Where do you draw the line, that is the big debate. At school there were always some who made the astounding assertion that you could count *pictures* of engines, without having seen them in real life – a definite taboo with most of us. As to whether you can count a numberplate, I would need to consult the ethics committee. I said no, but after all, it is the number, and the number is what trainspotting is all about. Does it matter if the loco is no longer attached? Spare parts surgery is a straightforward debate in comparison.

There was one small compensation back in April 1966. Strolling past Horninglow station a couple of days later, I glanced towards the signal box – and there, standing upright in one of the dustbins, was the signal box nameplate, dumped and unwanted. There was no hesitation. I grabbed it – all five feet of it! – and scurried home. This time there was no ambush and the souvenir is still intact.

006

Bristol Temple Meads

Bristol Temple Meads has always been my favourite station. Seen from outside, the castellated honey-coloured stone and the clock tower give it the look of a minster in the English shires. Even now, five decades after the end of steam there, its vaulted roof encloses a classic railway space: vast and light and dusty, full of familiar smells and echoes of the past.

Bristol Temple Meads … the name rolls around the mouth like an English plum. It's impossible to say without thinking of freckled girls in Thirties hats, or small boys in sailor suits. Every time I come here it seems as if I am struggling to remember things – people, conversations, trains – that dance just beyond the reach of memory. Perhaps I was a porter here in the Thirties, or a tea-trolley boy who fell in love with an aloof, ringleted girl glimpsed through the window of a first-class compartment.

The gateway to the west, Bristol is the junction where routes from Paddington and the north-east meet and holidaymakers who still choose the train start to get excited by the thought that they're halfway to the seaside now. In steam days, Blackies from Manchester and Jubilees from Leeds would be uncoupled from their trains and exchanged for something more exciting, a Castle or a Hall in lined green, with copper piping and a gleaming brass nameplate.

The perspective of Temple Meads lends itself to mystery. The tracks bend sharply westwards from the station and disappear under a road bridge. On my first visit, in 1965, I could only stand and watch as trains pulled away for Taunton,

Exeter, Plymouth and Penzance, imagining a soft seasidey land somewhere far beyond my ken.

The train fare to Bristol was beyond my modest pocket money, but the pull of the city became too strong and even though my mum didn't earn a lot, I managed to wheedle enough out of her to afford a ticket. It was my first long-distance spotting trip, a gruelling three hours from Burton, via Birmingham, Worcester and Gloucester. Near Bristol we passed through an unusual triangular station called Mangotsfield, where Arnold Ridley of *Dad's Army* had once found himself stranded for the night and been inspired to write his play *The Ghost Train*.

The great days of the GWR were over by the time I got to Bristol. But I found it didn't matter. I wanted to see engines in their prime and didn't feel ashamed about chasing diesels – the Warships, Westerns and Hymeks. I knew these same diesels had usurped the Castles and Kings, but I wasn't as sad about that as I made out. I loved steam as much as my friends did, but I'd had my fill of charity cases. This was *my* era and it did no good to be stand-offish about dieselisation. Even so, I was glad to be there on my own – it meant I didn't have to explain myself to anyone.

With maroon paintwork and beaky yellow noses, the Warship diesels were charming. I loved the names: *Magpie*, *Benbow*, *Zambesi* and *Pegasus*. Steamers were named after dusty old writers, British colonies or celebrated warmongers, and I hated those values with which we boys were brainwashed. The times were changing. We didn't have much of an aristocracy any more, so why did we need trains named after past glories? Kids were rebelling and no longer gave a toss for the likes of Lord Kitchener or Clive of India. Yes, the Warships were named after the very same destroyers and battlecruisers that upheld British rule, but at least the names were colourful and ambivalent, free of pedagogy.

In time I grew to love some of those 'dusty old writers', but it's worth noting that no locos had ever been named after Jane Austen, George Eliot or the Brontë sisters. The only woman deemed worthy was Boadicea, no doubt because she was half naked and drove a wild chariot!

The Western class diesels had a sharper, cleverly contoured profile, with windows like oversized versions of Yves St Laurent's specs. Livery aside, what charmed me were the cast-iron name and numberplates. That was why so many people loved the Western Region: it was a railway Ruritania, clinging defiantly to its own colours and traditions, living by its own rules. Even the names were a final act of defiance: *Western Queen*, *Western Pathfinder*, *Western Stalwart* – all 74 named *Western* something or other, like a last two-fingered salute to British Railways management.

As late as 1966, nearly twenty years after nationalisation, BR was still struggling to impose its rule on a culture defined by past glories, on men with long family allegiances. The railways had been nationalised, yet they remained a loose affiliation of small republics, each with its own identity and history. Footplatemen and stationmasters didn't think of themselves as British Railways staff at all, but as men of the Somerset and Dorset or Great Central.

It seemed like a harmless tradition (and an honourable one), but the bosses were determined to squash it. They succeeded in the end and the railways have never again had that same *esprit de corps*. There is still loyalty, between the staff at least, but 'corporate ethos' is a vastly different thing to company pride. No one has a job for life any more, and a railwayman's boss is no longer someone older and more experienced, but just as likely a fresh-faced tyro from university. Grumbling was always part of a railwayman's life, but in the old days he knew who to yell at and could get it off his chest without risking his pension or being labelled a whistleblower.

Bristol's main depot, Bath Road (82A), was entirely die-selised and packed with Warships, Westerns and Hymeks. I walked round to it from the station and stood on the bridge trying to get as many cops as possible. I didn't dare try bunking it. Security was far too tight. Unlike the ramshackle steam sheds of yesteryear, Bath Road had been purpose-built, with unwelcome visitors factored into the design. Even the cheekiest trainspotter would never have got past the glass-fronted office strategically sited at the entrance, let alone made it down the stairs into the depot itself. Bath Road was a showcase of a shed, and quite apart from the usual objections to trespassing, trainspotters would have made it look untidy.

But probing its defences became a challenge – 'extreme spotting' if you like – and there was always someone who claimed to have cracked it. I was told of one well-built lad with a deep voice and precocious sideburns who'd donned a BR jacket and slipped easily past the defences with a cheery wave. It sounded like a splendid wheeze, but I couldn't help wondering what would have happened if the foreman had handed him a job sheet and told him to take a Hymek out to pick up some empties from the goods yard.

Still, if Bath Road was impregnable, the former Midland sheds at Barrow Road (82E) were more spotter-friendly. And they still had steam there. With the depot in its final days, no one cared much about trespassers. The locos here were mainly workaday freight engines, nothing I couldn't have seen back in Burton, but there was a smattering of GWR veterans, stripped of their name and numberplates of course, but still plodding on. I had sneaked in under the wire. Within a few months the Western Region would be entirely steamless and these locos just any old iron in the nearest scrapyard.

You might wonder why my mum let me wander so far at such a young age, considering how much she cherished me. We only had each other, after all. The fact is, she didn't let me.

Knowing she'd only worry and grumble, I didn't always tell her the whole truth. I would just say I was nipping over to Derby, when I had every intention of travelling a hundred miles in the opposite direction. I dread to think what would have happened if anything had gone wrong. Poor Mum, she wouldn't even have known where I was! Britain seemed a safe enough place in the Sixties, but I wasn't entirely naive and from the newspapers I knew that all the kinds of bad things could – and did – happen to children. Between the accidents and the abductions, I was just one of those fools who rushed in.

By the age of thirteen I was getting around far more than any of my schoolmates, each trip taking me further and further away in ever-widening circles. I was the ripple – but who had cast the stone? No one else at school had ever gone as far as Leeds or Bristol, and certainly not on their own. They had their excuses, of course: Andy had had enough of the so-called Great Western, and Pipsqueak hated diesels more than any of us. Not that it stopped me showing off all my Warship and Western cops during morning break. I knew they were jealous, but then they turned their envy on its head and threatened to blackball me – it looked like Whittaker was turning into a diesel lover! Why all this enthusiasm for what they called tin boxes on wheels, when there were still plenty of steam engines worth looking for!

Much as I enjoyed the camaraderie of trainspotting, I cherished my solo ventures too. Crewe, Derby and Snow Hill were team efforts, but Bristol, like Leeds and Oxford, I wanted to keep for myself. I liked going solo, but there was no shortage of company when you needed it and I always found someone to talk to. Most of the kids I met in Bristol came from odd little West Country places like Ilminster, Yeovil or Carmarthen and they'd grown up in a totally different railway environment. What was a novelty for me was common as muck to them. They had classed their Warships and Westerns by the time they hit puberty and couldn't see why I got so excited over *Zephyr* and *Ramilles*!

Much as Bristol was exotic to me, local spotters regarded me as an interesting specimen in my own right. A sucker for flattery, I was more than happy to sit on a luggage trolley hamming up the northern grittiness. 'Gissa fag then,' I'd say. And there'd I'd sit, smoking and basking in their envy as I told them about Peaks D1 to D10. Since they were restricted to taking coal from local mines to local power stations, Burton was the only town where you could regularly see the ten locos (*Scafell Pike, Helvellyn, Skiddaw, Great Gable, Cross Fell, Whernside, Ingleborough, Penyghent, Snowdon, Tryfan*) that gave the Peak class its name. They were an everyday sight to me, but these kids would have had to mount a major expedition – and even then they would be unlikely to see the whole set in one day.

It wasn't until 1968 that I finally went west, heading out under the road bridge behind a Western. Aged fifteen, I had bought a Western Region railrover, which enabled me to go all the way to Devon and Cornwall, travelling the coastal line at Dawlish and bunking sheds like Newton Abbot (83A) and Laira (84A) in Plymouth, which until then had been just a dream.

My love affair with Bristol has endured for half a century, and yet apart from those walks to the railway sheds in the 1960s I've never been out of the station. My affection was based solely on what I'd seen from the train: the red-roofed suburbs, terraced houses climbing the hillsides, Clifton Suspension Bridge and mental images of the docks taken straight from *Treasure Island*. I had never even considered that the city could have a darker side, so the St Paul's riots and the debate about the city's underclass came as quite a shock.

Temple Meads today looks as grand as ever, and they can't take that away, but there are signs of neglect nibbling at its edge. Apart from Birmingham or the London termini, no city seems busy enough nowadays to need fourteen platforms.

Temple Meads is stuck with them though. They get used on the odd occasion, but it's not worth keeping them spruced up or providing loos or refreshments for anyone. The small outpost serving tea and biscuits, which seemed mostly for the benefit of trainspotters, was boarded up many years ago now.

007

Waterloo Sunset

There were steam engines working in London until the summer of 1967. It hardly fits in with the Swinging Sixties myth, but while the Flowerpot Men were suggesting a trip to San Francisco and exotic scents hung over Fitzrovia and Soho, the expresses from Waterloo were still hauled by steam. Across the river, barely a mile from Carnaby Street or the King's Road, Waterloo stood out as the last of London's old-fashioned termini. British Rail had just invented InterCity and were busy splashing everything with corporate blue paint. But the slick modern image was belied by the sizzle of steam and the primeval smells of coal. It seemed mutinous, a last stand against the tide of dieselisation. While Hendrix sang of a purple haze, the one over Waterloo was defiantly grey.

I had been up and down to London several times since 1965, and I was there in that summer of love. With ten bob pocket money and £1 from my paper round I could just about afford the fare. A child return was only 17s 6d (the booking clerk didn't even have a proper half fare ticket, so would improvise by snipping an adult one in half diagonally). My remaining funds would just cover bus and tube fares to the various MPDs, plus something to eat. The barrow boys were selling three peaches for two bob and with a couple of bags of crisps it made an admirable lunch.

Waterloo fascinated me – wooden and smoky, with the constant clatter of indicator boards and pigeons which flapped and fluttered in between an endless parade of shoes: the polished brogues of city gents in pinstripes and bowler hats, and the laceless cast-offs of tramps on the lookout for cigarette butts and discarded sandwiches. They would sit on their benches all day long, waiting for night; then bed down on them, snatching sleep before they were upended by cruel policemen.

Waterloo had not yet been sterilised and Dixonised, turned into the much blander place it is today. Like many of the big stations, Waterloo was a sprawling bazaar, full of tobacco kiosks, newspaper stands, flower stalls – and shoe-shining machines with whirling dusters.

The furniture of railway stations has changed drastically over the years, but up until the Sixties travellers could indulge in some eccentric amusements, like the foot-massage machine which promised to bring the tired commuter's feet back to life. It looked similar to the weighing machines found out-side chemists' shops, but a nasty shock awaited any latter-day Colonel Blink who stepped on it to check his weight. You put a shilling in the slot and it started to vibrate. I always had the strangest sensations, as my legs and feet seemed to turn to goo and slide away from underneath me, something like the melting watch in that Salvador Dalí painting.

Less alarming, especially for would-be pop stars (and which of us weren't?), were the booths, not much bigger than a phone box, in which you could cut your own record. On one occasion, when I took Mum to London with me, we squashed ourselves into one for an impromptu recording session. But while Mum took it all seriously, singing a passable rendition of Ken Dodd's 'Tears', I just spoiled it for her by sniggering and making silly noises.

It was at Waterloo that Ian Allan, the patron saint of train-spotting, came up with the idea that would change the face of boyhood. In 1942, while working as a railway clerk, he invested his savings and published the first-ever *ABC* spotting book, a list of Southern Railways locos. Despite initial opposition from the railway companies (it was halfway through the war and fear of spies was rampant) Allan's enterprise was a great success, so much so that things soon seemed to be getting out of hand. 'Train craze sweeps the country!' exclaimed the *News Chronicle* in 1944.

Like most crazes it was frowned on by older people. Quite apart from simply not getting it, the sight of others having fun always rankles with some, doubly so if those others happen to be youngsters.

'During school holidays as many as 200 boys at a time go trainspotting at Tamworth', said a police inspector during the court appearance of two dozen Brummie lads up for trespassing on the tracks. The event must have seeded itself in folk memory, for even when I started some twenty years later, Tamworth was cited as an example of railway yobbery and the station remained strictly out of bounds to trainspotters, even those who had splashed out on a platform ticket.

Quite apart from the dangers of trespassing, the authorities must have been unnerved by the idea of 200 working-class youngsters gathering in one place. The trespass wasn't just physical, for it must have seemed to many that these youths were intruding on middle-class territory. Railways had been of 'scholarly interest' for gentlemen since Victorian times, but far from welcoming a wider audience the old guard were horrified. This number-collecting craze threatened to bring the genteel study of railways and locomotives into disrepute.

Soon after the Tamworth rampage, in an effort to avoid being tagged as the Pied Piper of railway hooligans, Ian Allan formed his eponymous Locospotters Club and from then on every *ABC* spotting book came with an application form. (Since this was often printed on the inside back cover, joining up could entail making a real mess of an otherwise cherished book!) Members received a badge (de luxe chromium 9d extra), a membership card, a pencil and a one shilling voucher.

But first you had to sign your pledge:

> I, the undersigned, do hereby make an application to join
> the Ian Allan Locospotters Club and undertake on my word
> of honour if this application is accepted to keep the rule of
> the Club. I understand that if I break this rule in any way I
> cease to be a member and forfeit the right to wear the badge
> or take part in the Club's activities.

This effort satisfied the authorities, but I wonder how many
club members kept to a rule that would have destroyed half the
fun of trainspotting. The more timid ones probably thought it
best to obey, but peer pressure would soon win the day. Quite
how Ian Allan would have gone about getting the badge back
from renegades is unclear. Perhaps this would entail some
kind of public humiliation – Ian Allan badges ripped off school
blazers in view of one's peers, lifelong banishment from trainspotting venues, one's name listed in a monthly Roll of Shame
in one of the railway magazines.

Southern Region drivers were well aware that they had the
honour of being the last men in Britain to drive steam-hauled
expresses. They could still cling to the idea that driving trains
was an important job, and at the end of a trip to Bournemouth
or Weymouth, children would still come up and say goodbye
to the crew.

I never had enough money to travel down to the south
coast, but I did get steam-hauled over the suburban lines to
Clapham Junction. I couldn't help feeling sorry for the local
trainspotters. With the Bulleid Pacifics on their last legs, they
would soon have nothing worth spotting apart from the
crummy electric units, thousands of them, all the same drab
green. The south-east was infested with them already and soon
they'd be coupling up into twelve-coach trains and pretending
to be holiday expresses. The Southern never had any diesels to

speak of, only the Cromptons shedded at Hither Green, and they were far too boxlike to attract admirers.

Nine Elms is today better known as the location of London's fruit and veg market, but in 1967 the site was home to the last steam depot in London. Nine Elms, Old Oak Common, Hither Green, Cricklewood – why did so many of London's railway places sound so misleadingly rural? Here, right below the windows of council flats, West Country and Merchant Navy Pacifics were turned about, polished and coaled, and fired-up in readiness for their trips to the south coast. With their squared streamlining and distinctively spoked wheels, the Bulleid Pacifics – named after West Country places and Battle of Britain squadrons – were one of the most popular classes. I'd seen my first West Country in Oxford in 1965 when it arrived with a northbound Pines Express, and I'd been chasing them ever since. I loved their seasidey names: Appledore, Lyme Regis and Clovelly.

Nine Elms was a top-notch depot, yet none of the staff seemed too bothered by kids (and adults) wandering around. British Rail cared little for these wonderful steam engines now and couldn't wait to get rid of them. But the drivers and cleaners still took pride in their charges and in themselves. Far from ordering us to get out, they stood back and let us look; they wanted us to see the twilight's last gleaming.

Things didn't always go so smoothly for me, though. I'd had a few minor scares over the years, but none like the one I was destined to get.

Nine Elms and its lovely steamers apart, I'd always thought there was something a little sinister about the Southern Region, all those joyless electric units and that throwaway footnote to Stewarts Lane (75D) in the 1965 *Locoshed Directory*: 'Note. There are conductor rails in the shed yard.' For the careless trainspotter, death would be instantaneous. For me, even today the name Stewarts Lane brings a touch of nausea. No,

I didn't get electrified (or I wouldn't be writing this book) but it was here that trainspotting lost some of its William Brown playfulness in a sickening way.

As long as you did avoid the live rails, bunking Stewarts Lane was quite easy. There was a small gatehouse just inside the entrance, but I'd walked past without being nabbed. It looked like it would be a textbook bunk. It wasn't until I was on my way out that things turned nasty.

As I passed the gatehouse, a fat Cockney bloke jumped out to bar my way, herding me inside by tactical use of his beer gut. His fingers looked like uncooked sausages, pink and hairy, but they had a grip like iron. The sun shone, but he had a two-bar electric fire on and the room stank of armpits and sour milk.

He took my spotting books from me, put them on a high shelf, then sat down in a suspiciously stained office chair and looked me over. I stood, frightened and contrite as he reached for the telephone.

'You know what happens to trespassers, don't you?'

I shook my head. He couldn't take my Ian Allan badge off me – I wasn't even a member.

'First I'm calling the police. They'll lock you in a cell. Then you go to court. Then they put you in a home with other delinquents.'

The most dastardly part of my 'crime', so it seemed, was that since he'd not seen me go in, he assumed I must have got into the sheds by walking across the main lines. Did he really think I was that stupid! To walk across the busiest railway lines in the country – eight or ten tracks, side by side and in constant use? I assured him I had simply walked in past his stupid gatehouse, but my protests fell on deaf ears. He took pride in his job and simply refused to believe anyone could dodge his hawk-eyed watch. I'd exposed a flaw in his security and he meant to punish me for it.

He dialled a single 9 with his sausage/finger and let the dial spin back, watching me all the time. At this point I began to cry. I said I was sorry and begged him to let me go. I wanted my mum. I wanted to be at home, lying on the carpet and filling in my books. Years later, reading a transcript of horrific tapes made by the Moors Murderers, the memory of Stewarts Lane came back to me. It would be flippant to put my experience in the same category, but for a moment I really felt the existential panic of being separated from loved ones and the safety of home, the dawning terror that they knew nothing of your situation and could not help and you would never see them again. I cracked. Panic-stricken at the thought of never seeing Mum again, I did everything except get on my knees. I cried and wailed and blubbered, so loudly that he started to get embarrassed. His cruel taunts had got out of hand and he couldn't control the anguish he had unleashed. Any passing railwayman would surely have intervened. Chucking kids out was part of the man's job, but you couldn't torture them! Reluctantly he thrust the spotting books back into my hands and pushed me out of the door, glad to be rid of me. I was relieved, but he had scared me too much for any feeling of triumph.

My legs still felt weak, but as I walked slowly back to the station I thought over what had happened. As worldly as I felt myself, I had been too naive, too in awe of adult power to realise what he'd been threatening was highly unlikely. Dialling 999 to report a junior trespasser, for God's sake! If it had happened today, I'd have been straight on the phone to Claims Direct and a solicitor would have sued the fat bloke for causing unnecessary mental distress to a minor. The police would have confiscated his hard drive and found all sorts of trainspotting torture videos on there.

The name of Stewarts Lane haunted me for years afterwards. Ten years passed before I dared go back, and only then because I didn't want to look foolish in front of Jinx, one of my regular spotting friends. I'd told my tale many times over the years and it had become less of a horror story and more like a joke. All the same, walking through those gates again gave me a heavy heart, for no one really understood the genuine terror I had felt that day in 1967.

But the fear soon went. The gatehouse had gone completely, with nothing left except some tiled flooring cracked open by weeds. Hard to believe that some fat sadist had ever sat there in a chair, smirking at a young lad's terror. The whole area seemed so much smaller. I relaxed – until I saw two railwaymen coming towards us. I fought the urge to run. Silly me! They were just two guys coming off shift and they nodded a greeting to us as they passed.

008

The Black Cities of the North

On our travels we often met kids from Manchester or Liverpool or Leeds. We couldn't help but envy them. They'd been born lucky: what wonderful spotting lives they must have had. They lived amidst a dense maze of urban lines, with dozens of depots to bunk – from four in Leeds to a couple of dozen around Liverpool and Manchester. Yet they always seemed paler, thinner and not so tall as the rest of us. They were obviously poor, too. Why else would they have to wear their school trousers at the weekend? Or blazers with elbow patches?

Still, however superior we might feel, one look at their Ian Allan books – page after page of underlined Scots, Jubilees and Britannias – was enough to knock us sideways: rarities such as *Hereward the Wake* or *Abukir*, locos that always eluded the rest of us.

'*Coeur-de-Lion*?' they'd scoff. 'That effing wreck? It's been farting about down Edge Hill yard all last week!', they'd say – as if to them the fabulous beast was no more than a workaday shunting engine.

Steam buffs eulogise the 'grime 'n' glory' steam days, but as a pale green liberal, I can't help a ripple of disapproval. The old puffer trains may have looked lovely on the Somerset and Dorset or in the midst of the Derbyshire Dales, but as far as I know no one ever studied the effects of steam engines on the folks of Lancashire and the West Midlands. Some of these people – generations even – spent their entire lives under a speckled grey duvet of sky, despairing at their washing day whites (which never were) and breathing a haze of coal dust and sulphur. It would be naive to think that it did not have some long-term cumulative effect on their health.

Merseyside 1966

On my thirteenth birthday Mum delighted me with a big blue £5 note. The following Saturday I set off to conquer Merseyside. This would surely be a trip to boast to my classmates about …

My first stop was Warrington Bank Quay, from where I walked towards the outskirts and made a neat, unchallenged bunk of the sheds. Heading north again, I changed at Wigan. This time I was less successful and simply got lost in the back streets. These things happened, but I didn't usually tell anyone about the cock-ups. Disappointed, I made my way back to town and the smaller Wallgate station, where my mood picked up again with the arrival of a steam-hauled train to Southport. This was a real treat, since steam-hauled passenger trains were becoming a rarity. A three-coach local, it had plenty of empty seats and I found myself a place close behind the blackened tank loco. With my head out of the window, I sniffed my way across Lancashire, from the grey fug of Wigan to the salty sea breezes of Southport.

I'd had my head out of train windows for most of my teenage years and sported a weekend hairstyle similar to a chimney sweep's brush. I often wonder why I didn't get it knocked off. There were enough signs – 'Do Not Lean Out Of The Window' it said on every door – so I couldn't say I hadn't been warned. Morbidly I tried to guess how I'd feel if my head got knocked off by a signal post and landed on the trackside. How long would I be conscious for? Long enough to be frightened? Would my optic nerves carry on working for a moment, enough time to see a headless schoolboy leaning out of the rapidly disappearing train? It was a horrible idea, one which fascinated and repelled me. Even so, it never stopped me tempting fate.

After a successful bunk of Southport sheds (8M), I headed off along the coastal line towards Liverpool. The trip was going like clockwork – until I arrived on Merseyside around teatime and found myself caught up in some kind of Scouser rush hour. I was a weedy sort and got quite scared as I was dragged along in a stampede of burly dockers in donkey jackets and lumberjack shirts.

Teatimes in January can be pretty gloomy and, intrepid as I was, my thoughts strayed again to the safety of home and baked beans on toast. But I still had Birkenhead sheds (8H) to do and I wasn't going to give up the chance of a bunk when I'd come so far.

Birkenhead was huge, and had it been daylight I'd have been overjoyed by the scores of engines; but in the winter gloom, walking between the long rows of engines seemed overwhelming and claustrophobic and I had difficulty in making out many of the numbers. Ironically, for once, it was an absence of any other people – spotters *and* staff – that unnerved me. Frustrated and spooked, I gave it up as a bad job and made my way back to Lime Street to catch a train for Crewe. It had been an epic trip, but only half-successful and I was more than glad to sink into a seat on that bog unit back to Derby.

Leeds

Travelling on a Sunday was always dodgy. From a trainspotting point of view, though, the Sabbath had a great advantage: the depots were always packed, full of locos back at base for the weekend, and with few staff at work bunking was easy. Getting to a far-off place on Sundays could be a nightmare, though, and trains held up or diverted by engineering work were inevitably late. I recall the horror of one Sunday in Bristol, when they announced a delay to my homeward train – not ten minutes or even half an hour but three hours!

So, I knew it would be a risk taking a Sunday trip to Leeds with the intention of bunking the four depots there. I mentioned my idea to others, but no one else wanted to forgo their Sunday roast and risk being stranded on a windy station for hours. I didn't mind. I liked being on my own, and that's partly why I had so much success with shed bunking. No matter how quiet any gang of kids tries to be, it simply defies the laws of nature. Boys make noise! Going solo made it much easier for me to slip through fences, tip-toe over crunching expanses of clinker or duck into the shadows whenever I was in danger of capture.

My first stop was Holbeck (55A), Leeds' main depot, which still had a fascinating mix of steam and diesel. Star cop of the day was 72008 *Clan Macleod*, one of a class of only ten and the first one I'd seen. They were all shedded at Carlisle, so no one in our gang had ever copped one. Flushed with success, I headed off to see what I could find in the city's other depots, my next target being Farnley Junction (55C), a half hour's bus ride away.

You might wonder how a stranger to Leeds (or anywhere else) found their way around, how they knew which bus to catch and where to get off. It was all made possible by the *British Locomotive Shed Directory*, an essential pocket book from Ian Allan, compiled by the respectable-sounding Aidan L.F. Fuller FCA. Although the publishers took pains to warn against trespassing, everyone regarded the book as a 'bunker's bible'.

Some sheds you could easily work out yourself. They were hard by the station, or you could discern the plumes of smoke over nearby buildings. But other depots might be up to an hour's walk away and Fuller's well-researched routes were essential. To get from Holbeck to Farnley Junction I would need a 31, 32 or 47 bus. On alighting, I had only to 'walk along Royds Lane and bear right along a rough road just before the railway bridge'. I still have that 1965 shed directory and often browse through it to relive some of my exploits.

It would be a salutary experience to repeat them now: following the same instructions would probably see you end up in the middle of a housing estate or a B&Q car park, with nary a clue to tell you that a railway depot had ever existed there. Nearly all the old steam sheds have long since been razed to the ground, though a few survive, adapted for various industrial purposes.

By the time I'd bunked Stourton (55B) and Neville Hill (55H) and made my way back to Leeds City, night was closing in. Waiting for my train, inevitably late, I had plenty of time to sit and think. Railway statistics are fascinating and I couldn't help pondering questions like: how could there be so much coal? Think of it: ten million trainloads of it, trillions of tons of black glittering coal, all cracked into useful pieces. I tried to work out how many sleepers there were on the whole of British Rail. This involved extensive calculations of which my maths teacher would have been proud. I knew there were about 1,500 sleepers per mile, so that needed to be multiplied by the total mileage of tracks up and down the country, from single-line branches to busy four-track stretches. Plus all the dozens of sidings and marshalling yards! Not surprisingly I always gave up after a couple of minutes. Today's PCs could have come up with an answer in less than a minute, but I still think the hard disk would have given off some serious grinding noises.

The Manchester trips
By the end of 1967's 'summer of love' steam was in retreat all over Britain, banished from the west and the east, from Scotland and from Tyneside. Its last stand was in the cities

of Liverpool, Leeds and Manchester, and in Lancashire's 'Clinker Triangle' between Lancaster, Blackburn and Preston. That Christmas my mum bought me *The Decline of Steam*, a huge book costing three guineas, full of black and white photographs depicting the vanishing world of steam engines. The size would have defined it as a 'coffee table' book – but tombstone would have been more apt. There were no words – none were needed – the grainy pictures said it all and were an urgent reminder that we still had some serious trainspotting left to do.

It was around this time that I first met Jinx. I knew him by sight, since he lived in the same street, but he was older and went to a different school. Our paths would never have crossed if I hadn't got a paper round at the same newsagent's. One day he asked if I fancied going to a pop concert at Leicester's de Montfort Hall. We had a choice of tours. One had the Spencer Davis Group, The Tremeloes, Paul Jones and The Hollies; the other offered Jimi Hendrix, Cat Stevens, Engelbert Humperdinck and The Walker Brothers. Jinx was a Hollies fan and after picking up on his hints, I agreed to go to the first one. We had a great time, but I've always regretted not taking the chance to see Hendrix. The trip only cost 17/6 (including the fare to Leicester), and it wasn't until we got talking on the coach that I found out he was a fellow trainspotter.

Summer is the season most often recalled with nostalgia, yet a simple check of the records often belies people's memories of balmy days and herb-scented evenings. I'm the same with winters: the ones I remember are white with snow, full of coloured parcels, smelling of herbal cough sweets. Belisha beacons blinking vainly in freezing fog. The railways have a starring part in these imaginary home movies. Each station we pass through, ragged smoke hangs in the air, a tantalising clue to an unseen loco. 8-Freights, Ozzies and Blackies struggle bravely through Peak District blizzards, slipping on ice-covered rails, spraying snow and sending clouds of multi-shaded grey over a countryside as beautiful as a Christmas card.

Yet the winter of 1967/68 was exactly like that. Jinx and I would catch the train from Derby to Manchester. We'd strike off early, with sandwiches and flasks of Heinz soup tucked into our tartan duffel bags. Our train was a four- or five-coach affair, yanked along by a plucky Bo-Bo diesel. Some minimal warmth seeped into the compartments, but whatever you did with the star-shaped knob marked HEATING it never made much difference. Water pipes froze, and in the toilets there would be a huge pitcher of water for flushing. As for washing hands with the postage-stamp-sized bars of soap – it wasn't worth bothering.

We would drink from our flasks to warm our insides, but as the journey progressed things would start to get cosier. The heating under the seats kicked in and as it toasted our socks and wafted up our flared trousers, the journey became a treat. More than a treat: as we rocked and rolled through the snow-covered hills, in and out of scary tunnel mouths and over bridges, Derbyshire became a breathtaking experience.

And then the heating would get too much and we'd smell the elastic in our socks burning. One of us would leap up to adjust the HEATING knob – but again it made no difference.

These Manchester trips had started in a rather unexpected way. Jinx had persuaded me to accompany him on a coach trip to see Manchester United one Saturday (I was indifferent to football, but easily swayed). With an hour or so to kill before kick-off, we'd caught the familiar whiff of coal and smoke and it didn't take long to find out where it was coming from – Trafford Park sheds, only a few hundred yards away.

In recent months we'd become distracted by pop music and girls and neglected our trainspotting duties. This trip reawakened us, reminding us of what was still left and how soon it would all be gone for good.

Forget the anorak myth. We were cool guys in 1967, bang up to date with the fashions. I sported a chocolate and cream polo neck sweater and a pair of hipsters with check so loud it wouldn't have disgraced a Yankee tourist in Stratford. True, my shoes were school-issue lace-ups, but even with my paper round I couldn't afford Chelsea boots. I was aware of the mismatch, but considered hip footwear was hardly suitable for scurrying over the accumulated dirt of railway yards. If Jinx wanted to risk splashing his Chelsea boots in a puddle of diesel oil, that was his lookout!

If we had a favourite among the Manchester sheds, it would certainly be Patricroft (9H), if only for the bird's-eye view. There would often be several ways of approaching an MPD – officially, or most often unofficially – but no spotter crossing the footbridge that led from the street could fail to be excited by the smoky panorama. Patricroft was always busy, mostly with workaday freight locos, but it had its excitements too and we often saw Britannias there.

Newton Heath was one of the biggest and busiest sheds. But, in common with many depots at that time, it had a shameful corner – a 'scrap line' where they kept locos not officially withdrawn, but too clapped-out to do any useful work. It was there we found Britannia 70023 *Venus*, cold and lifeless. It had been there some time, apparently. The depot staff didn't seem to care when we clambered up and posed for snapshots in the driver's seat. These knackered express locos were fit only as playthings now. How could this be happening? *Venus* was only 25. Was it possible that only a year ago we'd seen her at Crewe station, sleek and green, a British Railways pin-up girl at the head of a Carlisle express? Even the passengers thought they were getting good value when they saw a beauty like her on their train.

Pop songs, especially of the Sixties, are inextricably tied up in my railway memories. Without them I could never have

1. Spotters enjoy the sunshine at Birmingham New Street, while passengers wait for trains in the station's Stygian shadows.

2. Visiting Stanier 8F 48196 alongside the water column in the shed yard at Burton (16F) in April 1965.

3. An old-style DMU at Birmingham Snow Hill
on 5 March 1967, the last day of its use as a mainline station.

4. My first-ever Bulleid Pacific, Battle of Britain 34057
Biggin Hill at Oxford sheds (81F) in 1965.

5. Andy's dad may have stopped us bunking Crewe sheds that day in 1965, but this photo of 'Scot' 46128 *Lovat Scout* is a cherished memoir.

Walter Parker

Andy Parker

Eileen Dover

6. (*above, top*) On a more 'free-range' visit to Crewe in late 1966, we bunked Crewe South (5B) – where I posed on the front of 'Duck Six' 44525, on the scrap line awaiting its fate.

7. (*above*) An unidentified Britannia in the 'muck hole' – officially the freight avoiding line – alongside Crewe station.

Bill Wright

8. A sign of the times … Crewe North (5A) in December 1965, already looking totally dieselised, the only smoke visible coming from the railwaymen's hut.

Walter Parker

9. An unidentified BR standard runs light engine beneath Crewe's trelliswork of electric wires. Absolute 'railwayness'!

10. My best friend Andy Parker, standing alongside Deltic D9005 *The Prince of Wales's Own Regiment of Yorkshire* at Grantham in 1965.

11. Deltic D9002 *The King's Own Yorkshire Light Infantry* passing through Grantham on a northbound train in 1965.

12. Steam lovers unite! Andy and I at Horninglow station on a wet morning in April 1966, the day the Burton–Tutbury line closed.

MIGHTY
FIRESTONE
MIGHTY SAFE

13. 'Blackie' 44847 crossing over the main Burton–Derby road as it heads for Wetmore Sidings.

14. Western diesel-hydraulics D1031 *Western Rifleman* and Hymek D7004 at Bristol in August 1965.

15. Spotters young and old admire Bulleid 'West Country' Pacific 34018 *Axminster* at Waterloo on 5 May 1966, a year before the end of steam there.

dated all these tales so accurately. 'The Last Time' at Steamer Gates, 'I Feel Free' at the Iron Bridges and 'Ticket to Ride' at Crewe. 'Elusive Butterfly' recalls a trip to Doncaster, and 'Monday Monday' instantly brings Sheffield and Tinsley to mind – even though I went there on a Saturday. Yet what has always mystified me is: where did this music come from? I didn't have a tranny and Radio One had yet to start up. I like to think that the music was in the air, threading through my various adventures like the soundtrack of a film. It's a nice thought, but admittedly impossible. The only explanation I can think of is that I memorised the tunes from *Top of the Pops* or *Two-Way Family Favourites* and hummed them to myself when I got bored. On my first trip to London, in late 1965, I vividly remember standing by the door, wiling away the miles by humming 'Guantanamera' by The Sandpipers, 'Il Silenzio', a mournful trumpet solo by Nini Rosso, and the wishful-thinking 'Almost There' by Andy Williams.

Ten years later, when there were only diesels left, I would sit on a luggage trolley at Taunton or Plymouth, working through a medley of Seventies hits by Cockney Rebel and Typically Tropical and getting mildly tipsy on the diesel fumes that drifted across the platforms. Sixties, Seventies, Eighties … the music has always been there. And whenever one of the old songs is played (usually on Smooth or Gold) I'm immediately back in my trainspotting past, in one particular place, on one particular day, and I can almost smell the smoke or the diesel and hear echoes of tinny platform announcements.

009

Yesterday Has Gone

August 1968: a date etched in our memories. Cupid's Inspiration were in the charts with 'Yesterday Has Gone' – something of a sad synchronicity in the month that steam locos were finally banished from British Railways.

We'd had years to prepare ourselves, but the 1968 Ian Allan *Combined Volume* came as a shock. There was hardly anything *to* combine! My first had been plump and shiny, with that petrolly smell of fresh-printed books. But in the four years since it had shed thousands of numbers. By 1964 they'd already stopped issuing a separate steam book for each region. They all fitted into one, which then got progressively thinner until they stopped that too – after 1967 it would have been a piss-take, no more than a flimsy pamphlet. Even with this 1968 *Combine* they had been forced to pad it out with a twenty-page puff for the rose-tinted future of the railways.

Not that steam fans cared. As far as they were concerned there *was* no future. It wasn't only the darling steam locos that were destined for history's dustbin, but the whole caboodle, our great smoky playground – the wooden signal boxes, sidings, men in denim jackets and greasetop caps, station porters – anything that made a noise or cast shifting shadows. The future railway scene would not be rosy, but eerie and soundless: clanking signals would be replaced by winking lights; countless rattling wagonloads would be transferred to the roads; and even the track was being welded into long continuous strips, so we would lose that evocative diddly-dee, diddly-dee, diddly-dee that had formed the backing track for our exploits.

If the British Railways Board had had any decency they might have let the lads enjoy one last glorious railway summer, six weeks kicking about in the dried grass, drinking pop and sniffing out those last ragged clouds of coal smoke. But the school holidays had hardly started before steam was wiped out. At least the weather was good. If the end had come in winter, the last Blackies and 8-Freights would have slunk off to the scrapyards veiled in drizzle and smog. When it came to it, we had carnival weather and the crowds came out to pay their respects.

Rose Grove, Lostock Hall and Carnforth – these three names are inextricably linked with those final days. For some time already these Lancashire depots had been the last bastions of mainline steam, points in a 'Black Triangle' that had Preston, Blackburn and Lancaster as its corners.

This is where they all came, a steady stream of spotters desperate for a last glimpse. The railwaymen made them welcome: there was no kicking ass, no harsh words about trespass. Visitors were even invited to help out, and happily set to with rags and polish. British Rail may have wanted it over as quickly and quietly as possible – but the shed staff and steam fans were determined to make an occasion of it.

The railway equivalent of the JFK question is: 'Where were you on the last day of steam?' The faithful are able to testify that they were somewhere in Lancashire, visiting the three depots, chasing up rumours of steam workings, snapping every possible photo. Some had been hanging around for months, and there were so many turning up at Carnforth in those last few weeks and days they had difficulty parking their cars.

I know where I was. I wasn't there. And I've always regretted it. It destroys my credibility. I shouldn't even be writing this book, not this chapter anyway. For four years I had chased steam locos around as much as pocket money allowed

– yet I couldn't even make it to Lancashire to attend the wake. How will I explain that to my grandchildren? I'll feel like a soldier too ashamed to admit I didn't fight on D-Day. But it's true: while the diehards were mooning around the sheds at Rose Grove and Carnforth, chasing the last freights up the Calder Valley, I was more interested in attending the youth club disco, eyeing up girls, and shaking my bum to 'Jumpin' Jack Flash'.

If one of the gang had suggested going, then I'm sure we'd all have made the effort. But no one did. Pipsqueak was too proud: he would have hated to see 8-Freights and Blackies limping from one humble duty to another, leaking steam, covered with a blistered rash of limescale that no one could be bothered to clean off. Andy seemed more into football at the time and had ambitions of managing his own team of juniors …

There might have been another, more sombre reason for our absence. Earlier that summer, Jinx's mum and dad had been killed in a car crash. A tragedy that had thrown a shadow over us, especially Andy and me, because we'd been round at Jinx's house swigging his dad's beer and bopping to the Dansette when the police called. That it was a tragedy for Jinx goes without saying, yet it made us all feel vulnerable. Part of trainspotting was the coming home at night to security and a hot meal, clearing the table and sitting down to do the paper-work. Kids take their parents for granted. I loved my mum and the idea of her not being there was too awful to think about. The event had destroyed our worry-free childhood world, made us newly timid, a little less adventurous.

So how can I write about '68 with any authority? Maybe I can't – but steam's final days are part of railway mythology, so well-documented in words and pictures, in film and sound recordings, that everyone knows the story.

I doubt if I was the only one who didn't go. Old spotters

are like old soldiers – they all claim a share of the glory and it would be hard to disprove them now. But if everyone who said they were there had actually been there, the county of Lancashire would have sunk down two inches, like a smoky Venice.

Arguments have raged ever since about whether the end of steam was necessary. To spotters and socialists it had the smell of a political fix. While hippies had been high on pot, the establishment was high on modernisation, and they'd had a vision: a wonderful future full of high-rises, supermarkets and comprehensive schools. British Rail had invented InterCity, painted all its carriages blue and white and put whole trainloads of freight into one container. Steam engines had no place in this utopia; they were too dirty and clunky and emitted embarrassing smells. Yet some of these steam locos were barely ten years old (the last built as late as 1960), and might have lasted another fifty, even a hundred years. Getting rid of them was a shocking waste. Even the diehards accepted that steam engines had to go one day – but not this way, so hastily and with such disgraceful lack of gratitude. Britain's wealth owed much to the invention of the steam engine and its century and a half of loyal service, but at the end of the day loyalty counted for nothing.

Dr Beeching – a name even now accompanied by an oath – had chopped the railways by a third and if he'd had his way there'd have been none west of Plymouth or north of Edinburgh. The scale of the change can be gauged from the fact that 20,000 steam engines were replaced by a mere 5,000 diesels and electrics.

There's even a domino theory, that the end of steam marked the end of our industrial society. Without the railways to supply, the strength of the coal industry was considerably weakened. The railwaymen and the miners had always stood shoulder to shoulder, but that symbiosis had gone. Shunters and dockers were dead against containerisation – but they got it anyway!

The weekend of 11 August 1968 saw the famous '15-Guinea Special', hauled from Merseyside to Carlisle and back by a couple of Blackies and the one remaining Britannia, 70013 *Oliver Cromwell*. It cost £15.75 – about two weeks' wages then – for the privilege of travelling on the last-ever steam-hauled train. British Railways were going to milk tearful trainspotters for their last penny. There was no shortage of takers. I suspect that the thousands who stood at the lineside and watched it go by had a better view. The vision may have lasted only a few seconds, yet it was all the more poignant for that, more dignified than actually being on the train, fighting for a window space.

For me, steam had lasted only four short years. It had seemed such a long time, and in a way it was – a quarter of my life then. And yet, emotionally, spiritually, it's always seemed more like the whole. I still have recurring dreams. I'm back in the Sixties (or steam has been revived for some reason), walking across a bridge when I hear a whistle. I jump up to see over – and it's all there: the whole of my childhood, all my summer holiday viewing pasted onto a long and vivid frieze – an Ozzie rattling past with a coal train, a Blackie coupling up to a trainload of mixed wagons, a faithful little Jinty shunting in the sidings. I've had this dream in various forms, on and off, for forty-odd years. I once plucked up the courage to tell Andy Parker about these sentimental visions, and to my surprise he confessed that he had them too.

Carnforth was also famous as the location for one of the smokiest and moodiest of railway films, *Brief Encounter*. It's hard to believe, looking round there today, that this tale was possible and believable – all that passion, betrayal and eroticism, the whisper of steam, the rhythmic beat of pistons and the thunder of the non-stop express that brought with it a hint of *petit mort*. That happened here?

Much is made of the eroticism of motor cars, but it's tacky phallic symbolism. The railways could never offer that, but they have certainly provided the setting for romance and eroticism over the years. Could a brief encounter still happen at Paddington or Birmingham New Street? There's no Beryl at Carnforth to serve our star-crossed lovers with tea and penny buns today. But the world keeps turning and the sweet Polish girl behind the counter in Costa Coffee knows many secrets, even if the ones glued to their mobiles see nothing at all.

010

Barry: Graveyard of Steam

The steam age had its elephants' graveyard in South Wales, in the Barry Docks scrapyard of Woodham Brothers. It was an eerie, windswept place. On sidings overgrown by grass, pot-holed by dirty orange puddles, stood row upon row of dead and rusting steam engines waiting for the cutter's flame. Not just a few but over 200 of them, parked up buffer to buffer. There were no privileges here. 'Battle of Britain' Pacifics and Great Western Kings shared the same fate as humble freight shunters. With the smokebox doors yawning, you could see their guts were all the same. It was heartbreaking to see them for what they really were – just scrap boilers cluttered with limescaled pipes.

Not that Barry was the only place. Britain was full of scrapyards – Cashmores near Tipton, Birds of Bridgend, Wards in Sheffield. Business had been booming. Many times over the last five years, looking out from a train, I would see one or two derelict locos on a siding. Pilgrims went to these places even then, picking their way through a ferric shambles – wheels, axles, buffers, bit of whistle, piston rods, cylinders and, hopefully, a cabside with a number just discernible. In the 1980s P.B. Hands began to catalogue the slaughter: these booklets were the parish registers of the steam age, an archive where spotters could make a desperate search for their loved ones, read about their earlier lives, their withdrawal and places of death.

For nearly two decades, from 1968 until well into the 1980s, when it was finally emptied and closed down, Dai Woodham's scrapyard was an essential pilgrimage for those mourning the glories of steam. Not that there was any glory here; it was as joyless as any cemetery. Many steam fans kept well away: better to stay at home with your memories, your slides and a few beers to cry into. Why on earth would you want to go to that awful place? they demanded. Without the living tapestry of railway life as a backdrop, these engines were just scrap metal. Better to get them cut up quickly, anything but this lingering shame …

But we had to go and have a look. For one thing, Barry had engines which we'd never been lucky enough to see in action. Like the Kings, withdrawn before I even began spotting. It was a form of necrophilia, I suppose, but I still wanted to cop them. In years to come my grandchildren might say: 'You saw the Great Western Kings, didn't you, Grandpa?' And there'd be no need to add they had been orange with rust at the time, flaking like cream crackers. I'd not only seen them, I'd say, I'd been up on the footplate – but I wouldn't mention the bird's nest in the chimney and the dog shit on the footplate. (How had that dog got up there anyway? It will be forever a mystery.)

The 1968/69 period marked a watershed. Steam had gone and with it a large part of childhood. We'd become cocky sixteen year-olds, our thoughts of girls and illicit boozing as much as railways. But trainspotting wasn't something you could throw aside like a game you'd got bored with. It had got into our bloodstream. Even if we were no longer so obsessed with collecting numbers, there were other things we could do, grown-up things, like paying homage to our past.

Six of us went on that 1969 trip to Barry. A pilgrimage, maybe, but that didn't stop us messing about. Like most teenagers, we were often cruel and thoughtless to each other. But we always played fair and used a rota system. Today it was Andy's turn to be tormented. While he was in the loo we knotted the toggles of his parka to the string luggage rack – a trick he only discovered as our train drew into Cardiff station, where we had to change for the bog unit down to Barry.

'You twats!' he screamed, desperately fumbling with the knots while we leaped out onto the platform.

Before he had time to undo them all, the guard was waving his green flag to send the train on to Swansea. Hearing the whistle, Andy flung the window open and shrieked.

'Emergency … stop the train!'

The guard blew twice to alert the driver. It was turning into a major incident now. Everyone stopped to see what was happening, anticipating some tragic spectacle – a heart attack perhaps, or someone's leg trapped twixt train and platform – so they were annoyed and disappointed when Andy stepped off, red-faced and furious, with his coat. By now we'd stopped laughing, having been collared by the guard who told us that holding up trains was a very serious matter.

The atmosphere on the local DMU to Barry got a bit nasty. It wasn't just the luggage-rack trick that Andy was wound up about – he suspected Jinx of stirring up mischief and division. I ought to have expected some trouble: Andy and Jinx had never been best buddies. Andy supported Leeds and Jinx Man United; Andy liked Traffic and Atomic Rooster, Jinx liked the Hollies and Elvis Presley. It was a volatile chemistry. With as much care as a society host, I'd always made sure that my different friends were kept in separate compartments, so I'd been uneasy when so many people expressed an interest in the Barry trip. Two or three was the optimum number. Six people would have been anarchic at the best of times – with arch-rivals in the mix it was asking for trouble …

Once at Barry we sobered up a bit. This was no place for bickering. Now and again, stumbling along iron-sided gullies between locos, dodging the orange puddles, we came face to face with other spotters. But there was no bonhomie, just a courteous nod and a typically British shuffling past each other, avoiding glances. This was a weird landscape, painted every imaginable shade of decay. Some of what we saw was disgusting: strange formations of fungi and rust, the cancerous growths that had taken down our lovely steamers.

Climbing up on the footplate, we could sit in the driver's seat (if it hadn't been nicked for a souvenir), our hands on the controls. But when you looked through the shattered windows the illusion vanished: what you saw wasn't the road for Waterloo or the right-away signal from Snow Hill – just those rows of dead engines. This was the reality: no more damp steamy days like those we'd known, no long summer holidays at the lineside swigging pop and seeing who could spit out their chewing gum and kick it right over the tracks all in one go.

A kind of demob fever took hold of us. Let loose in this rusting playground we could do whatever we wanted: climb up on onto the cab roofs and walk along the top of the boiler, stick our heads down a chimney and shout four-letter words into a loco's iron belly. Was this any way to behave? It was hard to imagine that chaps from the Railway Correspondence and Travel Society would act so wild. But maybe we'd spent so long in awe of the railways, been told off and chased off so many times, this was our way of getting our own back.

We weren't to know, but as things turned out, we needn't have been in such a rush to get here. Dai Woodham, the amiable scrap dealer who'd bought all these locos and corralled them here, had no idea that he would end up as the patron saint of steam preservation. He'd bought these wrecks to make money out of. If his men had got to work with their blow-torches straight away, as intended, the whole lot would have been gone within a year and Britain would never have had the working steam heritage it has today. But he had decided to cut up the wagons first …

Spotters were able to carry on with their pilgrimages for another twenty years. Amazingly, only a handful of the 215 steam locos at Barry were scrapped – the rest were sold off to some hastily-convened band of preservationists or a millionaire railway enthusiast. For years we were bombarded by appeals, from the 4247 Preservation Society, the Stanier 42968 Fund, the MN Appeal, and scores of others. Penny by penny, decimal coin by decimal coin, cheque by cheque, these ad hoc societies scraped up enough to save their precious engines from the bite of the oxy-acetylene. Penny by penny is about right too, since it took some of them twenty years to save up enough.

It wasn't just a matter of towing away a crippled engine. There were spirits in that wasteland – dead drivers and lost boys – and they couldn't be abandoned. We had to guide them back towards the light. The last of the wrecks didn't leave Barry until 1988, but it's as if they knew they'd be rescued one day, that their friends would never let them down. Rescued, reboilered, re-engined, repainted, every one is now in steam somewhere, spanking new and better looked after than ever. We can congratulate ourselves that, between us, with a quarter century's loose change, we've saved so much of the steam age in working order.

On the way back to Burton, as Andy grumpily hid himself behind a football paper, one of us put a match to it, forcing him to leap up and shove the flaming sheets through the window. For all we cared, this prank could have scarred him for life, turning him into some disfigured Phantom of the Platform, haunting stations with his spotting book and sandwich bag, his face hidden by a pulled down woolly hat.

We had some great fun on our trips. Yet when I look back at the railway magazines that I read in those days, I'm dismayed by their lack of humour. Not that anyone read *Railway World* for a laugh, but the language always seemed so formal and correct. The most remarkable thing is that the word 'train-spotting' was rarely mentioned. These magazines had loftier ideals, hence the emphasis on historical study, locomotive performance and timetabling. They couldn't quite shake off the tradition that railways were something for Edwardian gentlemen to dabble in (and after all, the magazines had their origins a good half a century before trainspotting was invented).

Not that there was any lack of loco information for the trainspotter, but it tended to be presented in a matter-of-fact way, without comment or irony. Lads like us bought the magazines for the pictures and the info on withdrawals and reallocations, but they didn't talk our language and their learned articles, however carefully researched, were rarely read by us or any other spotters we knew – we just weren't interested in long-winded technical waffle about 'LBSCR Train Services of 1905' and suchlike.

This refusal to acknowledge the average trainspotter as a real person is worth remarking on. Ian Allan's *Locoshed Directory* gave directions to every railway depot in the country. It was a 'bunker's bible' and every roving spotter had one in his pocket. It had been produced with bunkers in mind and profited well from their pocket money – yet it had to go through the motions and stress that the book in no way sanctioned any trespassing or shed visits. As if it had been produced for purely academic purposes!

This formality and denial was in inverse proportion to the real-life fun involved in spotting. Since Ian Allan had already been in trouble for encouraging trespassing and vandalism, he had to tread a thin line between giving schoolboys what they wanted and being accused of incitement to trespass. He had to keep in with both factions; not an enviable position.

The reminiscences in today's *Steam World* tend to prove my theory, with all kinds of petty crimes and reckless antics coming to light: but the passage of time has given them a *Just*

William quaintness. It also lends support to my assertion that the trainspotting of the Fifties and Sixties was much more light-hearted than it is today.

Back home in Burton I got out the steam books I thought I'd never use again and began to mark off what I'd seen in Barry. There were lots of cops: Castles and Halls from the Western, Battle of Britains and Merchant Navys from the Southern. I sat down with my ruler and lined them off, but couldn't feel the same joy I'd always felt before. It felt more like a duty that had to be done, that was all – my final audit of the steam age.

THE SEVENTIES

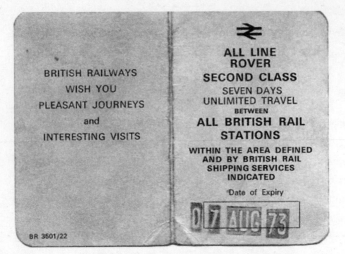

BRITISH RAILWAYS
WISH YOU
PLEASANT JOURNEYS
and
INTERESTING VISITS

≠

ALL LINE
ROVER
SECOND CLASS
SEVEN DAYS
UNLIMITED TRAVEL
BETWEEN
ALL BRITISH RAIL
STATIONS
WITHIN THE AREA DEFINED
AND BY BRITISH RAIL
SHIPPING SERVICES
INDICATED

Date of Expiry

0 7 AUG 73

BR 3601/22

BRITISH RAILWAYS BOARD

SECOND CLASS   N° 3363

FROM   0 1 AUG 73

TO   0 7 AUG 73

AVAILABLE BY TIMETABLE,
RELIEF AND ADVERTISED EXCURSION TRAINS
between
ALL STATIONS
on
BRITISH RAILWAYS

also by
BRITISH RAIL SHIPPING SERVICES
to the ISLE of WIGHT and on LAKE WINDERMERE
and by
THE CALEDONIAN STEAM PACKET CO. LTD.
between the CLYDE COAST PIERS and LOCH LOMOND PIERS
also on the
TILBURY/GRAVESEND, KYLE of LOCHALSH/KYLEAKIN
and HUMBER FERRIES

NOT AVAILABLE by Continental Boat and Ocean Liner Trains or
by services operated by London Transport

The usual supplements are payable on Pullman and
Observation Cars

Issued subject to the Conditions and Regulations in the Boards
Publications and Notices.

Name of Holder   A Whitaker

NOT TRANSFERABLE

An Itinerary of Despair: Our All-Line Rover, 1973

For Andy and me, the All-Line Rover of 1973 turned out to be our last trip as trainspotting buddies. It was an inspired but crazy idea, born out of the desperation of our last teenage summer. I had turned twenty that January, but Andy was still nineteen. We were both working – me in a crummy factory, Andy in the Parks Department of Burton Town Hall – but we spent most evenings together, cruising the town's pubs and chip shops in Andy's battered Escort van. 1973 was proving a remarkable year for music – *Dark Side of the Moon*, *Cosmic Wheels*, *Six Wives of Henry VIII* – and the sublime *Tubular Bells*, which seemed to thread those mellow days like a silver ribbon.

The planning took weeks. Each of the British Rail regions issued a separate timetable, so we had to buy them all before we could even make a start. If we were going to get our money's worth, every trip had to be carefully planned, with no time wasted going along the same routes twice. The word 'itinerary' cropped up an awful lot: one of us had found it in *Roget's Thesaurus* and it gave our jaunt extra gravitas.

We didn't want to waste a minute of our time, which is why we took the 00.49 Burton–Bristol, the first train out of town. The last time we'd set off on a spotting trip, Burton station had been a grand Victorian building, proud with filigree and importance, coiled around with the thick brown aroma of history. But someone didn't like the smell – so they knocked it down and replaced it with a Lego kit. How could this be the same place where we'd had so much fun? The long platforms with so many important doors opening off – Station Master,

Porters, Parcels Office – and the waiting room with the big oval table and coal fire – all gone now. And in its place a horrid brick square, a refrigerator of a waiting room with an electric fire rigged to provide exactly thirty seconds of heat before switching itself off. The new station had an air of meanness about it and no fine words about modernisation could dispel that view.

Across from the southbound platform lay the sausage and pie factory, a place where 'dead of night' had a horribly literal meaning for the truckloads of pigs who'd just arrived. Their panicked squeals echoed in the dark, a distasteful start to any holiday. But once on our way we soon forgot it …

> A star has followed our train to Bristol
> Playing peek-a-boo behind trees and houses
> Before dawn's early light
> Puts it back in the wizard's hat

I can't really believe I wrote that in my notebook, and I only include it now in the name of frankness. The early Seventies were still tinted with hippy ideals; we'd been corrupted by Tolkien and grown men were often heard talking about elves, ents and dwarves. Perhaps, secretly, we saw ourselves as brave Hobbits setting off on a quest. We were still trainspotting – I have the numbers written down – but there seemed to be another more spiritual dimension to our odyssey.

Neither of us said as much, but I think we both suspected this would be our last railway trip together. Adulthood had caught up with a vengeance. Andy had just split up with his girlfriend. Fussy about his women, he thought he'd hit the jackpot when he met Lynn. With crinkled hippy hair and a love of books and poetry, she was the girl he'd been searching for all his life. Now she'd slipped from his grasp and he was deeply depressed. To make it worse, I was on a high. A married woman (all of nineteen years old) had told me only that day that she was madly in love with me. For the first time in my life I was on a genuine promise – even if I had to wait until the end of our holiday to take her up on it.

As our train rattled through the night, I stared out at the shadows and the colour signals which blinked from green back to red as we passed. Whoever coined all that stuff about love and hearts had been way off course: it was the guts where it hurt most. Andy was trying to lose himself in *Watership Down*, the latest tome (we called all books tomes just then) for hippy types. But my mood must have annoyed him.

'What the heck's up with you? We're supposed to be on holiday …'

I was bursting to tell someone.

'I've just met this girl. Well, I didn't meet her exactly, I knew her already. She fancies me rotten. Can't keep her hands off me.'

'Oh yeah?' Andy had heard enough of my tales before. 'Who is it then?'

'Jean.'

'Jean! She's bloody married. What are you playing at? Colin'll slay you.'

I repeated everything Jean had told me: about how boring her husband was, how he left her on her own too often, how unromantic he was. But Andy didn't give a hoot. It was immoral.

'You're playing with fire,' he warned.

'It's a good job I've got a sturdy poker then!'

It seemed, sometimes, as if Andy hated to see me happy. The trip had got off to a bad start.

After a couple of beers and a fitful doze, we arrived in Bristol around half past four, just as the sun started to gleam through the clouds over Temple Meads. The station was busy with parcels and newspaper trains. Bristol was one of the few stations with an all-night buffet and it attracted an exotic mix of nutters, oddballs, winos, insomniacs, kids recovering from all-night parties. And trainspotters.

Our first stop after that was Weston-Super-Mare. It was still barely seven o'clock and we'd envisaged a quiet stroll on a deserted beach before the plebs arrived. Instead we were greeted by an even worse sight – a banana-yellow bulldozer and bin-men stuffing ice-cream wrappers and empty Lilt tins into black bin bags. Disgusted, muttering about the end of the world, we hurried back to the station and jumped on a westbound train which took us through Devon and on into Cornwall. At Liskeard we changed for a two-coach bog unit, which squirrelled down the exquisitely quaint branch line to Looe.

The bickering started up again. I'd been content to bring a small khaki knapsack with a spare T-shirt and Y-fronts, my notebooks and a packet of fags, but Andy had brought a huge steel-framed contraption. It was proving a constant source of embarrassment: every time we got on or off a train he'd be knocking the spectacles off a pensioner's nose, poking a toddler in the eye or, even more dangerously, sliding one of the protruding poles against the buttocks of some hard-faced labourer.

At Looe, we dived into a harbourside pub and with our luggage stowed safely out of harm's way, had a shandy and a ploughman's. Tiredness had caught up with us and after a quick look around, we lay on a grassy bank near the station and managed to catch a couple of hours' sleep.

Back at Liskeard, we connected with the Cornish Riviera Express and arrived in Penzance just after six. We parked our stuff in the Left Luggage office, and followed our noses to the nearest chip shop. Hurrying back along the beach with our hot parcels, we spread them out within view of St Michael's Mount. Our fish 'n' chip supper was a paragon of its kind, good fresh cod and fluffy chips stained with vinegar – all washed down with Strongbow cider. I have some snaps of us on the beach there. We don't match anyone's idea of trainspotters, that's for sure. Our hair is long and unkempt and we're sitting with fags dangling, surrounded by empty cider bottles. We look like tramps, or stragglers from a hippy convoy of old buses. Today we'd certainly be questioned by police, our claim to be trainspotters met with a sneer, our protests met with a jolt from a Taser …

At 21.30 we were on our way again, hauled by 1041 *Western Princess* over the 325 miles to Paddington. We had the compartment to ourselves as far as Plymouth. Some chap came in then and I had to make room, but still managed a good six hours of kip.

We snatched a so-called 'Continental' breakfast at Liverpool Street, and boarded the train to Norwich. After ticking off the cathedral, we looped back to London via Ely and Cambridge, thus taking in, at a fairly leisurely pace, two cathedrals and a university in a few hours. My cultural notes for Norwich and Cambridge read 'Plenty of nice chicks around' and 'LOADS of chicks!' It's so sad to think that most are now nearing retirement age …

We had supper in the King's Cross buffet. A steak and kidney pie would be nice, I thought, but as I picked it up from the foil tray, the bottom bulged and burst, splashing me with gravy. I put it back in the tray and fetched a plastic fork. It had been a hot day, and stayed warm right into the evening. The bar of chocolate I'd bought for afters was so melted that it dropped gobbets of brown onto my trousers as soon as I unwrapped the silver paper. I looked like I'd fallen into a cesspit. In the end it had to be crisps, good old Golden Wonder, always a reliable standby.

Those were the days when you could get from London to Aberdeen without having to fork out for a sleeper. But let's not get carried away with the hobo romanticism: it could just as often be hell. This 20.00 King's Cross to Aberdeen should have been an epic voyage, but it turned out like a club outing for all our most-hated travelling bugbears – nattering women, bawling babies, drunken soldiers playing cards in the gangways. We had seats, at least, but how could we sleep?

We didn't. Staring out of the window, we wished death and dumbness on the lot of them. But fatigue caught up with us and by Newcastle we were barely awake.

'Newcastle,' I said to Andy. 'Where's the Tyne?'

'Twenty to twelve,' he said, glancing groggily at his watch before slipping back into a stupor. I soon followed him, my head cradled on the table. We woke to find the carriage quiet and half empty, but by then we were almost in Aberdeen. We carried on napping on the connecting DMU to Inverness. I'd wanted to see Scotland so much … and here we were just sleeping through it all!

Andy's constant harping on about the glories of nature started to get on my nerves. We couldn't pass a pine tree or a duck pond without some comment about how lucky we were to be alive. I knew he was just trying to distract himself from being jilted, but I'd rather he got mad and kicked cats or chucked lightbulbs out of the window – anything but the 'pawns of a higher destiny' crap. To avoid being his nodding dog, I deliberately took up a contrary stance, pooh-poohing the rural idyll and thinking up a defence for every factory and eyesore we passed. To me it was a revival of our old LNER vs. GWR rivalry, a fun way to pass the time – but Andy took it seriously and despised me for my flippancy.

But the rows were soon forgotten when we reached Inverness. This was intended to be the highlight of our trip – the train to the Kyle of Lochalsh, a sedate 30mph trip along what was considered the most scenic line in Britain. It had the whole package: hills purple with heather, sky-scraping pines, streams of liquid silver, majestic stags, and isolated stations where no one got on or off. Andy was overjoyed, and I eased off with the wind-ups. I was still half asleep, so the scenery passed like a pleasant dream, all blues, greens and silvers flickering across my eyelids. At Achnasheen we had to stop for a while, unable to continue until a train came the other way, this being one of the few places where they could cross. The station stood in the middle of nowhere, and beyond all was stillness and wilderness.

We'd gone the whole day without trainspotting. There'd been a shunter and a handful of BRCW Type 2 diesels in the sheds at Inverness, but that was all. The Type 2s were Scotland's 'maids of all work' and we had D5316 chuntering away at the head of our train.

And there, at the end the line, the Isle of Skye. We got off the train and straight onto the small ferry for the five-minute crossing. The rain was coming down in sheets, so we took shelter in a solitary phone box and tried to smoke damp cigarettes. When the rain cleared, we headed off along the beach, clambering over slippery boulders and peering into rock pools, gasping at the size of the crabs. I had to admit, Nature was pretty wonderful, and pretty pretty too.

On the way back to Inverness we were joined at our table by two angry Glaswegians. They'd been hoping to get home from the southern end of Skye, crossing to Oban for a train to Glasgow. But they'd missed the boat, literally, and had to hitch-hike to Kyleakin and catch this train, to get home via Inverness. It seemed like a reasonable Plan B – except they hadn't got any tickets. They had been able to afford a bottle of whisky each, and with drunken generosity they urged us to have a tot. We sipped, not wanting to offend but anxious not to exchange spittle with them.

'What will you do when the ticket inspector comes?' I asked one of them.

'I'll fucking slay the bastard,' he growled, and he rained a torrent of karate blows on the table to make his point. The whisky bottle danced dangerously and his friend made a grab to stop it from falling.

And here came the ticket inspector now, good-naturedly clipping the tickets offered to him by the honest passengers. Should I warn him that Bruce Lee was on an awayday? The Glaswegian glared at him.

'This is ma fucking homeland, man, and no guy's telling me I can't go where I please. One word of Sassenach law and I'm going to put him in a coffin.'

Andy wanted us to move to another seat, but this was just the kind of thing I wanted, to sit and talk with nutters and thugs, not simper about mountains and lochs. Still, I hoped the man was joking. I wasn't sure what I'd do if things got rough. At the same time I had this mad idea that if I somehow saved the hapless inspector from a slaying I'd be lionised in the press and rewarded by British Rail with a go-anywhere ticket for the rest of my days.

I watched the ticket inspector get nearer. One of the men got up and headed for the toilets. The angry one suddenly came over all dopey and dropped into a dead sleep, head on the table. We watched in horror as the inspector shook and poked him, convinced that the Jock would leap up and snap the poor man's neck with his horny fist, or smash his lovely British Rail hat with the whisky bottle. But the man's coma seemed so deep and genuine that waking him was impossible.

'He's been drinking,' I said helpfully.

The inspector shrugged and moved on. I expected the Scot to wake up straight away, but he slept the rest of the way to Inverness.

We treated ourselves to a supper of pie 'n' chips and pints of Tartan, then mooched around the station until it was time to board the 23.45 overnight to Glasgow. Our two Scottish pals came weaving down the platform, shouting and singing, but luckily they didn't see us. Andy and I were looking forward to getting some sleep, but this train too seemed to be full of bickering Glaswegians and we heard a couple in the next compartment threatening to kill each other, but not before they'd listed all the relatives who were to blame for everything.

'Ya drunken git, I am telling ya, if ya dad looks at our Gina again like that I'll stick him wi his own breadknife.'

Glasgow Queen Street – Carlisle – London – Portsmouth – Brighton – London – Swansea – Reading – Exeter – the station signs passed our window in a blur. When we got back to Burton we'd be boasting that we'd been to all these places, but we'd have precious few details as proof.

I did my best to cheer Andy up with a 'plenty of fish' pep talk. There were dozens of nice hippy chicks at Burton's 76 Club, I reminded him; he'd soon find a replacement for Lynn. But he didn't want to know. He was also increasingly irritated by my expectant smirk, which got harder to suppress whenever I thought ahead to the treats in store after we got back to Burton.

On 'Day Five' we were back in Devon again. Not the sunny Devon of clotted cream teas but the more sinister county famed for pirates and smugglers. As we approached Dawlish, the rain came slamming in off the sea, splotching against the windows and leaving salt crystals stuck to the glass. But we stuck to our plan to get off, and recklessly walked out onto the breakwater, ending up so sodden and bedraggled that the layered soles on my shoes began to peel off one by one. There was no way of fixing them, and if I hadn't had a pair of plimsolls in my rucksack I'd have been stuck.

This was the pits, the lower depths of friendship. The six years of trainspotting camaraderie were well forgotten. We were lovesick, unwashed, hungry, tired, and hated each other's guts. If we'd had the cash or the credit cards we might have stopped off at a B&B, had a bath and a meal and a good sleep and started afresh. As it was, trains could go to hell – we just wanted to get home and sort out all our problems …

But despite the tiffs it had been a memorable trip, and worth writing about. We'd both kept diaries, and I set about sending off accounts to newspapers and magazines. I was utterly naive about the ways of journalism and thought talent was enough to get me published, so I felt hurt when they rejected my 5,000-word travelogues. Slowly I learned the value of conciseness, and after each rejection I got less hurt and did more cutting, until I had whittled down the whole odyssey into 800 words, which I finally managed to sell to *The Observer*.

012

A Highland Fling: Women and Trainspotting

Railway excursions, once a part of British life, are virtually extinct. The idea seems as old-fashioned as charabancs and bobbies in helmets. Yet we still had them up until the 1980s. The Merrymakers (named when marketing men still had a British sense of humour, or had just returned from the pub) ran from the Midlands every weekend. As well as seaside trips and the 'London shoppers' they offered a variety of high-brow choices – Haworth for the Brontë Museum, Canterbury for the cathedral, Edinburgh for the festival. But it wasn't only normal people the Merrymakers appealed to: they were perfect for trainspotters who wanted to go a long way on the cheap …

Scotland tantalised us. Burton spotters were lucky enough to see locos from Bristol, London and East Anglia, but had next to no chance of seeing anything from Dundee or Aberdeen. If you inspected anyone's spotting books, the yawning gaps were always the Scottish locos. Going Caledonian wasn't a whim but a necessity if you wanted to fill up your *Combine*.

We had bought our Edinburgh tickets back in June. Jinx and Aidie Parker (younger brother of Andy) were using the Merrymaker as a cheap way of doing a Scottish bash – and that had been my intention too. But I had a different set of priorities now and trainspotting was the last thing on my mind. Still, the trip seemed an ideal way of escaping from all the hassle I'd detonated with my extra-marital affair.

Not many husbands would consent to a rival taking their wife to Edinburgh for the day, but I was full of youthful arrogance: Jean and I were in love – why shouldn't we go on a day trip? I had to lie shamefully to get my way, though. Colin had begged me to end the affair, and so I told him I needed time alone with Jean so I could break it off gently. Desperate to have his wife back, he agreed.

Many years afterwards I came to realise how tolerant Colin had been: anyone else with my cheek would have been met by a gang of in-laws after closing time and taught a bloody good lesson.

Colin looked a lot like the stereotype trainspotter – harmless, bespectacled and anoraked – but was, in fact, a model aeroplane nut. His marital strife was all down to this hobby: if he'd spent more time with Jean instead of gluing bits of balsa wood together she probably wouldn't have strayed. How ironic that it was with a trainspotter, even if this one wore a purple hippy jacket and two-tone shoes. To give Colin his due, he was willing to sacrifice his hobby to save his marriage and burnt all his precious planes in the back garden. The neighbours watched with open mouths as the flames licked up from what looked like a scale model of *Apocalypse Now*. It was a great spectacle, and a grand gesture, but a mite too late.

The Edinburgh Merrymaker departed at five on the Saturday morning. Colin came to the station with us, in the forlorn hope that Jean might give him a farewell peck. (A peck with a machete, I thought more likely.) He waved as the train pulled out, but Jean ignored him, gazing out of the opposite window and feigning interest in the coal depot. I felt awkward and guilty, so I waved him a cheery farewell. He was about to flash two fingers in reply, but Jean turned and he just managed to change his clenched fist to a wave.

While Jinx and Aidie jumped around the compartment to catch loco numbers en route, Jean and I sat and cuddled, relishing our time together. We didn't care about Colin – we'd forgotten him already – but felt self-conscious in front of Jinx and Aidie. To be fair, they took it quite well. It had been meant as a boys-only trainspotting jaunt after all: no one was expected to turn up with a woman. It just wasn't the done thing. Not that they'd have been rude, and if they weren't exactly allies, at least they hadn't turned snooty and censorious on me like Andy had. But our lovey-dovey moves obviously made them uncomfortable. It was partly guilt. What if Jinx's wife had found out? Wives may well put up with their menfolk going off trainspotting, but only on the understanding there are no women around!

In thirty years of trainspotting, I've come across very few female trainspotters. The only one I recall clearly was at Crewe in 1965 – a pre-pubescent tomboy dressed in jeans and patched school blazer. With her sexless figure and the patina of smoke and chocolate that smeared her unkissed face, she blended well into that male territory. There may have been some mild teasing from other lads, but not much, because her brother looked like a mean bugger. In any case, she knew her stuff and had a spotting book with an enviable score of Scots, Jubilees and Britannias underlined. I remember being allowed to look briefly and feeling madly jealous. She came from some backside part of Liverpool, so it was natural for her to have all those top-class locos whistling by at the bottom of her terraced street.

The trip was long and arduous, even for seasoned spotters, and sleep had crept up on us all before we got to Newcastle. By the time we arrived at Edinburgh Waverley station, the four of us had managed to get ourselves tangled in an indecent knot, legs akimbo, clothes disarranged. I opened my eyes to find one of my trainspotting chums getting an eyeful of Jean's legs.

Tumbling out onto the platform along with a motley collection of shoppers, festival-goers and trainspotters, we adjusted our clothes and arranged to meet up at teatime. Glad as I was to have time alone with Jean, I couldn't help feeling envious of Jinx and Aidie as they set off to bunk the sheds at

Haymarket. We'd come such a long way and I might never get such a golden opportunity. The Brush 4 diesels, since re-dubbed Class 47s, were the most common diesels on British Rail – 510 of them – an all-purpose workhorse found every-where from Penzance to Inverness. After ten years' diligent spotting, I needed only eight – and five of those were Scottish, shedded at Haymarket.

I'm sure if I'd suggested a bunk of Haymarket sheds to Jean she'd have agreed – anything would have been romantic just then. But how could I think of exploiting her loyalty like that? And it would have been unfair on Jinx and Aidie: they must have been glad to stop being gooseberries. From the looks Aidie had been giving us, it must have sounded as gross as slugs mating in a cracked saucer.

One of the sub-plots of the trainspotter myth is his failure with women, made worse by the lack of female trainspot-ters. While modern women take charge in the boardroom or form their own rugby teams, none have yet demanded acceptance in the world of trainspotting. Alone at the end of the platform, notebook in hand, the trainspotter ploughs a lonely furrow. Any who haven't got a girlfriend already are in a difficult spot. Dating agencies are one answer. Dateline are regular advertisers in the railway magazines (but to be fair, wherever there are men there is always a market, and most hobby magazines are good territory). These are men who know all about diesel transmissions and modern signalling, so they have faith in technology. Why rely on stupid Cupid in the age of the microchip? They fill in their questionnaires with great confidence. But if finding them a date melts the motherboard, they can always send off for introductions to 'Attractive Filipino Ladies'. Grateful to escape Third World poverty and willing to please, who better to trail behind hubby carrying the camera tripod and the Tupperware box full of sandwiches?

In 1993 there was an almighty rumpus when the *Sunday Times* 'Culture' section ran a cover feature entitled 'Trainspotters – A National Joke?' It touched a raw nerve among the fraternity and they protested fiercely against yet another re-run of the same tired jokes. What hurt the most was the accusation that trainspotters – dullards of the first degree – could never hope to attract a girlfriend.

In the deluge of protest letters, much was made of wives and girlfriends. One Lancashire spotter even claimed to have half of the local hospital nurses in his harem. Lack of girlfriends? I get my 'exercise' with a staff nurse from Blackburn and a casualty sister from Manchester! A trifle exaggerated perhaps, but no more so than the jibe that provoked it. A one-off joke made sometime in the mid-Eighties had been filed away for use by any lazy journalist. Now that the *Sunday Times* had put its weight behind the joke, what hope was there? It had become part of our folklore.

The weather in Edinburgh was perfect and, for a few hours, we managed to pretend that the world loved us as it should. By six o'clock we had assembled at Waverley for the train home. Jean was tired and had nodded off in my arms by the time we reached Carlisle, leaving me to be the gooseberry as Jinx and Aidie compared notes. I looked on as they slapped their plastic rulers across the shiny pages of their *ABC*s and underlined their cops. I asked Jinx for a glance at his book and my gasp of annoyance made Jean jump. They'd seen four of the five Haymarket 47s that I needed! They thought this highly amusing: that would serve me right for deserting the brotherhood for the sake of a bit of nookie …

We got back to Burton about half past midnight to find Colin waiting for us on the platform. I'd totally forgotten about my promise to let Jean down gently, but he'd been expecting to find his wife in tears, all ready to return to happy domesticity. Seeing this was not the case, he flashed me an evil look. He grabbed his wife's arm and marched off with her. I didn't even know if I would see her again.

I walked back from the station with Jinx and Aidie, but I still felt like a bit of a pariah. If only I'd had the simple pleasure of going home to mark off my numbers.

013

Whoa! I'm Going to Lostwithiel

1974 had been a year of self-pitying solitude, and 1975 didn't look as if it would be any better. Jean had long gone back to her husband – we'd never stood a chance against the combined forces of in-laws, do-gooders and nosy neighbours – and even after a year I was still upset. Andy, in the meantime, had patched things up with Lynn and they'd nested down in a small flat above a handbag shop.

I spent all my wages on Penguin Modern Classics, but Sartre, Camus and Herman Hesse were hardly the chaps to cheer me up. I felt like Steppenwolf and 'the Outsider' rolled into one, with a dose of Sartre's nausea thrown in to keep my nose up against life's cracked toilet bowl. I prayed for someone to knock on the door – just like Jinx did one day in May – and ask me if I fancied a trainspotting jaunt. Good old Jinx! He'd stood by me when the chips were down, offering Jean and me sanctuary from small-town gossips, covering for us when necessary. I owed him for that, and happily agreed to join him on a Western Region railrover in the summer.

Popping out to stock up on notebooks and pens, I had a renewed spring in my step. Back home I put away all the miserable existentialist crap and sat down with the latest *Railway Magazine* to try to catch up on what I'd been missing. Mum, for one, was pleased to see the old me resurface.

Jinx's loyalty to the railways had never wavered. The end of steam hadn't bothered him that much and he found plenty of interest in Seventies diesels. Not only that, he was on the team now, with a job as a guard, a proper railwayman's hat and a whistle. My sights were set on a life in London, but I couldn't help feeling some envy. Sitting in a guard's van sounded like my ideal job – frowsting by the coal stove in winter, contemplating life from the end balcony in summer. And the job came with that ultimate perk for trainspotters – cut-price or free rail travel. If I hadn't had a bee in my bonnet about 'making it' in London then I'd probably have been quite happy as a guard.

It looked like being a great summer! 'Whoa! I'm going to Barbados' sang Typically Tropical – and it felt like the right thing to be doing, heading west again to see some of those lovely Western Region hydraulics while they were still around.

It had been only seven years since the end of steam, yet some of our favourite diesels were now under threat too. Diesels had been intended as a stop-gap between steam and nationwide electrification. Many had been built in a rush, some hardly more than prototypes, barely tested in the rigours of everyday service. British Railways had commissioned dozens of classes, some successful, others far from it, some loved by the drivers, others loathed for their temperament. The Westerns and the Warships were good runners, but being diesel-hydraulic rather than diesel-electric made them non-standard, so that many railwaymen hadn't got a clue about how to drive them or service them. Consequently these locos never made it into the grand British Rail scheme. Other diesels did survive, even into the next millennium – a testament to their good design, but also highlighting British Rail's ongoing struggle to find finance for its electrification programme.

When we set off on the 00.49 on the Friday night I felt as if I was beginning a new life, and it didn't take long for the humour to return. Sometimes – with hapless passengers yanking the communication cord because they'd got the wrong train, or buffet staff telling us off for stirring our teas too fast – the railways seemed like a 24-hour comedy routine. We had a whole week's trainspotting laughter to look forward to.

The Warships had all gone by 1972, some of them only ten years old when withdrawn, and the last half dozen Hymeks went just a few months before the start of our rover. The Westerns had survived remarkably intact, but were gradually being usurped by Class 50s transferred from the London Midland. They were as boring as vacuum cleaners by comparison (hence the nickname Hoovers). Jinx hated them and cursed 'shit English Electric' whenever one came along, especially when he'd spent ten minutes setting up his tripod and camera in the hope of a Western. I refused to get riled. I was there for the Westerns, true, but I could find my pleasure just as easily with the incidentals, smoking a meditative cigarette at Starcross, drinking a cuppa in the buffet at Exeter, or marking up my books while sitting in the sun on a Cornish station shaded by yellowed palm trees.

Our trip from Exeter to Barnstaple behind Bo-Bo 25219 took us along a sadly neglected route (since rebranded as the Tarka Line in an attempt to attract more passengers). For me, perversely, the dereliction was part of the charm. A summer shower had wet the old stations and they smelled of rust and rotten wood. Two decades previously, when these stations had been full of life, children from Bristol and London would have been peering through the train window, impatient for the woodland to disappear and the horizon to broaden out as it does when the sea lies sparkling over the next hill.

I boasted to people that my railway trips made me into an observer and chronicler of life, that alongside the numbers in my notebooks I made pithy comments of all aspects of British culture. 'Barnstaple – scruffy brown dog chasing plastic carrier bag. Plymouth – had a cup of tea. Exeter – man asleep on seat. Newquay – cup of tea and digestive biscuit. Cardiff – Bounty and orange Fanta.' I even jotted down snatches of conversation too. Cockney lad: 'They've got to move the train cos it's too long for the platform.' Posh woman with hairdo: 'If I can't get a sleep I shall go in the first class …' The oddest thing is, I can remember all these people quite clearly.

Further west, after a trip down the Gunnislake branch, we paused for lunch. Despite the self-incriminating evidence in my notebooks, a trainspotter's life wasn't all Kit-Kats and BR tea. We were capable of modest attempts at self-catering. A small sliced Hovis and a pack of cheese slices will provide sandwiches as easily as shuffling cards. I'd given up on flasks, though. You set off with good intentions and a warming pint of cream of chicken soup, but it calls for self-discipline – washing it out thoroughly, asking for a refill at a station buffet, swilling it out again. I'd never got past that first step and ended up carrying the empty flask around all week. Tightly sealed, stewing in its warm bacteria-rich fumes, that remaining spoonful of chicken soup soon turned itself into a salmonella time-bomb. A week later, when the flask was opened, the mould sprang out like a magician's bouquet.

In some ways this trip was a reprise of the one we should have made in 1968. It wasn't the last steamers we were chasing this time, but the last hydraulics. I had at least seen all the Warships and now I needed only four more Westerns for the set. Steam or diesel, the urgency was the same. The chase was the thing, the mission to record an endangered species before it went for good. This time, though, we were more involved, old enough to appreciate the occasion, and solvent enough to afford all the chasing up and down between Penzance and Paddington. Yet for all that, we remained totally powerless. Nothing could halt the march of progress. 1968 came and went, and there wasn't much we could do about the Westerns either, which would all be gone in a couple of years.

I'd always wanted to make the ferry trip across the River Exe, from Starcross to Exmouth. I just liked the name. Starcross had a mythical sound to it, the kind of place elves lived. We sat in the sunshine to wait for the ferry while the holiday trains clattered alongside the mudflats, a blur of happy pink faces and summer colours moving above our heads.

Jinx and I were unanimous about our affection for Warships and Westerns; there was no dissent, no argument. It made for a quiet life, but if I was totally honest, I missed all the LNER–GWR rivalry and the teasing about each other's love lives that I'd shared with Andy Parker.

Jinx had been married for three years by then, but his wife was tolerant of his trainspotting urge. It didn't cost him any money, so she could hardly attack him with the standard (and justified) complaint of many wives: that hubby was squandering money better spent decorating the kitchen.

There was another thing I wasn't happy about. Unnoticed by me, British Rail had gone and changed all its loco numbers. The new system, TOPS, was supposed to make life easier for everyone. Some of it appeared logical enough – Deltic 9001 became 55001 and 8100 became 20100 – but much seemed random and baffling to me: 9000 became 55022 (because the primitive computers of the time couldn't recognise 55000), 1783 became 47301 and 5536 became 31118. It made me very uneasy. How could I be sure it was all bona fide, that the renumbering hadn't been massaged or cocked-up? I might be chasing numbers, unaware that I'd really seen them before, thinking an engine was a cop when it wasn't. It seemed dangerous to me, like meddling with the holy code, force-feeding the digits of the computer age into the ramshackle homeliness of the railways. They hadn't bothered renumbering the Westerns though, because they weren't going to be around long enough to take part in the computer-age railway.

Regional railrovers like our Western one, while limited in scope, had a lot of advantages. With a smaller area to cover, we had time to take it easy and look properly at passing scenery. Unlike the All-Line Rover I'd been on with Andy, we didn't feel we had to see every inch of Britain in seven days and make ourselves sick doing it.

I'd been to many of these Western places before, but Jinx and I broke some new ground, like the three branch lines to Fishguard, Pembroke and Milford Haven in west Wales. We didn't expect to see many locos this far west, apart from the occasional shunter and a Brush with a trainload of oil tanks. But it wasn't really locos we were after, merely the status of having covered these remote lines, not so much branches as twiglets.

Despite boasting an overnight sleeper service to Paddington, Milford Haven turned out to be little more than a halt, no bigger than the old Horninglow. It had no comforts to offer, not even a drinks machine. The single luggage trolley was chained to a drainpipe and looked as if it hadn't been used for ten years. Anyone tugging at it would probably snap the rusty drainpipe and bring down the rest of the station on top of it all. Yet I liked forgotten corners like this and always thought of Buggleskelly in the film *Oh, Mr Porter!*

A couple of sedative pints in the pub across the road set us up for a pleasant overnight kip to Paddington. The train consisted of two sleepers and three ordinary coaches. We had a compartment to ourselves and everything seemed set fair – until we arrived at Swansea, and 300 people off the Cork ferry tried to cram in alongside us. It's the worst thing, that awful moment when you're woken from a pleasant doze by a load of strangers and — smiling, of course, in that English way — you know you've now got to sit up all the way to your destination. Even if you manage to get any sleep your head will be lolling, swinging around like Linda Blair's in *The Exorcist*, before you wake up with a jolt, dribbling, everyone else smirking at your embarrassment.

Why did I still pretend this was a 'holiday', when so many of my old schoolmates were jetting off and spending two weeks relaxing in Greece or Spain? How could I argue that tea and crisps in the Swindon buffet was in any way comparable to cocktails by the pool?

Two nights later, in a similar situation on an overnight to Paddington, we baled out at Exeter St David's and bedded down in a small waiting room on platform 2. It was about as big as a garden shed. But no one disturbed us and, despite the hard wooden benches, we managed to get some sleep before catching a London-bound train the next morning. My back was killing me. Even at the tender age of 22 I was already thinking that I was getting too old for these nocturnal adventures. Still, unlike my ill-fated railrover with Andy, at least Jinx and I had managed to see this one through to its conclusion.

I haven't been on a railrover in Britain since 1975. These trips of 1973 and 1975 would be impossible to repeat now – not least because there are scarcely any overnight trains left. There are posh sleepers to and from Scotland, and one to Cornwall, but none of those meandering, unhurried trains. It's one more part of railway life that's changed out of all recognition to us old-time bashers. Twenty years ago the railways still had a night-life. Insomniacs and wide-awake children who lived by the railway could still sit by their windows and see the yellow-lit compartments and the dark outlines of passengers. Spotters could still find plenty to occupy them at places like Bristol, Leeds or Manchester, and there were plenty of trains they could doss down on. It wasn't just the major routes: there were all kinds of eccentric overnight workings, mail and parcels trains with a couple of carriages tacked on behind just in case. As recently as 1980 you could travel overnight from York to Aberystwyth, via Huddersfield and Manchester, arriving at 7.00am, or go west-to-east on the night train from Manchester to Cleethorpes, arriving at the awful washed-out hour of 5.00am.

The overnight trains have gone, and with them much of

the railways' mystery and sense of adventure. Sure, waiting around for them could often be cold and uncomfortable, but those midnight stations had a definite magic: the deserted platforms, the ticking clock with its burping springs, the sudden rush of a three-tank milk train, the red and green signal lights, the boxes of flowers to be delivered to London by dawn, the mailbags dragged along the platform like murder victims to be disposed of …

Lying flat out on the dusty seats, there was something comforting in the lingering smells from years gone by: mackintoshes and newspapers, cigarettes and orange peel. The old sound of wheels on a railway track still has much in common with the ticking of clocks or the sound of steady rain; it slips in with the rhythms of the body, a syncopated slow-burning jazz session that lulls you to sleep, to dream of travelling ghosts.

014

King's Cross Solitaire

In 1975 I got a lowly clerical job in the Department of Trade and went off to live in London. One Saturday in September, my mum stood at the window and watched me go, dressed in a new blue suit, lugging my suitcase to the station for what must have been the saddest train journey of my life. She'd seen me off for the station so many, many times in the past ten years, but this time I didn't have Dairylea sandwiches and I wouldn't be home at teatime with a book full of numbers to sort out.

Newly-installed in a hostel for young civil servants in Highbury, I felt lost and homesick. Everyone else seemed to be pals already, and I was too shy to speak up and join in. The options for socialising were stark: games of snooker or ping-pong, sitting in a smoke-filled TV room, or getting drunk at The Cock. None of these appealed.

Feeling lonesome, I naturally turned to the trains. Every evening, after a dinner of chicken supreme or mince stew, I left the others to their ping-pong and pub crawls and took the Victoria line one stop down to King's Cross. At the end of platform 8 with fag and notebook I felt at home. The Deltics still had charge of the Scottish expresses and I remembered the thrills as they'd roared through Grantham. That was partly why I found King's Cross such a comfort: it connected me to home, not just physically – knowing I could always jump on a train and escape – but spiritually too. Alone in a city of eight million people, just another lone figure on a London station, I could still reach out and touch the green paintwork of the same Deltic that had thrilled me as a kid.

I wasn't totally alone. Like most hobbies, trainspotting has an underlying social function, offering all kinds of people an excuse to talk. Not that I'd ever been a chatterbox, but I wouldn't ignore anyone if they talked to me. There was always someone who wanted to know what loco had been on the 7.30 to Leeds, or whether any Scottish-based Brush had been sighted, and I was happy to provide answers. But I resisted any further plays for friendship; even a simple drink in the buffet might lead to all kinds of complications. I could tell that some of these people were lonely – but while I rather enjoyed my solitude, others wore their loneliness like a torn badge.

I remember one who scared me, a quietly-spoken middle-aged man with smelly breath. He'd latched on to me, persisting with all kinds of questions, and I was getting bored, wishing him away but scared to move myself in case he followed me. I was just plucking up the courage to be rude to him when I happened to glance at the trainspotting book he was holding. It was totally blank except for three diesel shunters. That rang alarm bells and I felt I was in the presence of somebody quite deranged.

From the suburban platforms on the west side, I watched the last commuters of the day heading back to the dormitory towns of Hertfordshire. I no longer bothered taking 'bog unit' numbers, but I was fascinated by this twilight exodus from the city. And jealous. Bathed in the yellow light of their carriages, they were all going home to their neat suburban houses, their pretty wives and cuddlesome children. It made me awfully homesick. My inner feelings can be guessed from this snippet of an unfinished novel which I recently found scribbled in the back of my spotting book:

Mark sat in the buffet at King's Cross station with a pint of bitter and a half full pack of cigarettes. A cartridge player was churning out pop music. Mark spent many of his evenings at King's Cross, primarily to watch the trains, a joy since childhood, but also because it was a comforting haven, an easy reference point in London, a city of 8 million assorted egos.

After the eight o'clock had departed for Aberdeen (the same train Andy and I had been on just two years previously) I made my way back to the hostel, stopping off for egg fried rice from the Chinese takeaway at Highbury Corner. Back in my room I sat on my bed and gobbled it quickly with the plastic fork. Since food wasn't allowed, I had the choice of opening the window and freezing, or risking discovery because of the smell. The warden had a room just along the corridor and had a nose like a beagle.

Being ever the dutiful son, I rang Mum every other night – but I didn't tell her about my evenings at King's Cross. There'd been a TV programme about runaways and the seedy sexual nightlife centred around the station. I'd never seen anything untoward, but to avoid worrying her I told her I went to Paddington, as if that was somehow more respectable.

Being whisked away by a gay press-gang seemed highly improbable, but what did scare me was the thought of being blown to bits by the IRA. The mid-Seventies were a nervy time, and even when the bombs weren't real we had lots of false alarms: at least once a week my trainspotting seemed to be disrupted by an order to evacuate the station. The world of railways seemed not so safe any more: I could be happily jotting down numbers one moment and simply ceasing to exist the next.

Everyone had the jitters and when I went to the Deltics' home depot at Finsbury Park one evening I got short shrift from the Cockney foreman who nabbed me.

'How do I know you're a bloody trainspotter?' he challenged. 'You could be a bloody IRA terrorist for all I know.'

He was right, of course, and couldn't be blamed for being vigilant – though I refrained from pointing out that he'd hardly be ticking me off if I was a real terrorist. After years of carefree trespass on the railways it came as a shock to realise that my harmless hobby could be liable to misinterpretation. I felt it was a slur – as if I'd ever do anything except simply walk round and jot down numbers.

In retrospect I suppose I should count myself lucky not to have been jumped on by the Special Branch and given a good kicking.

This enduring fascination with stations helped keep me loyal to the railways when I eventually stopped collecting train numbers a couple of years after this King's Cross period. However indifferent people have become to trains, anyone with a smidgin of poetry in their soul can't fail to be fascinated by the comings and goings of a railway station. Or am I just dealing in clichés? I know that was the case for me: all the years I'd been a trainspotter, I'd always felt I saw something my mates didn't. The railways had a transport function, of course, but they had a poetic function too. It's this poetry that no politicians or marketing men have succeeded in killing off or privatising.

A few years later, I finally got myself a job with British Rail. It may have been a humble clerical post – in the Traveller's Fare offices at King's Cross – but it meant precious travel concessions. Like Jinx, I'd soon be able to travel to Inverness for a couple of quid or shoot off to Poland to get a last whiff of steam. That was the theory anyway.

This vital part of BR's catering operation was housed in a crumbling slum at the back of King's Cross station, in a corner notorious for its drug addicts, prostitutes and inner-city decay. What had once been a bustling railway quarter full of parcels offices and railwaymen's houses had become a windswept rat-run. Grass grew through the pavement and the downstairs door of our offices bore the boot-prints of down-and-outs who'd tried to break in for a kip in the hallway.

The job entailed collating the dockets from the dining cars and checking them off against the cheques and credit card slips. Besides me, there were two other clerks: Moira, a moody girl from Newcastle, and Myra, an old biddy who wore cardigans and had a stick through her greying bun. The similarity in names didn't help much: every time I called to one, I always got the other. It led to a lot of irritation on all sides.

Our boss was a gentlemanly Indian from Bombay who proudly considered himself anglicised, but I couldn't understand a word he said. He'd had to go through the job routine twice with me, but at the end I was none the wiser and I never did quite twig it. The offices were grim and Dickensian, a century away from the gas-powered chairs and ergonomic desks of the modern scene. The desks we worked on were wooden, scratched and stained by decades of ink blots. I couldn't help but be fascinated by the ownerless trilby on the stand: Myra said it had belonged to a previous employee who had jumped under a tube train in 1971 and they were all too superstitious to touch it.

Bored silly, I was prone to daydreams that even Billy Liar would find embarrassing. Even a luncheon bill could set my imagination off. I made up little conversations in my head, whole scripts even for murder mysteries which I would type up that evening and send off to the BBC the next day.

BILL: I'll get this, Fred. (He gets up from the table.) Must visit the little boy's room.
FRED: If this Vienna deal's going to go through, Tom, we'd better make sure McGinty doesn't talk.
TOM: He won't, Fred. I'll make sure of that.

I don't know whether my mouth moved as I made up these *Murder on the 5.15* screenplays, but I often looked up to find

Moira giving me some very strange looks. Moira looked at me quite a lot, if the truth were told: sometimes in a mooning sort of way, which I thought might be lovesickness, but other times it looked more like pure contempt. But being young and male I couldn't fail to notice her charms. Unlike Myra, in her old cardigans smelling of Mothax, Moira had the desk nearest to the electric fire and wore blouses thin enough to show her lacy bra. All in all we seemed to spend a lot of time looking at each other, then looking away when caught out.

In the end, I decided she did fancy me and resolved to take a chance …

The next evening I caught her at the bus stop after work. She was glad of my company: a couple of days previously she'd been kerb-crawled by a creep in a Cortina. She'd been seething about it all week: couldn't a girl wear nice clothes without some perv getting the wrong idea? I made sympathetic noises and tried to crank up my courage before her bus came.

'We could nip in the pub for a drink,' I suggested, knowing quite well we'd have a stiff walk before we found a decent pub around King's Cross.

'I've got to get back. I've got to wash my hair. And *Coronation Street*'s on tonight.'

'You don't need to wash it. It looks lovely as it is.'

Moira looked at me pityingly, curling a finger round a lock of hair and letting it go as if in disgust. 'It's awful.'

A friend had once told me that compliments always worked, but he hadn't given me Plan B, what to do when the compliments were rejected out of hand. Moira's disappointment was tangible: what kind of boyfriend would I make if I couldn't tell when a girl was fed up with her hair?

Moira was one of those people who always seemed to live in the most obscure parts of London – Palmers Green or Walthamstow or Dulwich. They thought they lived in London, but they were always too worried about getting home to have any fun. If I'd had a car I could have given her a lift and I'd have been halfway there with her. As it was I had only my wits to rely on.

'You could always come back to Belsize Park,' I said.

She thought for a while. 'That's miles away. What about me getting home?'

'You can stay over. Not so far to travel in the morning then.'

That tore it! My clumsy suggestion that intimacy might take place obviously shocked her. Spoiled by the easy morality that prevailed in Belsize Park, I naturally assumed that everyone was dying for it. Moira may have been making sheep's eyes at me, she may not, but she was happy to share her bus stop with me and be persuaded. But I'd blown it. She wanted flowers and candlelit meals, not a bedsit one-nighter in NW3.

I dreaded going in the next day. From the dirty looks as soon as I walked in it was obvious that Moira had told Myra about my clumsy advances. The kerb-crawler had been knocked from No. 1 spot in the pervs' gallery by the sex-mad clerk. I kept expecting Myra to whip the stick out of her hair and stab me, but she contented herself with ignoring me when tea was made.

The atmosphere festered. Unable to face their silent reproof and the sheer boredom of the job, I jacked it in and went back on the dole. If I'd had a hat I might have left it behind as a memento, but I have a feeling that Moira would have taken it off the peg and chucked it in the bin.

015

Trans Europ Express: Paris, 1975

Anyone who sets store by poets or holiday brochures would probably choose springtime for their first visit to Paris. But when I received a surprise tax rebate in my wages one Friday in late November, I knew I had to take a chance. There was no planning: I just walked round to Liverpool Street station in my lunch hour and slapped down twenty quid for a big white ticket to Europe.

That same evening I was at Victoria, queueing for the overnight ferry service via Dunkirk. My fellow passengers had sensible rucksacks bright with souvenir badges or suitcases with squeaky wheels, but my only luggage was an Argos carrier bag containing an *Evening Standard*, a Topic and a packet of Embassy. If I looked eccentric I was happily unaware of it.

It was my first visit to Victoria and I'd always imagined that this 'gateway to the continent' would be a grand place. In fact, it looked dreary and suburban. Like many, I had a romantic idea that crossing to France would mean the Golden Arrow and Wagons-Lits sleeper carriages. But back then, twenty-odd years before Eurostar, the boat trains to Dover were the same common bog units used by commuters, two or three of them coupled together, rarely swept, often unheated, no refreshments – nothing to mark them out as special at all. But if there were banana skins in the ashtrays and dirty newspapers on the floor, I didn't care. The adventure blinded me to the grubbiness, and to the dreary suburbs through which the train rattled on its way to the coast.

It wasn't until I was on board the ferry that I remembered – Mum had no idea where I was. She'd have had a fit if she'd seen me. In my haste to get going, I hadn't given much thought about what to wear and all I had on was a thin maroon jacket, not much protection from the freezing mists that swirled around the boat. 'Daft as a brush,' she would have said. Mum might have had a point, but in those days when I still smoked, the glow of a cigarette was enough to make me feel warm. The boat train may have been a disappointment, but this was exactly how I had imagined the crossing: leaning on the deck-rail as a lighthouse beam swept across the lapping waters, watching the smudge of French coastline getting nearer and ever clearer. At last, the mists blew aside like torn net curtains, revealing what looked at first like dinosaur skeletons but turned out to be the dockside cranes of Dunkirk.

Off the ferry and through customs, I scurried down echoing corridors to the station, eager for my first sight of French railways, determined to get a good seat. Dappled by greasy shadows from the docks, the carriages that stood waiting for us were drab green and austere. There was no Flèche d'Or this end either. But as I walked the low platform to see what engine would be pulling us, the carriage signboards – 'Dunkerque–Lille–Arras–Paris' – worked their magic on me. I muttered these foreign place names to myself, like a mantra, excited and nervous of the promised adventure. That was the great attraction of travel: the dangers, the risks, the novelty – why did it matter if the train was clean or not?

I found a compartment and sat there shivering, with no idea when the train might depart. A faint breath came from the under-seat heater but hardly enough to make things cosy. Still, as a trainspotter, I accepted these rigours as par for the course. What did I expect, a Pullman armchair and a brass light to read the FT by? With the same old touchstones – sliding door, luggage rack, squeaky seat arms – I felt perfectly safe, cossetted in my natural environment. So I felt secure enough to stretch myself out on the slippery brown seat and slip into unconsciousness, dozing my way as far as the Parisian suburbs.

I'd never seen French people *en masse* before, so it came as a shock when the train jerked to a halt at a suburban station – St Denis, I think – and I woke to see miserable commuters lining the platform and staring straight at me. Wiping the dribble from my mouth, I ducked down out of sight until the train moved on. I had half a mind to let sleep claim me again, but no, I couldn't miss leaning out of the window for my first views of Paris. The suburbs of cities have always fascinated me, the way that houses, shops and factories start to congregate alongside the tracks, sparsely at first, then accumulating and jostling for space, spreading sideways, backwards and upwards until suddenly there's a full-blown city there, honking and smoggy, decorated by giant billboards.

Minutes later I stepped down from the train at Gare du Nord. Walking down the platform, I was full of it, like Sinatra in one of those American musicals. 'My kinda town, Paris is …' My Argos carrier bag didn't matter here: to the natives it must have looked foreign and chic. I skipped down the steps to the Metro and made straight for the map of lines, quickly sussing out how it all worked and which line I needed. Hovering by the ticket window, I watched to see what everyone else did and how much they paid – then I walked up and followed suit, slapping down five francs and scooping up the change. This was all part of trainspotting pride, this rapid assimilation of knowledge and the ease of picking up a routine.

It's easy to get caught out, though. When the Metro train came in I waited for the doors to open with a hiss and a bang, just as they did in London. I waited and waited, until the Parisians behind me exploded impatiently and barged past me to flick the door handle. Another lesson learned.

I loved the Metro. The cream and blue carriages had rubber tyres, so things seemed clean and quiet after London's grubby Northern Line. It wasn't just the trains, but the whole ambience: the bready smell, the warning hooters, the sad Africans with their lazy brooms. What charmed me most were the posters. Instead of far-fetched promises like 'Your firm will love moving to Peterborough ...' there were naked women luxuriating in perfumed soap bubbles. You couldn't smell the lather, yet you knew it was gorgeous and sensual. Even the housewives advertising frozen peas looked chic and sexy. The Paris Metro was an erotic wonderland!

With so much travelling behind me I considered myself worldly-wise, but I was often caught on the hop. Convinced that Rue Montmartre station was the one for Montmartre, it was a blow to my confidence when I came up the steps into an anonymous-looking street that I knew straight away was not the famous bohemian quarter. Still, I was happy enough to wander at random. I tried out my French on an old woman in a tobacco kiosk, but she gave me a baffled glare and then started shouting. To get myself a packet of Marlboro I had to resort to pointing like a toddler in a tantrum. I held out my hand for the change – *un faux pas très grand!!* – and with another curse she banged the francs and centimes down in a saucer.

I hadn't gone to Paris for the trainspotting (would anyone be such a dullard!) and started off with the best intentions, walking the scrunchy paths of the Tuileries, clocking the Eiffel Tower, pacing the rooms of the Musée d'Art Moderne – yet some homing instinct drew me towards the Gare de Lyon.

We collude in the pretence that 'purée de pommes de terre' is tastier than mashed potato, and that 'café au lait' is superior to bog-standard coffee, but why should the Gare de Lyon be any more exciting than King's Cross or Paddington? Why romanticise it because of its foreign name? But the Gare de Lyon *was* different. I stood at one of the nodal points of

Europe here, and every clattering of the indicator boards signalled adventure. Le Mistral, Le Capitole, Puerto del Sol, not to mention what was left of the Orient Express – this was where all those grand expresses left from. You could get on a train here and alight in a land of fezes and minarets.

Even the commuter trains looked different. Instead of Sharons and Tracys gum-chewing their way through *The Sun*, the grey electric units were full of bright-eyed Parisian girls reading Gallimard paperbacks.

I didn't bother to write down any of the loco numbers (without the French equivalent of an Ian Allan *Combine* in which to mark them off, they'd have been meaningless to me) but I couldn't resist wandering along to the far end of the platform to take some souvenir snapshots. Some of the French locos were as drab and utilitarian as drain covers, but others were more exotic. I loved the silver-and-orange electric ones. With their angled front ends they looked like sprinters poised at the blocks, ready for the starting pistol and a graceful dash down to Avignon.

The drivers eyed me warily. I didn't think the French would be as paranoid about trainspotters as the Soviets notoriously were, but decided not to push my luck. After my feeble attempt to buy Marlboro, how on earth would I explain trainspotting to a bunch of cynical French *flics*?

The Gare de Lyon wasn't the only place I visited. I was into Jean-Paul Sartre's *The Age of Reason* at the time, the opening sentence of which read: 'Halfway down the Rue Vercingetorix, a tall man seized Mathieu by the arm …' Like any daft tourist I wanted to go and see the street for myself. Nearly four decades had passed since Sartre had written those words and I found the street half-derelict, full of empty houses and boarded-up shops, a real let-down. I thought of asking someone to take a souvenir shot of me, but the few people I saw hanging about looked more likely to run off with my camera and pawn it for a Pernod.

The novel also said: 'A railway engine whistled and Mathieu thought "I'm getting old."' That meant there had to be railways close by – the line out from the Gare Montparnasse, I guessed. Turning the corner, I found myself by a bridge, next to a goods depot where a sage-green BB loco shunted wagons up and down. The Gare de Lyon was grand and exciting, but busy and public too, lacking in privacy. But this was just the kind of spot I could have made my own – a Parisian Wetmore Sidings!

After ten minutes watching railway stuff, I came to my senses. I hadn't come to the City of Light to look at trains. Worse, I was probably a trespasser. I could end up in the 14th arrondissement clink. Even here, I found trainspotting stuck in my head, not something I could leave behind at Dover.

I quickly reoriented myself and got back on the tourist trail: Notre Dame, the Louvre. By early evening, I was back at the Gare du Nord with plenty of time for beer and a station hot dog before getting my train back to England. I'd managed to get myself coffee and croissants, beer and hot dogs – all of which were easy enough to pronounce – but the Marlboro confusion had dented my confidence and I felt too timid to try booking in to a hotel. It had been little more than a day trip, really, but I'd broken the hold of Britain, the first of our old trainspotting gang to do so. From then on the whole of Europe lay at my feet. I would be Trans Europ Express Man, whizzing from København to München (it had to be the authentic spellings), smoking international brands and humming Abba's greatest hits …

016

Commuting: Just a Way of Getting From A to B

I've never been a proper nine-to-five sort of commuter, but during the mid-Seventies I found myself travelling by train so often that railways came close to losing their charm. Every Friday I caught the 4.10 from Euston to spend the weekend in Burton. I had a great time – Friday nights at the 76 Club, Saturdays mooching in town – and Mum's Sunday lunch, of course, especially welcome after a week of hostel fare.

But I hated the Monday mornings: up at 6.00, fighting for a seat on the 7.18 from New Street with an army of Brummie businessmen. They thought they were early birds, but to me they looked more like Christmas turkeys. Yes, I could sneer at them, with their identical ties and shirts and their panic to find a seat. But my laughter had a hollow edge – why should I think myself any different?

What I disliked most was not the routine, but the crowds. We don't like each other much *en masse*, if the truth's told. We'd all like four seats and a table to ourselves, then we could take off our shoes, pick our ears and noses, sing songs without feeling stupid. Nostalgia merchants will go on about the Golden Age of rail travel, sharing compartments, talking to each other, enduring delays with stoical Blitz spirit. There may be an element of truth in it, but that was just our British reserve – we hated the smell of each other's lives really. What everyone yearned for all that time was the freedom that cars would eventually bring.

These businessmen had no time for chatting anyway: they were preoccupied with finding ways to look important. Mobile phones and laptops are favourites now, but back then things were more modest. The snap of locks on a briefcase, the click of a Parker biro, ticks and scribbles on a document – these simple gestures were enough to mark you as a vital cog in British commerce. I always wondered just what all these papers were. Top-secret MOD files are always turning up in skips or being left on the Tube, but those businessmen never left any evidence behind. Perhaps it's for the best: I'd have been most disappointed to find out that those documents were nothing more than paperclip sales by region or the marketing strategy for a new vacuum cleaner bag.

Faced with all this self-importance (though I could never take Brummie businessmen completely seriously) I felt self-conscious about trainspotting. I no longer had a valid excuse. I wasn't a kid any more, beardless and eager and safely ignored. Whenever I looked up from jotting down a number or two on the edge of my newspaper, people smirked and looked away. Or was it just paranoia? Was it really a smirk, or perhaps a smile of recognition, a secret signal that he was part of the brotherhood? A man who could tell an 86 from an 87, a 33 from a 45? I didn't dare take the risk: to start talking to strangers about trains might have marked me as a kind of nutter.

Having to hide my interest was perhaps a first step in letting things slide, intimidated by public opinion. On my own, I'd have enjoyed myself and my observations; instead I sat and pretended I was just another commuter with nothing better to do than read the paper.

To be honest, there wasn't so much to see anyway. I still needed a few of the electric locos on the West Coast main line, but apart from what I saw in the stations at Coventry or Rugby, everything flashed past too quickly – a thump of squashed air against the window, a blur of blue and white livery – and no chance of getting numbers.

Someone had shifted the gears and moved trainspotting into the fast lane. But this speed wasn't there to thrill trainspotters, its purpose was to blur, to marginalise everything between A and B. These trains had windows, but you weren't supposed to be that interested in the outside world: businessmen had better things to do than look at sheep and canal boats.

Things were certainly improving on the railways – but at the same time they were getting less interesting. The new Mk II carriages were comfy and warm, double-glazed and brightly upholstered, but as sterile as a DHSS waiting room. I felt sorry for the men who were trying to catch forty winks in these seats – they'd never been designed for dozers. This was the future, though, designed by committee, democratic open-plan, purpose-designed. The trains were starting to look identical now and so too were many of the passengers.

I missed the past: the seats smelling of dust, luggage racks of knotted string and compartments with curtains and framed pictures. I wanted those long seats I could sprawl out on and those little windows that could be snapped open for a reviving gust of wind.

Why was I being so churlish? That illuminated 'Vacant' sign at the end of the carriage would eliminate wasted journeys to the toilet. True – but did we really want everyone else to know we were going for a wee? Whenever the light went off, people naturally looked up to see who had been in there, wondering if it had been a No. 1 or No. 2. Anyway, all the new technology couldn't stop men losing their aim whenever the train swayed.

Wasn't this what we'd all dreamed about – railway management and trainspotters alike – the train of the future, wired up with shaving-points and a PA system to keep passengers up-to-date?

'This is Coventry. This is Coventry …' Did travellers no longer have eyes? Couldn't anyone see the rather large station just outside the window? British Rail were grooming us for a new railway age … but it meant treating us all like babies.

'Ladies and gentlemen, we will shortly be approaching Rugby. Next stop Rugby …' Was anyone really impressed by an old guy from the steam age self-consciously fiddling with technology? This was supposed to be the future, but it had the stuttering and breathy sound of the past, like when Jinx and I would play rock stars in front of the mirror, hollering 'Paint It Black' or 'Tin Soldier' into a dingy tape-recorder mike with fluff in the grooves.

I always perked up as we passed the loco depot at Willesden in London and even muttered 'Yes!' if I copped anything. The suits were too busy to take any notice of me, getting ready for the race, locking their briefcases, folding newspapers, edging their way down the train. Some made for the nearest door, happy to be first out of their carriage; but a few would make their way right down the train to the very endmost door. Window down, hand on handle, tense and ready to twist – each was desperate to be the first person to step off at Euston. Sad little triumphs. Yet it would be frighteningly easy to become like them. I could see myself all too clearly, just another shop dummy on the escalator as it went deep deep deep into the ground to deliver me to my job in the City.

Was this it then, the end of adventure? Train travel no longer a lark, but just a way of getting from one concrete station to another?

This was all in 1976, but it's not so very different now. Only the faces have changed, and the sad thing is that not all of them have. Some have been shuttling up and down this line for the past twenty years.

One day a guy sat down and plonked a radio-cassette on the table in front of him. They were as big as suitcases in those days, but he'd wired it up so he could listen to his music through heavily padded ear-cooking headphones. The suits from Tipton and Walsall stared as if he was a freak. But not me, I had only admiration. This man, bearded and anoraked, was a herald of the future. If only they could miniaturise that, I thought, they'd be on to a winner. Everyone will want one. Even the suits had James Last and Carpenters tapes they'd rather listen to than read the *Daily Telegraph*.

Sure enough, just five years later, the Sony Walkman arrived. It came as no surprise to me. I've conjured up reams of philosophy during my travels, but that was the only time I'd safely predicted the future.

Strangers on a Train:
The China Clay Special, 1976

Living in London now, I had new friends, new interests. I attended fringe theatres and went to see French films at trendy Islington cinemas. I hadn't seen Jinx for ages, so I was surprised when he got in touch to ask if I wanted to go on a train trip with him. The 'China Clay Special' was a spotters' bash, a twelve-coach train ('408 tons approx' boasted the brochure) hauled from London to Cornwall by one of the last remaining Westerns ('5400 h.p. gross' we were reminded).

These details were important to some people. Trainspotting involves a lot of punter's maths. Here, for instance: how well would a 5,400hp Western cope with a 408-ton train? What would be the optimum speed, and how would that be affected by gradients, signal slows or wet rails? There were a lot of parallels with horseracing. Just as racegoers get excited by the sweat glistening on a panting horse, so trainspotters would get a thrill from the effort of a loco, the growling, throbbing and kicking of those 5,400 theoretical horses under the bonnet.

I wasn't interested in those kind of details. After taking a roundabout route via Bristol, Plymouth and Falmouth, the China Clay Special would visit Newquay, with the promise of a fish 'n' chip lunch. After a year in London I needed a refreshing blast of ozone, so I told Jinx to get me a ticket.

I'd been happy with my job at Companies House, until they said they were transferring me to Cardiff. They even sent me there for a week – a whole week, during which I lived in a B&B

and spent lonesome evenings at Cardiff station, half-heartedly spotting, supping Worthington E and listening to Frampton's 'Show Me the Way' on the buffet jukebox. Cardiff held no charms for me and I refused to relocate. So they transferred me to Millbank Tower, a horrid glassy monolith overlooking the Thames. My office was so high up that the morning mists didn't clear till midday. When they did I could see trains going in and out of Waterloo – but it brought no pleasure: they were so far below I felt I was looking through the wrong end of a telescope. This wasn't much better than those awful factories I'd worked in. In fact Millbank's self-importance made it worse: in the factories you could always have a laugh and stick two fingers up at the bosses; at Millbank such mutinous familiarity would have cost you your career and a black mark in the files of Special Branch.

Jinx was flabbergasted when I turned up to meet him at Paddington. Instead of the regulation rucksack, I had a bulging suitcase. I'd jacked in my job, done a flit from the hostel and was heading home – via Newquay. The China Clay was as good a way as any, and on the return trip I could jump off at Bristol and get a train to Burton. Despite curious glances, no one wanted to know why I had a suitcase on the luggage rack. And if I looked a bit glum, no one remarked on it or tried to cheer me up. They were too excited by the forthcoming trip and I should have known better than to bring along a load of emotional problems to embarrass everyone with.

As we passed Old Oak Common sheds at half past midnight, everyone rushed to the windows for a glimpse of 50s and 31s parked under the floodlights. This was what many wanted to be part of – a 24-hours-a-day man's world – walking the tracks with their lamps swinging, loosening couplings, connecting air-brakes. But I couldn't join in this collective envy of railwaymen. Nor was I in the mood for sticking my head out into a rushing slipstream. I'd got more fussy during my time in London and didn't want to arrive in Cornwall looking like Worzel Gummidge.

Trainspotters' specials are still hugely popular. They come in all shapes and sizes: non-stop runs from Paddington to Penzance; loco endurance tests on the Settle–Carlisle ('Listen to that beast!'); or specially routed excursions which travel via freight lines that no normal passenger ever sees. These trips have been going for decades, pre-dating trainspotting itself, when an interest in railways was a suitable pursuit for educated gentlemen, a history reflected in names like the Stephenson Locomotive Society and the Railway Correspondence and Travel Society.

The China Clay reached Bristol at 2.35. I was just beginning to doze off, but Jinx and the others were in no mood to waste good bashing time. We had an hour's wait, plenty of time for them to fetch tea and Kit-Kats from the buffet, then set up their cameras to take time-exposures of 31s on newspaper trains and natter about old times. Trainspotters are a scattered tribe, but they all get to know each other sooner or later. Most of the passengers were Western Region nuts and had known each other for years, sharing tea and train stories at Taunton, Plymouth and Swindon. As more and more spotters chased fewer and fewer Westerns, they kept ending up in the same places at the same time. The China Clay wasn't just any old trip, it was a club outing and old boys' reunion rolled into one.

Unlike the majority of my fellow travellers, I'd never been interested in the mechanics of trains. Exactly what a diesel-hydraulic was, I hadn't the foggiest, nor any inclination to find out. I didn't know what a torque converter was (a Western had six, apparently) nor did I give a toss that the driving wheels were 3ft 7in as against the Warship's 3ft 3in. It must have made some difference, but I didn't care. I liked Westerns because they were maroon … but that wasn't what I was expected to say. Imagine their faces if I'd chipped in with airy-fairy non-sense about maroon livery caressed by scintillating coastal lights, or ragged clouds of diesel floating above bright-faced holidaymakers. I couldn't understand men who liked the Westerns just because they were diesel-hydraulic, nor could I understand why, as a result, they despised diesel-electrics. But it actually mattered to them and they could keep up fervent conversations with each other about the most obscure details.

TONY: The MD650 does more revs than the 655.
LES: Yes, all that thrashing about's no good.
TONY: Warships have got a 30-ton advantage.
LES: But smaller driving wheels, don't forget.

Was it any wonder I often felt excluded? Not only did I not have a mechanical mind, I certainly didn't have a mechanical soul. Why did it have to matter how things worked? I loved the Westerns and the Warships every bit as much as they did, but they were only interesting as part of the whole: on their own, analysed by spotters with X-ray eyes, stripped down and turned back into blueprints, they were as uninspiring as council dustcarts …

Eventually, after taking an obscure freight line, we arrived in Newquay. Not that anyone cared. Newquay was just the excuse: even trainspotters have an inkling they ought to make an effort to look normal. The beach was out, the prom was slashed by cold drizzle, and we only had an hour anyway … so we grabbed fish and chips, then retreated to the station bar for a beer while we waited for the Western to reverse round to the front of the train.

At the end of one freight branch, the China Clay drew to a halt and we all had to get out. It wasn't compulsory – wives and girlfriends usually stayed behind to chew toffees – but it would have looked odd for me to stay on the train with them.

The women would have made me feel awkward and the men might think I was I trying it on behind their backs or something. So I resigned myself to getting off, feeling oppressed by the pressures of conformity. Even in your leisure time you couldn't escape from it. And so there I stood, in the cold mist, while the rest set up their tripods and took snaps of *Western Fusilier* trundling up and down the sidings. The driver sounded his hooter for the hell of it and each metallic blast was greeted with a loyal cheer.

'Listen to that!' said Jinx.

I couldn't help but listen, since the close-proximity hooting had shaken the wax from my ear.

'Are we getting back on yet?' I asked.

They stared, baffled by my impatience. They were having a whale of a time, but I had realised I no longer had the same commitment. I wasn't a wimp, I'd paid my dues in rain, snow and freezing fog. What was getting to me was the madness of doing it in *en masse*. I felt surrounded by faces lit by a light I couldn't understand any more. I felt like an impostor, a cynical observer at a cult rally.

So why on earth was I here? Unlike many of them, I'd never needed the comfort of an all-male environment. I had no need to beg acceptance with dirty jokes or to display my knowledge of hydraulic transmission. I'd always hated the locker-room mentality – so why had I chosen this most boyish of pastimes in the first place? I had this nightmare: I'd rush along the train, slamming open compartment doors, looking for company, someone to talk to about cinema, theatre, books, anything but trains. But there'd be no one, just trainspotterish faces, grinning and ballooning out at me like a scene from a bad trip.

But I didn't see why I should be elbowed out. Enjoying the railways was a private pleasure, and I did it in my own way. I'd never minded when there were just three or four of us, but this restless mass of railway enthusiasm unnerved me. If I wanted to look hypnotised by the lovely syncopated rhythm of wheels on the track, I wanted to do it without being poked in the ribs by some chap telling me about that night in 1969 when he took a picture of D1037 on a milk train.

I wanted to join in the fun, but there was something troubling me and I couldn't at first work out what. Then it hit me – there were hardly any kids. Apart from two or three ten year-olds out with their dads, the whole twelve-coach train was full of grown-ups. Suddenly, so suddenly, I saw the weirdness of it all and felt out of place. I was the same age as the rest of them – physically – but I didn't feel like one of them at all. It was the *Just William*-ness of trainspotting that had always attracted me: the grime, the sauce, shinning over fences, putting pennies on the line. But these people had grown up and put all that behind them.

Not that I really expected them to act so recklessly now, but what bothered me was the fact that they seemed to have reinvented trainspotting as something much more serious.

The trip back was less joyful. We were in mourning for the Westerns and I suspended my scepticism out of respect. How long would it be before any of us got to see a Western again or heard those Maybach engines echoing over the Devon combes? Who would have thought we'd have been so sad to see diesels go? Here we were, glum and reflective, trying to cheer each other up with stories about sunny days at Exeter and Newton Abbot. They were bloody good engines, people insisted, none more than fifteen years old – why did they have to get rid of them? But they knew the answer already: railways are businesses, not theme parks.

Anyway, the agonies were all part of the spotting game. We knew all along that steam was doomed, and that Warships, Peaks and Deltics would one day follow them to the scrapyard. Everything ended up as paperclips in the end. This is the elegiac end of things, the bit that some trainspotters find so hard to put into words.

They all pretended to be sad. But no one shed real tears. When the China Clay Special was finished and *Western Fusilier* gave them all a farewell hoot, Jinx and the rest of them simply went home and filed their slides of the occasion and looked around for another class to bash.

018

Fare-dodging

I've always loved St Pancras for its style, but trainspotting-wise it was always something of a dead loss. Admittedly it gave sanctuary to the Peak diesels in the Sixties and Seventies, but those days are over and Panky's all about Eurostar now. That lofty roof that we all love so much was built to resound to the bark of steam trains and the phlegmy growl of diesels. Midland Mainline has its 125s to Derby, Sheffield and Nottingham, but they're nothing to shout about either, even if they do have a fan club boasting a membership of 850!

Still, St Pancras is the station I always choose when travelling home to the Midlands. Never Euston, not if I can help it! Of all London's stations St Pancras has the most relaxed and homely feel. Despite the arrival of Eurostar, the shopping mall and the champagne bar, it has managed to cater for the 21st century without sacrificing too much of its Victorian charm.

There's a story that an American tourist once wandered into this wedding cake of a station in the belief that it was Westminster Cathedral, surprised to see a ticket inspector instead of a bishop. They could never build a St Pancras today. The last time British Rail built a big station, they came up with Milton Keynes Central, a concrete folly which proves my point. It's a prime example of Eighties excess, a six-platform station at which there is little chance of two trains stopping simultaneously, let alone six. It must have looked great on the drawing board, with colourful matchstick figures dotting the pristine platforms, but Milton Keynes will never be the setting for a Brief Encounter. And come to think of it, you don't see spotters very often either.

I often wonder how different my life would have been if I'd had a job on the railways. What better for a trainspotter! It would have given me even more time – paid time too! – to look at trains. But being a BR employee would have meant taking orders, and I was never any good at that, so I held on to my pride and kept telling myself that some other kind of fame lay just around the corner.

Yet how much more of my life was I going to fritter away, wearing clumsy boots and working in a Wellington boot factory in Burton, day-dreaming the life of a writer and putting myself at risk by not looking what I was doing? The money wasn't bad and there were factory girls to flirt with, but I needed something more ...

Greg, my best friend from the hostel, was still at drama school but he'd moved into a crummy flat above a kebab shop in the King's Cross hinterland. It was just the kind of bohemian life I hankered after, and to get my fix of it I would head off to London whenever I could. What fun we had – the boozy pubs, the girls from drama school and the all-night cafe off Regent Street where a one-armed waitress performed wonders with plates. Tanked up, drunk on beer and ambition, we'd walk back across London at all hours of the night. Sometimes, passing King's Cross at 2.00am and seeing a slow passenger train waiting to depart, I wanted to grab Greg and take him north, show him what adventures trains could bring.

But he had drama classes to go to, and I had to find myself a job if I was to jack in the factory and make a triumphant return to London.

Greg and I were from opposite ends of the country and very different cultures. He'd never been a trainspotter and regarded the hobby as a northern eccentricity, like whippet racing or black pudding contests. I'd grown up in the smoky

Midlands with its colourful mix of steam and diesel, but Greg came from Sussex, right in the middle of BR's most boring region. How could any lad have been turned on to trainspotting by the parade of electric bog units that prowled the south coast, never once showing any character or virility? A steamer, or a diesel in difficulty, always put on a show of emotion, rattling, roaring, whining, erupting with black smog – but the Southern's electric units were smug and inscrutable, totally without charms. Even when they went wrong they just stood there sulking or juddered along yard by yard. I could hardly blame Greg for being uninterested in railways. It hadn't stopped us becoming friends, though. I didn't want to spend all my time in the company of trainspotters and I suspected that he, in turn, sometimes got sick of all those gushing drama queens. We were chalk and cheese, but we made a good sandwich.

We often acted as if we were already famous, already the wealthy actor and writer we aspired to be. One time, in a reckless fit of high-living, I blew all my spare cash in an Italian restaurant in Camden Town. Bloated with pasta and tipsy on amaretto, we floated out into the cold air of NW1 and it was only when I woke the next day I realised I had nothing left for the train fare home.

What the heck … I'd just have to bilk it. British Rail surely owed me a loyalty bonus after all the money I'd put in their pockets since 1964. I'd never been dishonest, apart from paying a child's fare well past the cut-off point, kneeling at the ticket office window to make myself look smaller. And once, when I lost the return half of my ticket to York, I had climbed up a drainpipe to get out the station. But that was just to avoid embarrassment. I considered myself a seasoned traveller, and losing tickets was for old ladies and batty professors. Real dishonesty would have gone against the unwritten codes of trainspotting and respect for the railways.

On this occasion, though, it was a case of needs must.

Trainspotters often scorn people who aren't railway-savvy, sniggering at those who can't read timetables or turn up late for their trains. Most amusing are those hapless souls who settle themselves on a local stopping train to Watford in the goofy belief that it's an InterCity to Carlisle. How on earth could anyone possibly mistake an AM10 unit for Class 87 haulage? But if he despairs of the ingénues, the trainspotter despises the people who put tomatoes in the ashtrays or wee on the loo seats.

As for fare-dodgers, they're the lowest of the low and should be strung up, or put in the stocks and exposed to public disdain on the concourse at Euston. Maybe not! But that's how guilty I felt about it. I wasn't just breaking the law, I'd gone against my conscience and spoiled my record as an impeccable passenger. I was a fare-dodger now, depicted on posters as a furtive shadow – a criminal who could never evade the arm of the law in its officially striped sleeve. As a child I believed that even litter louts would go to prison, so this was totally out of character for me.

And so there I sat, miserable and unable to relax or enjoy a single moment of the journey. As each mile passed and I got nearer to home I began to feel more optimistic. Maybe I would get away with it after all. An element of pride attaches to the simplest of crimes if it meets with success!

Then the door at the end slid open and the ticket inspector appeared. I had a sob story ready, just in case, but my mind went blank. Had I meant to say the ticket was simply lost, or claim that my wallet had been snatched by a mugger? The inspector was just an ordinary chap with a clipper in his hand, but he might as well have been flexing a bull whip for the terror he induced. All those memories of Stewarts Lane came flooding back.

How bloody and unfair it was, when all I wanted was to be friends with the railways. Perhaps if I told him how faithful

I'd been, about all the years spent sitting on fences and waving to the drivers and guards ... Ridiculous! All he'd see was another fare-dodger trying it on. I'd rather have walked back from London to the Midlands than go through this torture.

As he got nearer I feared I might actually be sick. But then came a delay, an old lady asking him some long-winded question about her connection. I was busy praying, willing her to tie him in exasperating knots with her silly questions. Then I noticed we were slowing down, coming into Leicester. He clipped the old lady's ticket and moved down the carriage towards me. I couldn't even get up and move down the train, as we were in the final carriage anyway.

Then, with a screech and a jerk, the train stopped in Leicester station. The inspector heaved a sigh, shot a glance at the half dozen remaining passengers, then jumped off. His shift had ended at Leicester and I'd had the closest shave of my life. I was scarcely able to believe my luck! And then I was suddenly bursting with pride – for being so daring, for escaping by the skin of my teeth.

In later years, when I was better off, I was able to enter the grand stations with a fat wallet and a clean conscience. But I never forgot the fear. To this day I clutch my ticket fiercely, or keep it in a zip-up pocket. Even then I have to take it out and check it every ten minutes. I have this nightmare that when the ticket inspector turns up I'll smugly whip the ticket out from my pocket, only to find that I've been clutching a 20p off Persil voucher.

019

A New Agenda

Greg had landed a part in a play at the Theatre Royal in Worthing and, having nothing better to do, I went down to stay for a few days. He'd borrowed a small flat overlooking the railway. I'd always wanted to live by a railway line. Anywhere would have done – anywhere, that is, but on the Southern Region. We were in for what looked like becoming the coldest winter since 1962, but even a soft blanket of snow, white and twinkling, could never make this bit of railway look romantic.

We spent New Year's Eve in a backstreet pub. Greg copped off with one of the actresses and disappeared, leaving me to see in New Year on my own. There was plenty of kissing going on, but no promise of anything more. Towards 1.00am, I staggered out into the lamplit streets and took my first cold breaths of 1979, little suspecting that the year ahead would be full of change.

Back in London I got myself a job at the Belsize Tavern and managed to build up another kind of life for myself. Trainspotting hardly figured in it. I had ambitions as a journalist or novelist and didn't think that literature and train-spotting could comfortably co-exist. The paperwork would be a nightmare.

Jinx was still working at Burton station and I always stopped for a chat on my weekend visits home. We had our trainspot-ting past in common, of course, but whenever the conversation turned to railways, it seemed as if he was talking in a foreign language. Unlike me, he had remained up to date with it all. New locos had been built, new nicknames coined, and I didn't dare show my ignorance by asking for a translation. Trainspotting had changed. Sitting at the lineside jotting down numbers had gone out of fashion and 'bashing' was the order of the day, travelling up and down the country, trying to clock up a set amount of 'mileage' behind each loco – one thousand miles behind each Peak or Hoover, for example …

But I was pleased to see how much of the past remained. Horninglow station still stood, just about, and people still used my Wetmore footbridge. Burton's old steam sheds had been taken over by a local firm as a warehouse. On quiet Sunday afternoons I'd walk the bramble-strewn path from where the Steamer Gates had been and look around. The doorways were bricked up so I couldn't get inside, but walking round into the yard and looking up at the soot-blackened windows, the years dropped away and I felt twelve years old all over again.

Rumour had it that in 1963, Burton shed staff had buried half a dozen Jubilee nameplates in the yard, hoping to recover them later and sell them, but then they'd gone and forgotten the exact location. It sounded like another buried treasure legend, but as I crunched across the ancient clinker, I couldn't help wondering if those nameplates did indeed lie there just beneath my feet.

The only thing I found were some pages from a *Daily Sketch* of 1967, yellowed and oily, but still readable. One page had a picture of Twiggy and I imagined one of the old drivers looking her over and scoffing. 'Cor! Don't they make lasses with a bit of meat on 'em any more?' But maybe he had already guessed that the Sixties would belong to skinny girls in miniskirts and fops in kaftans, with no place for old men in overalls.

I visited the footbridge at Wetmore Sidings, but felt even more uncomfortable for lurking there. The signal box stood derelict, so I climbed the steps for a look inside. How strange it was to find these citadels and watchtowers of the railway kingdom deserted and in ruins: I felt like a soldier sweeping through an abandoned kingdom. Trespassing had always been a sport, but only as long as there was a danger of being caught. Now it felt quite wrong. Not that there was anything worth stealing. Every bit of scrap metal and souvenir had been looted. The vandals had soon got to work and the signal box was no more than a wooden shed full of broken glass and useless wires, too empty and windswept to offer shelter to ghosts.

My kind of nostalgia had no charms for Jinx. he was too busy chasing Peaks up and down the St Pancras–Derby line, bashing 37s in North Wales and building up his collection of colour slides. Andy Parker had always shared my poetic perspective on the railways and would have understood my feelings, but I hadn't seen him for ages. He had gone to Spain to teach English. He'd split up with Lynn and found someone more sensible and down-to-earth. Pipsqueak was still around, but he'd changed his name to Lord Fishfinger and fronted a band of musical wannabes. Darb had taken early retirement and gone to live in Dawlish, with a bird's-eye view of the line along the sea wall.

Burton-on-Trent was changing and I began to understand how much the railways had defined the town I'd grown up in. The main Newcastle–Bristol line had split it right down the middle, and from it the dozens of lines that ran through the breweries. Burton without railways would have been as lifeless as a body without veins. The factories gathered close to the railway as well, so it was no coincidence that the posher you were, the further away you liked to be from all that racket and muck. Few people had ever lived by the railway from choice, though and with so much of the clutter and activity now gone, those poky houses at Little Burton Bridge looked high and dry and twice as mean. No doubt their occupants were grateful for the silence at nights and the chance to hang out their washing without getting it covered in smuts. But at the same time, without the grey veil of railway smoke, it seemed that their poverty was even more exposed. They looked like people on a reservation, as if they didn't belong to our times at all.

THE EIGHTIES

020

A Grey Train to Fontainebleau

The grand railway hotels were before my time and out of my price range. Still, there was that weekend in the Café de la Gare in Fontainebleau …

1979 lived up to its New Year promise. With snow still on the ground, I had an article accepted by *The Observer* and made friends with Marie-Christine, a Camel-smoking French girl who worked as a cleaner for our landlord.

She was everything a French girlfriend could be – intelligent, cultured and sexy. We had a fun few months, but I knew she hadn't come to London for good. One day in July, a rep called at the Belsize Tavern and removed 'Je t'aime … moi non plus' from the jukebox – and the next day Marie-Christine had gone. I played the Rolling Stones' 'Love In Vain' over and over, and when it came to the bit where Mick sings 'I followed her to the station …' I blubbered like an orphaned seal pup. Stations, which had always held out the promise of an open door, were now places where the door could just as easily be slammed in your face.

A month later, when Marie-Christine invited me over for the August bank holiday weekend, I jumped at the chance. The station seemed like a place of hope again.

I'd become blasé about making the London–Paris trip and the Gare de Lyon, once so enchanting, seemed as familiar as Euston or Derby. Still, I was on a promise. Rattling through the Parisian suburbs on a grey train to Fontainebleau, warmed by the sun and listening to Jean-Michel Jarre on someone's transistor, the world seemed a grand place. Provence may be an old-timer with a beret and an accordion, but that day Paris seemed all romantic-techno and Jean-Michel captured it perfectly. I even had the cheek to pass myself off as a native and when someone thanked me for a light, I waved away the favour with a cheerful 'De rien'.

Marie-Christine hadn't bothered to fix up any accommodation. After meeting me at the little station, she marched into the Café de la Gare opposite and asked the patron for a room. He stopped drying his Ricard glasses and tossed her the key. Eight pounds a night for a love-nest – who could complain! It had a fluffy double bed, shuttered windows and a view across the railway. On the first floor, we were close enough to the cafe terrace to eavesdrop on the locals chatting. So close that if I'd wanted to I could have flicked peanuts into the old men's wine glasses.

Lying awake listening to the railways sing and chatter is one of the most comforting feelings I know. Unlike the honking cars and roaring motorbikes that jolt us awake, trains sync smoothly into nature's own rhythms. In Britain or France or Finland, it's as if we're all listening to the same metallic tides, reassurance that the world goes about its business while we sleep.

Readers might be expecting a funny story here. You know the kind of thing: how Marie-Christine lay naked and expectant on the bed while I leaned out of the window taking snapshots of a BB16000 trundling through the station with a trainload of mustard from Dijon. But no – I wasn't that easily distracted. Trains may offer compensation for middle-aged men in boring marriages, but for a young man with nine pints in his veins – eight of blood and one of Muscadet – trainspotting had to take second place.

Still, I couldn't completely forget that the railway was close by. During the day, when Marie-Christine had to work (at a summer camp for French teens) I was left alone to wander through the woods, where I soon found myself an eyrie over-looking the track. Did passengers get a creepy shock, I wonder, as they admired the forest of Fontainebleau, then suddenly caught sight of a watching figure, just like one of those loiter-ers they talk about on *Crimewatch*: 'It may well be that the man was an innocent trainspotter and if he comes forward we can eliminate him from our enquiries.'

Just as I adored Marie-Christine's accent – even her curses sounded sexy – she loved the sound of my English voice. Any nonsense would do. I only had to say 'Snug as a bug in a rug' to get her giggling and, for all I know, my ramblings about the golden days of British Railways probably sounded roman-tic to her. How could she have understood anyway? 'I had a love affair with steam' – how would that have translated into French? Outside of trainspotters, it doesn't even make sense in English. Taken literally, it sounds quite surreal and I can't begin to imagine what she thought I meant. Perhaps she imagined that I had been up to some sex games in the Turkish baths.

On Saturday evening we took the train into Paris to see a Jacques Tati film and have dinner in a little Greek place in the Rue Mouffetard. Hand in hand, we strolled back across the Pont d'Austerlitz, pausing to gaze on the twinkling lights of the *bateaux mouches*, for all the world like stereotype Parisian lovers. At the Gare de Lyon we found our local train humming to itself, as if it had been waiting just for us, anxious to be away before it turned back into a pumpkin.

As the station clock edged towards midnight, it looked as if we'd be the only passengers. Cheered by our meal, warmed through by pastis, we could sit and cuddle for the half-hour journey back to Fontainebleau.

But it wasn't to be ...

A couple of off-duty soldiers got on, then another two. Hearing shouts outside, I got up and looked out to see what appeared to be an entire battalion yomping down the platform.

Within minutes every seat and squatting space was taken. They were obviously conscripts and had no reason to be proud of their military service. They just wanted to get pissed and have a laugh before returning to barracks.

I started to get worried. We were the only civvies on the train – and Marie-Christine the only woman. Puffing on their Gauloises (it would have been suicide to point out we were in No Smoking) and swigging beers, the squaddies stared at us with bleary-eyed hostility. Who the hell did I think I was, taking one of their women? My imagination ran wild: they were going to knife me and throw me from the train, then molest Marie-Christine. They probably hadn't had a woman for months. Now they'd have the fun of killing an Englishman and screwing a healthy French lass. One wrong glance, that's all it would take to give them an excuse.

I kept my eyes on the floor but I heard and smelled it all: smouldering Gauloises, beery belches, the hum of unwashed male flesh. I listened closely to see if I could make out their words. Even when I tried to feign interest in the outside world, all I could see were their faces reflected in the window. Why did they have to keep staring! One by one the suburban stations came and went – Villeneuve Saint-Georges, Yerres, Boussy Saint-Antoine, Combs La Ville Quincy. I didn't fancy being buried in any of these places. How would Mum ever get to visit my grave if she couldn't even pronounce the name of the bloody station?

Every second became an agony. But at last the train slowed and I recognised the approaches to Fontainebleau. We got up to get to the doors, fully expecting our way to be barred by a tattooed arm ... but the soldiers all shuffled out of our way to make a gangway. They even wished Marie-Christine goodnight and gave me conspiratorial nods and winks.

It had only been a long weekend, but I went home on top

16. My friend Jinx poses alongside Blackie 44871 at Stockport sheds (9B) during one of our many Manchester trips in 1967 and 1968.

17. Manchester again – and a wonderful view from the footbridge as we make for a bunk of Patricroft sheds (9H).

18. A trio of ex-LMS locos – 45394, 43124 and 42622 – in the cathedral-like shadows of Leeds Holbeck (55A) on 1 August 1965.

Bill Wright

19. Britannia 70045 *Lord Rowallan* in the yard at Leeds Holbeck (55A),
along with Peak D33 and English Electric D396 on 30 October 1966.

20. An LMS Class 5 and BR standard 9F 92054 at Stockport's
Heaton Mersey sheds (9F) on 8 August 1965.

21. D6739 hauling condemned locos 45294, 48307, 48700 and
48740 through Wakefield Kirkgate on 17 May 1968.

22. Me, Andy, and brothers Andy and George Warrington
at Woodham's Barry scrap yard in 1969.

23. Kyle of Lochalsh station at the end of the line from Inverness. This photo was taken in July 1963, but it didn't look any different when we arrived on our 1973 Railrover.

24. Edinburgh's Haymarket sheds (64A) in July 1965 with Deltic D9020 *Nimbus* and workaday diesel D5308.

25. Western D1026 *Western Centurion* at the head of a Paddington
express express at Severn Tunnel Junction on 9 September 1965.

26. Hymek D7088 at Bournemouth with
a Birmingham–Poole express in June 1967.

27. A Deltic arrival at King's Cross in about 1980. I'd just bought a new Canon camera, which accounts for a better quality than my earlier efforts.

Proof House Junction

28. Class 86 'lekky' 86222 on a Birmingham–London train at Proof House Junction, just north of Birmingham New Street, in the mid-1980s.

Steve Burdett

29. Western 1056 *Western Sultan* brings the China Clay
Special back to Paddington on 4 December 1976.

Nicholas Whittaker

30. In between the youthful liaisons of Belsize Park and Primrose Hill there
was always time to stop off and peer over at the line out of Euston …

of the world. A month later I gave up my half of the flat I shared with Greg and set off to live in France full-time, in Marie-Christine's home town of Besançon. She had sorted out a flat and my plan was to get a dishwashing job to support myself while I wrote a novel. Blinded by love, I didn't even think how ridiculous I must have looked as I made my way to Victoria with a suitcase, a bag, a typewriter, and a dozen LPs tied up with string.

I knew something was wrong as soon as Marie-Christine met me at the station in Besançon. The twinkle had gone, replaced by a shiftiness. It wasn't another man, as I first feared, but another girl, which was just as bad really, despite what the sex magazines would have you believe. In between our bank holiday idyll in Fontainebleau and my arrival in Besançon, an old crush of hers had turned up and rekindled the lesbian fires. I stuck it out bravely, in the hope she'd change her mind, but it looked unlikely. I couldn't get a dishwashing job, but I thought I had struck lucky when I found work typing out a thesis for someone at the university there. I wish I hadn't. His writing was awful, and with me a two-fingered typist at best and a French typewriter keyboard somewhat confusing, I was lucky to manage a page a day.

One evening we drove over to Dijon to see Lou Reed in concert. Lou seemed to be in a foul mood, with 'fuck you' contempt for faithful fans who called on him to do old favourites. He simply had to agree to do 'Walk on the Wild Side', though. The audience were loving it – and so was I, until a thought struck me. With no sign of any beautiful black girls on stage, who would do the 'do-be-do-be-do'? Step forward three hairy roadies. Burly and boozy, they were no substitute for the black chicks. The world had been turned upside down: you couldn't even take comfort in the old songs any more!

Next day I caught the train back to London. With no return ticket, I had to borrow the fare off Marie-Christine but she'd willingly stumped up, overcome with guilt and relieved to see me go.

I felt numb, staring out of the train window, fidgeting in my seat and thinking about Marie-Christine and what a fool I'd made of myself. And interrupting my thoughts were those three fat drunks at the mike, turning my misery into some kind of camp sing-along.

What has all this self-pity got to do with trainspotting? Maybe very little, or maybe everything. If I'd had to go home by road, the endless tarmac, concrete walls and motorway lights would have turned me into a burnt-out case from a Jean-Luc Godard movie. But the trains helped keep me sane and safe, cocooned, tied to home by ribbons of steel. I'd gone wandering like a lovesick idiot, but inch by inch the rails would pull me safely home, through Paris and Boulogne and the sprawling suburbs of south London, all the way to the tube station at Belsize Park. By then I'd be feeling a tiny bit better.

021

East Germany: Steam Days Again

I'd always envied Jinx's travel perks – 75 per cent discounts and an annual quota of free tickets. Not just any free tickets either. Petty public restrictions didn't apply to him: he was quite at liberty to use his Burton-to-London ticket via Bristol, Crewe, Carlisle and Newcastle if he wanted. Yet these perks were a reward for conformity and I would never sell my soul for free travel, however tempting it was.

In the end, though, I found a way of getting my own free-bies. After my railroving article appeared in *The Observer*, I had several offers of complimentary tickets – coyly referred to as 'travel facilities' – from the Swiss, Italian and German tourist offices.

One small problem: I was on the dole. The freedom of Switzerland looked very tempting, but how did I get there in the first place, and what would I use for spending money? Not only that, a visit would have to be slotted in between signing-on days at the Camden Town Job Centre.

I asked if they could help me get there, but they said no, it would involve all kinds of complex inter-railway dealings and politics. British Rail were happy to give me a ticket to Dover, and the Dutch said they could offer a ticket as far as the German border. But who would pay the ferryman? Not Charon, but Sealink. No one seemed willing to pick up the tab. Perhaps if I'd explained my situation they might have made an exception, but they had been so nice to me I dreaded them finding out that their Sunday broadsheet travel writer was a claimant with frayed shoelaces and an overdraft of £14.

So, for the price of a ferry fare, the Swiss freebies slipped from my grasp …

A year later, when I had a bit more money, I wrote back to the Swiss people and said yes, I'd like that Alpine railrover after all. But my fame had evaporated by then and they couldn't even remember me.

Luckily the Germans had better memories of my *Observer* piece and were happy to give me a free rover – and a first-class one too. By that time, 1980, I'd more or less forgotten why I'd wanted to go in the first place. Germany had never appealed to me that much and certainly didn't have the same pull on me as France. But I went anyway, partly because it was free, and partly because of a trainspotterish urge to add some European place names to my collection, some stamps in my passport. The French were so laid back about it, they never bothered with stuff like that, but I thought that stamping things would probably appeal to German bureaucracy.

At one time I would underline all the cities I'd visited in my giant Reader's Digest atlas, and now I had a chance to add Hamburg and Munich to my cops. It sounds the worst reason for travelling and the kind of thing that gives trainspotters a bad name. Collecting engines, yes, but European cities? I'd even thought of working my way through Europe alphabetically, all the way from Aarhus to Zagreb. X would prove difficult, I thought, until I found Xativa in Spain and pencilled it in for future reference.

It was only the act of underlining stuff that marked me out as different. But not that different. Mankind is a collecting animal, a trait that manifests itself in a hundred ways. Football fans travel hundreds of miles to obscure grounds, just to say they've been; housewives fill pinewood racks with a complete range of herb jars, even though they have no intention of using more than five; and consumerism itself has distinct 'trainspotting' overtones – the must-have items, the necessity of collecting a complete set of football stickers, or every kitchen utensil including a lemon zester and boiled egg slicer, or the *Inspector Morse* box-set complete with outtakes and commentaries. The compulsion to collect, to tick off, to underline, to have the 'full set' – it is in each and every one of us. Anthropologists theorise about parallels with man the hunter, though that has always seemed a bit tenuous to me, as if Neanderthals went around ticking off woolly mammoths in a notebook. I incline towards the *Waiting for Godot* theory (made up by me). Trainspotting, like collecting Schwarz spice jars or building matchstick models of The Shard, is just an amusing way of passing an otherwise frightening stretch of time.

If I had to find a 'normal' reason for visiting Germany, then it was to see Berlin. The Iron Curtain was still in place and even if McDonald's had set up shop, Berlin could still claim to be full of Cold War intrigue. There was always the possibility that a glamorous Russian woman in a Burberry mac might step out of the shadows with a poisoned hat-pin … Ridiculous, perhaps, but these are the kind of mad fantasies which compel us to travel. But the real reason for going to Berlin was simply to say that I'd been: it might even merit a double underlining in the atlas.

My Hamburg–Berlin train was operated by East German Railways (DR: Deutsche Reichsbahn), green and drab, the perfect vehicle for a nervous peep behind the Iron Curtain. I had a first-class ticket, but East German first was worse than British second – hard on the bum, dismally decorated, stinking of wet dog-ends where melted snow had leaked through the window frames and into the ashtray. If it wasn't for the '1' on your ticket you'd never have known. What a superb trick to play on decadent Westerners: they paid extra into the communist coffers in the hope of dodging the rough stuff, but they got a salutary taste of austerity instead.

Our train squealed to a halt at the border-post and guards got on, tramping down the corridor, kicking dusty snow off their boots. Their dogs snarled at the scent of Western wealth and my heart thumped. What if there was something wrong with my visa, or they simply didn't like the self-satisfied British smirk in my passport? I'd joked about it back home, but now it all seemed a bit too real: what if I was taken off the train and never seen again, like the old dear in *The Lady Vanishes*? My body would be found by picnickers, who would speculate wildly about why my trousers were missing; meanwhile an off-duty soldier in Berlin would be picking up girls impressed by his trendy Levi's … I wondered whether to finger my name on the misted-up window just in case, when in they walked, slamming open the compartment door with well-practised menace. I fumbled for my documents and smiled politely.

In the event, the two guards were the politest young men I'd met for a long time. Even the growling dogs turned out to be more like Gnasher from the *Beano* than hounds from the Gulag, and made eyes at each passenger in the hope of a tit-bit. I couldn't help thinking this Cold War charade was just for the tourists and I wouldn't have been surprised if they'd passed round the hat.

Brown, frozen, lifeless, interspersed with grim-looking apartment blocks, East German scenery looked as dull as everyone had warned it would be. My thoughts were racing ahead to Berlin and I groaned as we came to a halt at yet another set of signals. Was it turning into a train journey from hell? No – a train journey into paradise! I thought I was hearing things at first, a hissing that sounded vaguely familiar, then a burst of steam and smoke that flattened itself against the windows. Through it, like the clearing mist of a dream, I caught sight of a steam loco. Black, rusty, leaking steam, it was busy shunting wagons. I could hardly move in case it vanished, in case I woke up. The past – my past – it still existed here. They'd changed the station names and the signs for the Gents and the Parcels Office, but I could have been back in Derbyshire in 1966, with a steam loco hissing by the water tower, railwaymen with greasy overalls and cigarettes, a beautiful monochrome tableau. It left a dull ache in my heart. But I fought the urge to stick my head out of the window for a closer look. This snow wasn't the soft, fairy-like stuff of Christmas cards, but vicious, splintery needles of ice which whirled in gusts and drove into your eyes. And I had to remember we were behind the Iron Curtain and I'd read enough scare stories about spotters being arrested by secret police and sent off to the salt mines.

Dampflok – the German word for steam loco – brings to mind a group of miserable sheep left out in the rain. But a horrible thought spoils the pun. What if every trainspotter who ever visited Germany made exactly the same lame joke? It's just the joke they would make, I'm certain. 'What, left your sheep outside again, Fritz?' The German wouldn't laugh at it, but the train buff would. 'Damp flock … get it? Ha-ha-ha.' No wonder they always ended up being arrested.

I felt disappointed, reluctant to let these steam locos slip away from me. But I had my limits and I wasn't going to risk hypothermia or arrest. What did they really mean to me, anyway, these odd-looking steamers with half of their insides on the outside? They were hardly in the same class as Castles or Britannias. For me to be truly hooked there had to be more, really, than the simple fact that they were steam engines. So I stayed huddled in my seat, staring out at the East German snow, until a concrete wall closed in on both sides of us and funnelled our train through the fog-shrouded suburbs of Berlin.

You wouldn't want to see my photos (though there is one in the plate section, if you insist). There's the obligatory snap of Checkpoint Charlie, of course, but why the hell did I take a picture of a railway yard covered in snow? There weren't even any engines at work: it was just a frozen fan of lines, a pointless photo – 'Berlin marshalling yard featuring no one'. I can't even imagine how I ended up there when I should have been in a cafe on the Kurfürstendamm, having a coffee and a bratwurst and keeping myself warm. Instead I'd wandered off the beaten track and found myself standing on a railway footbridge with ice biting my toenails, in a wind so cruelly cold I was on the verge of crying.

The most memorable trip of the week was the run down to Basel aboard the *Rheingold*. I don't know why it matters if a train has got a name, it just does. It lends impeccable romance. It's not, 'I went on the 7.24 or something to Basel' but 'I went down to Basel on the *Rheingold*'. Our Cornish Riviera is fine, but it doesn't have the same ring. While I'm being a travel-bore, I'll mention that I also had dinner aboard the *Rheingold*. Dinner in the diner is a magical experience (expensive magic, admittedly), one that car drivers and airline passengers will never share.

But I was glad to be heading back home. My abiding memory of that week was the bitter cold, the icy draughts that slashed at me like a butcher's knife and left me walking down the streets with tears in my eyes. The trainspotter who came in from the cold. But *The Observer* had expressed provisional interest in a piece about the trip. So I wouldn't be a journalistic one-hit wonder. At this rate I could see myself building up a brilliant career as a travel writer.

022

Love on a (Very Short) Branch Line

Most weekends in the early Eighties would find me on a train from Paddington to Henley-on-Thames. They were good days. I had a well-paid job, my first Barclaycard, and was in love with an English rose. Elaine was the girlfriend I'd always hoped to meet. She'd been privately educated, at a school where they wore straw hats, and lived in a Home Counties semi with two bathrooms and two sweet sisters. I'd had this daydream since the age of steam, an erotic and dubiously snobby fantasy that helped fill the gaps between trains.

Pretty, polite and educated, Elaine could recite the opening passage of Kafka's *Metamorphosis* in German and, in her sweet southern twang, it made me roll over like a pussycat. I never thought I'd meet anyone who could make an existential nightmare sound like an invitation to make love in a warm shower.

Trainspotting was definitely on hold. For one thing, I had bedded down well in London (in all senses of the word) and no longer needed trains as a comfort. And I'd got so many of them now, whole classes of Peaks and Deltics. I'd jot down a loco number if I saw one, but certainly wouldn't bother chasing around the country after the few I still needed.

Hold on, I hear cynics saying. The guy was a trainspotter, then he met a nice girl and decided that trains aren't so interesting after all. There you go! Isn't that enough proof for the nerd theory, that trainspotting is a displacement activity for clueless men?

Then again … as soon as I bought my first SLR camera – a

159

Canon AE1 – I would spend my lunchtimes snapping Class 87 electrics whizzing through Kilburn High Road station.

Elaine didn't care about trainspotting one way or the other, but certainly didn't think it weird. One of the 'character references' I used when we first met was my *Observer* piece about railroving, copies of which I carried around for just such an opportunity. I'm not saying it mesmerised her, but as a chat-up line it was at least original and lent me a touch of glamour. If I confessed to liking trains, at least I didn't fit the stereotype.

Despite my love of the Western Region, I'd never been to Paddington in my younger days and by the time I did, it had lost some of its mystique. I always associated it with Margaret Rutherford in the film *Murder, She Said*, based on Agatha Christie's *4.50 from Paddington*. But even in 1980, with honking taxis, rattling parcel trucks and clattering indicator boards, it could still deliver that big-station atmosphere.

I'd always thought of Paddington as a benign sort of place, free of the rent boys, prostitutes and runaways so often found at other London termini. And it was an exciting gateway. Euston could only offer boring destinations like Nuneaton or Coventry; Liverpool Street catered for Essex people; and Victoria was drearily suburban. Paddington was a holiday station, full of promises, the place you came for a train to Teignmouth, Paignton or Newquay. The tannoy crackled out a litany of a faraway forgotten England: '… calling at Saltash, Liskeard, Lostwithiel, Par, St Austell …' It stirred the blood and awoke old memories. You just wanted to walk up to the waiting train and go. Arriving in Penzance, you could walk out of the station and there'd be no more cities, just sand and sea and sky.

For Elaine and me, though, it was less romantic; a routine trip, sneaking away from the suburban platforms on a bog unit stinking of diesel and fags. I loved being with Elaine, but couldn't help wishing we were doing something more crazy, like running off to Paris or Lisbon.

'The Slow Train' – an old piano-and-whimsy song by Flanders and Swann – speaks of an England at its most leisurely and bucolic, and turns its junctions and branch lines into poetry. We British have always been a bit two-faced about our railways. Some insist they still miss the old steam trains and third-class compartments, slow-moving porters and cheerful drivers. It's a false memory that lies behind our contradictory attitudes; it's why we tut and smirk when the first-ever Eurostar is late or trains are halted by the wrong kind of snow. Trivial events, really, yet they will push war and famine off the front page, leading to countless jokes that are filed away in the folk memory to be trotted out again and again for the next fifty years, like the ones about British Rail sandwiches. 'They don't know how to run railways any more', grumble people who've never been on a train for twenty years and couldn't even tell you when steam stopped. Yet these same people all claim allegiance to the mythical English branch line and the Slow Train.

Today at any rate, branch lines and slow trains make a pretty boring combination. They may be just tolerable when abroad; on holiday you regard every little station as a postcard view, a sleepy *gare* or *estación* full of local characters. But there's nothing fascinating about Westbourne Park or Acton, no glamour in Southall or Hayes & Harlington – though I guess these same names sound strange and exotic to InterRailers from Madrid or Munich, who for years after cherish fond memories of the sunny afternoon their train stopped at West Drayton and an old man in a baseball cap spat in his handkerchief.

Getting to Henley-on-Thames called for a change at Twyford. The branch line experience has largely vanished from British life. Until Beeching went on the rampage, the railway map of Britain looked fascinating, an organic growth with scores of branches and twigs. But if it looked random, it had a beautiful logic, filtering passengers from the grandest of London stations, through country junctions, delivering them right into the heart of the cutest village or sleepiest market town. The branch line is a rural fantasy that refuses to die, as English as Elgar or sweetshops. Little wonder then that Edward Thomas's 'Adlestrop' is one of our favourite poems (it wasn't on a branch, I know, but it evokes that same feeling), and that *The Country Branch Line*, with its watercolour pictures, is one of the best-selling railway books ever. Since branch lines were pretty much a dead loss for trainspotting, one can only assume that its main readership is among the kind of people who spend their weekends buying grandfather clocks and spinning wheels.

Not that Henley branch had much charm. It's quite stumpy, in fact, with only two stops – Shiplake and Wargrave – along the way, each one a flyblown memorial to better days. Stations once busy enough to provide a living for a stationmaster and his minions are now just elegant ruins. Today, with no minions, let alone a stationmaster, and only rudimentary buildings to shelter travellers, the branch line stations of Olde England make perfect dens for teenagers to snog, smoke dope or swig 2-litre bottles of Strongbow. And if anyone has a felt-tip to leave their name behind, so much the better.

Elaine's mum approved of me, anyway. I don't know if she'd been fearing the worst, but now she could see I wasn't a punk or a druggie. I wore an M&S jacket, chewed food quietly and helped with the washing-up. Trainspotters were just as capable of getting a precious daughter pregnant, of course, but they could be relied on to make safe if uninspiring sons-in-law. In an ever-changing post-punk new-romantic world, trainspotting was a badge of normality and stability.

I wonder how many young women of today would be happy with a spotter as a boyfriend. Few know any in their own age group. The only ones they know are the stereotypes of the stand-up comic's routine, and perhaps their own fathers. It's an old guy's pastime, as dull as having an allotment. And what girl would want a boyfriend with the same interests (and the same ill-fitting jeans) as Dad?

Elaine admitted to remembering steam trains. She'd been brought up in Malaya, one of those countries where old steamers could still be found working the sugar and rubber plantations. I was intrigued. There had long been tales of British locos 'borrowed' during the war and never returned. Stupidly, I expected her to have fond memories, but however much I pumped her, she couldn't recall any details. How would she know if the locos were 2-8-2s with tenders or 0-6-0 tanks? They were just part of the foreign backdrop, no more important than the rickshaws or stalls that sold stir-fried dog. Listening to me talking about the Orient Express or my trip to Berlin was one thing, but she certainly wasn't prepared to reciprocate with the details of the 7.35 latex special to Ban Pak Phraek.

As well as two sisters, Elaine had a kid brother. He was a spotter (hooray!), but his stomping ground was Heathrow airport (boo!), training his binoculars on jumbos and Airbuses as they shot off over Hounslow. Spotters do have an affinity of a kind, but there are limits. We understand the need to spot, the satisfaction of collection and collation and the obsessive paperwork, but that's as far as it goes. Despite his invitation to visit Heathrow, I could no more get interested in plane-spotting than morris dancing or golf.

Our outward journey was invariably by bog unit, but on Sunday nights, when Elaine's dad gave us a lift to Reading, we got a fast train back to Paddington, as often as not one of the HSTs which were becoming common on British Rail. They'd been a novelty at first and we were charmed by the sleek lines and the gadgetry; you could walk along the carriage with coffee and sandwiches and doors would swish open for you, like magic. But these 'Flying Bananas' were fast taking over all the long-distance expresses once in the charge of Westerns and Hoovers. We'd surrendered the excitement and romance of loco-hauled travel for the simpleton's amusement of a sliding door. It looked like a bad bargain, and boded ill for the spotter's future.

023

'Return to Athens, Please'

What on earth made me want to go all the way to Athens by train? Adventure, bloody-mindedness, a chance to do some exotic trainspotting? A bit of each, probably. But a girl comes into it too, as is often the case. Suzanne, one of the girls from Belsize Park, had gone there to work in a bar and an innocent letter from her was sufficient to revive an old passion.

It was March 1982, I was fed up at work, and this sudden chance of travel made my nine-to-five routine weigh heavier than ever. If they wanted me to stay, I told them, I wanted a raise and two weeks' holiday to recover my *joie de vivre*. To my surprise they agreed. I wrote and told Suzanne I was on my way. The next day I went down to Victoria to get my ticket – and a wildly eccentric request it must have been from the way the ticket clerks stared.

'Return to Athens, please.'

'Ashford, sir? You need to go to the Suburban window.'

'No, Athens,' I said. 'In Greece.'

What followed resembled a scene from some old comedy: they had to blow dust off rarely-used manuals and then, still unsure, they rang their superiors for advice. Within minutes I had every one of the ticket clerks giving me the once-over. Yes, of course he's a nutter, they agreed. Not only would my railway trip cost nearly three times as much as a two-week package holiday, it took twenty times as long. I got my ticket in the end – paying a whopping £168 – but lost all claim to normality.

Elaine came to Charing Cross to see me off on the 13.00

to Boulogne. I kept asking if she minded me going, but she insisted she didn't. We'd been sharing a single bed for two years and she was glad of a chance to turn over. Still, I was full of regrets as she walked back to the Underground: I knew quite well that I was being a shit. But the tug of adventure was too strong. I bought a *Times*, a *Punch* and a *Railway World* from W.H. Smith and settled down in my seat. One or two couples looked to be on their way to Paris for a romantic weekend, which made me feel doubly guilty – I could have used that £168 to visit Paris with Elaine! But at the same time I longed for an excuse to say to people: 'Me? I'm travelling to Athens, actually.'

At the Gare de Lyon I shovelled a hot dog and a beer into my tummy, then bought a clutch of Kronenbourg cans and boarded the overnight train for Venice. I'd booked a couchette, so even though I had to share with an old guy who kept switching on his reading light and counting his coins, I managed to get a good night's sleep. So good, in fact, that I snoozed all the way through Switzerland without even noticing it and by the time I woke we were below the green hills of Lombardy.

Venice! One of those places everyone wants to go, but for me merely a junction, a place to change trains. I had a quick look round the muddy canals and scabrous houses for politeness' sake, but my main intention was to get something to eat, something authentically Italian, like a pizza.

The next morning found me behind the Iron Curtain yet again, further from home than I'd ever been before. As the train of drab green carriages snaked into Belgrade station – I couldn't believe it: steam engines! Not prettified painted antiques, but dirty workhorses banging trucks together in the station sidings, leaking steam and wheezing. As the train squealed to a halt in the terminus I jumped off and ran back to the end of the platform with my camera.

Suddenly there's a machine gun pointing up my nose and

I swivel round to see some kind of official shaking his head at me. He fingers his gun. I'm not sure what he is exactly – soldier, policeman, an armed stationmaster? – but I quickly get the gist. But even with a gun pointing at me I still feel sarcastic. 'Oh yes, I am a spy, the MOD are really interested in your old shunting engines ...' I don't say it out loud, of course. I just snap the lens cap back on my camera, park my backside on a luggage trolley and content myself by sniffing steam while our train is being prepared. It is being shunted into a new formation, having its restaurant car detached and two sleeping cars hooked on. Some American backpackers are filling their water bottles and washing their feet at a tap on the platform. Seeing their train move, they panic.

'Jesus Christ! Tony! The fucking train's going.'

Grabbing their shoes and water bottles, they sprint down the platform bare-footed, yelling, screaming, dancing on bits of glass and grit – hollering as only panicked Americans can. It's like the last helicopter out of Saigon. As the carriages disappear from view, they collapse on the platform. One of the girls is crying: wailing that her bag and her radio are still on the train. I suppose I could tell them the train will be back in a couple of minutes, but I don't. I just sit and watch, shamefully amused at their distress. After a while the train reappears from beyond the station. Tony lights up a Marlboro and laughs.

'Jesus Christ! It's fucking coming back. It's coming back! It's coming back!'

The girl is crying all over again, this time with relief. Their reactions are so childlike and I feel guilty for not telling them about the shunting. But really, why are Americans so touchingly innocent when abroad?

I haven't eaten anything since Venice, so when the train stops at Niš for twenty minutes, I go in search of refreshment. Beer bottles are pretty universal, so pointing is enough to get my desires known. The food is more puzzling, but some squares of golden pastry look quite appetising, so I point and the woman hands me two wrapped in greaseproof paper.

Back on the train, I unwrap my snack, only to discover that, in the warmth of my hands, the golden pastry is degenerating back to grease and flour. I bite into one of the squares and feel like throwing up. It's packed with an unappetising block of gristle and mince. I throw it out of the window and get stuck into my beers. I don't feel too guilty about littering, since there is a continuous ribbon of litter alongside the tracks, a blur of blue, red and yellow that stays forever at the edge of your vision whenever you look out.

After Leskovac I have the compartment more or less to myself. This is the life ... nothing to do but read, stare through the window and listen to the reassuring clickety-clack of wheels on track. Around midnight we arrive in Thessalonika. An old lady is struggling with her cases and I go to help her up the steps with it all, hoping I don't get caught out like the Americans in Belgrade.

After that I doze off, waking as we thread through the outskirts of Athens.

The suburbs of foreign cities – tediously familiar to their inhabitants – have an exotic quality for the newcomer. I'm intrigued by the pink-painted houses, sleeping shops and early morning bus queues. And more steam engines!

These ones are static, rusting in the sidings, but real steamers all the same. I grip the window and stare hopelessly as they recede from me. Even dead and rusting they still fascinate me, bringing back vivid memories of days out in Manchester or Leeds.

Athens station is a surprise. If we hadn't just come through those suburbs, I wouldn't even have thought of it as a city station. It's nothing like the noisy canopied sheds of Paris, London or Frankfurt, but quiet, unhurried enough for a tree to grow at the end of one of the platforms and for random patches of undergrowth that would never be tolerated at

Euston or the Gare du Nord. The effect is that of a country junction in the Fifties. Our newly-arrived train gives the place a temporary air of importance, and apart from us there is only an antique railcar, its engine rattling impatiently.

I draw a veil over my two weeks in Athens. Suffice to say I enjoyed myself, even if I didn't get what I'd hoped for – and it serves me right.

I'm glad to be going home. I'm feeling homesick and rather sentimental and long to be with Elaine again, to tell her how much I love her. (Like she's going to believe me after I've left her on her own for two weeks and spent 500 quid on a journey to Athens to see another woman!)

At the station I walk the length of the train looking for coach K – but there is no coach K; for some reason the letters only go up to J. I repeat the walk twice, as if the coach might suddenly appear, but it doesn't. So I try asking a railwayman what's going on. I have paid for a couchette, I tell him, and show him my ticket for coach K. He just shrugs and babbles in Greek. I haven't a clue what he's saying but the plain fact is that no coach K exists.

Luckily there are unreserved seats, a few of which remain unoccupied, and I manage to park myself in a compartment with a quartet of Americans. Luckily? I try to get to sleep, but they laugh and chatter all night long, about baseball, cars, *Star Trek*, pizza toppings. I hate them.

After a fitful night's sleep I set off to find another seat, waving a secret two fingers at my travelling companions. The train seems fairly full, but further along I come across a compartment with just one man, and he gets off soon after.

I think I'm doing all right – until we get further into Yugoslavia. Our train crawls now, stopping at every station, and at each one another hundred people crowd on board. Rowdy people, wearing a bizarre mix of fashions, the men in rough jackets and work boots or 1970s suits, the women either demure in black headscarves or tarty in Laura Ashley dresses copied onto the cheapest thin material. I pray no one joins me, but it's obviously futile. I end up sharing 'my' compartment with five young men.

'You Anglia?' one says.

I nod my head and trigger off a barrage of odd questions.

'You know Crystal Palace?'

'Pink Floyd – bloody good psycho band, huh?'

'You married to sexy English lady?'

They try their best to be friendly, but I'd much rather be alone. The worst thing is that none of them has any notion of personal space. Not only do they lean across me to talk to each other and pass sweets and cigarettes, one of them goes to sleep on my shoulder and his garlicky breath fans past just inches from my nose.

Another offers me a slice from some kind of pie. It looks suspiciously greasy and has a thumb-print on it, but I'm hungry and don't want to risk offending them. I nibble cautiously at it and smile diplomatically. Biting deeper, I gag on a lump of gristle. I daren't spit it out (actually seeing it would certainly make me feel worse) and for long unendurable minutes I move the thing around my mouth in an unconvincing mime, not daring to either chew or swallow.

Eventually, when the Slavic lads are distracted by some woman in the corridor, I take my chance and spit the mangled lump into a tissue, which I slip into my pocket for chucking down the toilet later.

Awful food is one of the hazards of travelling, but things get worse. I don't know what's going on now, but the lads are drinking and getting boisterous. One of them stands on the seat, straddling his friend and dangling his long fat penis over his head. They laugh uproariously and start bashing each other. I feign amusement and hope they don't get me to join in. The language is baffling enough, but I can't read the unspoken signs either. Are they just messing about, having a laugh, or am I in danger, trapped with a compartment full of gay gang-bangers? For the first time on this trip I'm feeling vulnerable, aware of how far from home I am.

Before I left Britain, someone at work tried to sell me a Walkman, but I'd refused indignantly. I wanted real life, I told them, not cassettes. But the Serbo-Croat babble is getting to me now and I'm desperate for the sound of English voices. I'd be so grateful for one of my Tony Hancock cassettes. I wish I'd stayed with the Yanks when I had the chance. If only they'd bless me with the sound of English. They can talk baseball, hamburgers and surfing all the way to Paris if they want and it will be as sweet as poetry to my ears.

Now I make my second big mistake. I nod goodbye to the lads and go in search of the Americans. The corridors are as jam-packed as the tube in rush hour. I squeeze along, peering into the crowded compartments only to be met by blank Slavic stares. There's no sign of any English-speaking people. There's no point in going back, though, so I end up in a cramped space by the toilets, alternately standing and squatting on my haunches. And there I am for the next eight hours, jammed up to the door. It opens inwards – and every time more passengers board, the door crushes my overnight bag down to the size of a wallet.

Crowded as it is, people still manage to grab territory. Two men have found enough space to spread out a newspaper on the floor and tuck into stale-looking bread and tinned sardines. But then we stop and as more people crowd on, someone kicks the tin of sardines along the corridor, splashing tomato sauce on people's shoes and coating the sardines in dust and cigarette ash. There's a right old rumpus and a half-hearted flailing of fists. But the two men manage to recover their sardines and after scraping off the skins deem them fit enough for eating.

Every time a woman goes into the toilet, some lads slip

a piece of wire through the door and undo the bolt, letting the door swing back to expose the poor woman to hoots of laughter. The flush isn't working properly. But people still go in, until I can see that the shit is brimming over the pan. The smell is overpowering. I'm beginning to feel almost hysterical with misery. This appalling behaviour and the babble of a hundred foreign voices is maddening. I've never thought of myself as a racist, but I hate these people, their dumb rural faces, ugly voices and stupid antics.

The train is far too crowded for passport checks. At Villa Opicina on the Italian border, the Yugoslav authorities make us all get off to have our documents checked. They treat us like scum, barking orders, pushing us into a line. It's frightening how a pair of boots and a peaked cap can turn men into fascist bullies. I'm beginning to feel sorry for my travelling companions now: poverty allows them to be treated like rats.

At Trieste the Yugoslavians alight en masse to spend their meagre wages on Western goodies like jeans and Walkmans. A troop of cleaners stuff bin bags with beer bottles, sardine tins, fag packets and banana skins. When they've finished, men in masks start hosing down the corridors, drowning the toilets in disinfectant. At least I'm on my own now, and I suppose I should be happy, but the train stinks of carbolic and there's a creepy silence. I imagine this is how the trains must have looked and smelled after delivering their frightened passengers to Auschwitz and Dachau.

By the time we get to Venice I'm calm again. I was so fed up for a while I thought of catching an aeroplane for the first time in my life, just to be back with people I know. But the panic has passed and I can last the 24 hours it takes before I'm back in London. Elaine … I'm so sorry. Once I'm home I'll start saving straight away, I'll take you for a weekend in Paris. We'll have a normal holiday, just like normal couples, just me and you and a little pink hotel on the Left Bank.

024

A Question of Class

The yuppie charades of the Eighties tainted us all one way or another. Like many people with more money than sense, I betrayed my socialist credo by regularly travelling first class between London and Burton.

We'd often sneaked a ride in first class during our train-spotting trips. It was a taste of forbidden fruit – fruit and a mouthful of dust left over from the 1950s. First-class compartments were defiantly elitist, with well-sprung seats padded in regal blue and creamy antimacassars. Instead of greasy roller blinds at the windows there were tasselled curtains. Sometimes there would be framed pictures of Highland stags or stately homes. Everything was imbued with the peculiar smell of old wealth: Parma violets, stale cigar smoke and denture fixative. Passengers' privacy was closely protected by ticket inspectors, and snotty-nosed kids like us were not even allowed to stand in the corridor, let alone sit down. As we were shooed away, we would catch a glimpse of old brigadiers dribbling in their sleep or ladies living out their autumn years on dwindling dividends. They travelled first class for the sake of their old bones – and because it was expected of them.

I always thought that second-class or 'standard' seats were comfortable enough for any reasonable human being. First class never had that much more to offer, apart from snob value. The premium is not for extra comfort – what really gives the first-class passenger a buzz is the leg room and the status. But it's all open-plan nowadays and even the smells are breezy and democratic, a haze of Lynx body spray and fresh coffee.

There's no pomp, no mystique, and the truth is that today's first class is something of an anachronism. We don't really need it and I'm not sure we deserve to have it.

I was never truly at ease cosseted in that rarefied atmosphere. I never felt I belonged there. It wasn't any kind of inferiority complex that made me think that, I just didn't like the idea of first class as a concept. I'd read about the five classes they'd had in Imperial Russia, and the first-class toilets they'd once had at Waterloo, and such things appalled me. I could blame all that on history, of course, but what on earth were we doing with first and second class in the last bit of the 20th century?

I enjoyed my socialist anger and spent the first-class journeys examining my fellow passengers for signs of snobbery. A combination briefcase, an Armani suit, a portable phone owner obviously so unimportant he had to resort to ringing out … these people weren't snobs or aristocrats or celebrities – disappointingly – just ordinary guys from semi-detached suburbia who liked the world to know they had money.

I nursed a constant fear of ejection. Not because I didn't have the money or the right ticket, but because I wasn't playing the game. A photographer commissioned to take a publicity shot of first class would have given me a wide berth. Among all the stripey-shirts with their briefcases and Parker pens, I was the worm in the bud. The one in jeans and trainers, a carrier bag full of newspapers and a bashed-in Pepsi tin rocking back and forth on the table. But however much I liked to imagine myself as some kind of fifth columnist, I don't suppose anyone took that much notice really.

My surliness can perhaps be traced back to an incident some years before, when Elaine and I took the train up to Burton to meet my mum. I thought we'd make an occasion of it, so splashed out on first class. We were lounging about waiting for the off when there was a sharp rapping at the window. I turned to see a chubby red-faced 'railman' glaring in at us.

'Come on, out of it,' he said, jerking his thumb at us.

Elaine and I exchanged glances and decided to ignore him. A minute later he was back, tapping on the glass again.

'I thought I told you to get out of there,' he snarled.

I stood up peered down at him through the open window. 'Why should we?'

'You're trespassing in first class,' he said, relishing the T-word. How lucky he was not to have a lisp.

'We've got first-class tickets,' I said.

He held a chubby hand up towards the window. 'Show me.'

'No,' I said. 'You're not a ticket inspector. You're only a porter.'

This slur had him stamping his feet with rage. 'If you don't show me your tickets I'll have this train blacked. Then you can explain to all the other passengers why they ain't going anywhere.'

I took out my wallet and hammed up a desperate search for the tickets, deliberately taking my time. Delight spread across his face. He'd nabbed two bilkers – he'd probably get a pat on the back for his vigilance. I drew out the suspense as long as I dared and almost felt sorry for him when I eventually handed over the tickets.

His face fell. He began to stutter apologies.

'Oh yes, first class, Euston to Burton-on-Trent. I'm sorry, sir. I must apologise.'

'S'alright,' I said matily. His hand-wringing penitence only embarrassed us. I'd just wanted to travel first class for a change, I didn't want men tugging their forelocks to me.

'Sorry, sir,' he insisted on saying.

'Forget it,' I said. I sat down with Elaine, anxious to be off and wishing him away.

'It's just that you don't look first class,' he added as the guard blew his whistle and the train drew away from the platform.

I'll never know if he was being quick-witted or whether he'd been so indoctrinated by the class system that the last remark had been said quite innocently.

I wasn't that much into trainspotting in the mid-Eighties. Since 1976, when I first started travelling between Euston and Birmingham, there'd been little to see anyway. Freed from the old habits, I started to take more notice of my fellow passengers – and I could always suss out the closet trainspotters. You always got a few in first class. They looked as if they were perusing office paperwork, and then all of a sudden a small notebook appeared from nowhere and you could see they were jotting down the number of a Class 87 electric or a humble shunter, nervously watchful for any signs of mockery from fellow passengers. Sometimes one of them would improvise a mini-confessional with the lid of his briefcase, enabling him to flick through the pages of *Railway Magazine* in peace. Further down the carriage other men browsed openly through *Mayfair*. They weren't ashamed: it was better to have a reputation as a randy executive than be branded a trainspotter!

One thing I did notice, though. I kept bumping into *Britannia* and *Royal Scot* and *The Black Prince*. Familiar names, but these weren't the magnificent green express locos from my childhood. The names had been hijacked for their nostalgia value and stuck on the side of the Class 87 electrics that shunted businessmen between London and Birmingham. Thirty years previously a name would have been something to remark on – 'Look, Dad, *Britannia*!' – but no one cared a toss now. It was a wasted exercise.

Another part of the first-class snobbery is the railway breakfast. Occasionally I had to visit Durham on business, seat paid for, food on expenses, so I treated myself. The eagerness with which my fellow diners tucked in was quite touching. From their waistlines it was easy to guess that their wives normally kept them on a diet of muesli and orange juice. What irony! The working man's bacon and egg fry-up had become both a kind of party treat and a symbol of first-class privilege.

I grew accustomed to first class and, despite my rebellious streak, no one so much as raised an eyebrow until some five years after the incident with Elaine, when I had another brush with a British Rail jobsworth. After buying a beer and a sandwich at the buffet I turned to go back to my seat – only to find my way barred by an official arm.

'Second class is back that way, sir,' the man said nastily.

'I am first class,' I spluttered. In no mood for games, I thrust my ticket at him straight away.

I wanted him to grovel, like the little fat bloke had, but he just shrugged and reluctantly moved aside to let me pass. But I felt no sense of victory, not with a queue of standard-class passengers behind me having a laugh at my expense. That'll teach him to be a snob, they were thinking. They were on the side of the British Rail ape, not mine. I was so upset that I wrote to InterCity to complain. I still have their letter.

I am sorry that you feel we have a 'stereotype' First Class passenger in mind. We are happy to see you travel in your denims and trainers, but you must recognise that this being the exception rather than the rule, people do tend to question this.

Our staff generally, I hope, do not take the action that you outlined in your letter and obviously we would be pleased to see you travel with us, whether it be First Class or Standard Class, and would not I hope make you feel awkward because of your attire.

I often wonder how many first-class passengers really enjoy their privilege. It doesn't take much to make them feel bashful or self-conscious, especially when some old dear totters through the carriage with her suitcase, heading for the hot and overcrowded standard class. There's a flicker of biblical guilt, just for a moment, until the old lady is followed by a family from a council estate with two chocolatey kids and a carrier bag full of snacks. These are the kind of interlopers, gloriously blind to the class divide, who commandeer a table and start sharing out the Penguins. Too scared of a knuckle sandwich, no one dares point out their mistake, so they sit and wait for the inevitable ejection by the ticket inspector, enjoying the show with self-satisfied smirks. The discomfort of others is a reliable source of amusement, but when it's all tied up with class it becomes particularly and distastefully British.

My foreign freebies were always first-class, of course, but I was happily conscience-free about those. Apart from the last time I went to France with Jinx. Even with his concessions, he could only afford a second-class ticket (the French still have the honesty to use the terms 'first' and 'second'). What was I to do? It would have been daft for us to travel in separate carriages, but on the other hand I was reluctant to forgo the luxury of first class on the TGV as it sped between Paris and Avignon.

In the end, socialism won the day and I sat in second with Jinx, much to the bafflement of the ticket inspector. I know he questioned me about it and tried to explain that I was needlessly discomforting myself. Since it would have been hard to explain it in English, let alone schoolboy French, I just smiled and let him do his Gallic shrug. But I can't help thinking that if the same thing had happened here at home, some of those BR inspectors (sorry, Revenue Protection Officers) would have insisted that I moved from second into first.

025

A Doomed Enterprise

The Sunday Luncheon Special was my new girlfriend Trish's idea. It wasn't real trainspotting, as such, more a way of showing off, spending money and convincing yourself you're having an 'experience' – like hot-air ballooning, bungee-jumping or 'murder weekends' in stately homes (though it seems odd that the murder weekend is the safest option there).

Trainspotters are often misunderstood, which is why mums, aunts and girlfriends think that anything to do with railways is a treat. You'll always get at least one birthday card depicting a steam loco. It's the thought that counts, of course, but the details can rankle, like when you get a card showing the LNER's *Mallard* in all its iconic glory. It's useless trying to explain that you're a Great Western man and you despise the LNER, and especially *Mallard*, ever since Andy Parker boasted about his granddad witnessing its record-breaking run. But women would never understand that at all. It's a train and you should be happy with it. How should they know the difference between one silly steam train and another! But that, you want to say but daren't, is the whole point of trainspotting.

Still, if someone else is paying for the tickets, I'm not going to say no.

Despite my good intentions, we get off to a bad start: I'm in my usual Millets casuals, but Trish is dressed like an Edwardian moll – waisted jacket, lacy blouse with a brooch at the throat, hair done up like the Duchess of Duke Street – the works. This is just what I dreaded. But before I get chance to tell her off for going over the top, I'm the one who gets it in the neck.

'Oh, for God's sake … couldn't you have worn something smarter? You don't go out for dinner in an anorak.'

As we get off the 159 in Ladbroke Grove and walk round to Marylebone station I catch a familiar sulphurous tang in the air and, as English as church bells, the wet sizzle of a steam whistle. The Bengali greengrocer patiently arranging satsumas in a pyramid is baffled: they told him that Britain had modern railways! But for two passing pensioners it's as if the whistle has signalled to them across the decades, giving them a chance to swap memories of when Marylebone was packed with evacuees bound for Leicestershire.

The station is swarming with steam fans, bodies festooned with video-cams and tape recorders. In the old days all a spotter needed was book, biro and duffel bag. Now, older and richer, he's fully equipped to record his memories and watch them on the home TV. And, you never know, if some dimwit (preferably a non-trainspotter) gets drenched by water from the loco there might be a clip worth sending in to *You've Been Framed* …

35028 *Clan Line* basks in the limelight, a gleaming green leviathan, wheels and pistons shiny with grease and loving care. I haven't seen this Bulleid Pacific since 1967, yet the years in between just fade away. The smell of smoke and hot oil makes me feel giddy with nostalgia, a yearning for those days at Nine Elms and Waterloo. If only someone could invent a process to can that distinctive aroma they would make themselves a fortune. Railway buffs would hold secret sniffing sessions in their club rooms and shrinks would pen papers on nostalgia abuse.

Men forget their wives and mortgages and become boys again, queueing patiently for a chance to climb up onto the footplate and listen to tales of gritty times on the iron road.

'Aye, I lost yon fingertip on *The Limited* back in '59,' the driver tells them. 'Me and Charlie were ten late out of Paddington, so we had to give it some hammer ...'

The men look fascinated, and then wistful, thinking: 'If only I could have been Fred's cheerful stoker instead of going in for financial consultancy.' Those who have brought their own children offer them up to be touched by Fred's heroic mutilated hand.

As we pull out of the old Great Central terminus, *Clan Line*'s wheels fight for a grip on wet rails, mechanical panic that sends clouds of steam billowing into the slate-grey skies. We wave to the lined-up spotters, but they have no time to wave back, for everything must be photographed and chronicled – especially a display like this. Snaking our way across the points, we leave them all behind and plunge into the tunnel that passes under Lord's cricket ground. Someone's forgotten to turn the carriage lights on, but the tablecloths are so fresh and white we can read our complimentary *Sunday Times* in the dazzle. Breaking daylight again, we rattle past hillocks of mangled cars and the backyards of kebab shops. In one an unshaven cook stands with his first cigarette of the Sabbath, dumbfounded by this eccentric intrusion.

Dismayed by the city's backside, we hurry on towards the leafy surrounds of Metroland. Flakes of soot come swirling in through the open windows. While a couple of trainspotters hang out with cameras and tape recorders, other passengers tut and glare. They want elegance without soot, they don't want their expensive taste of yesteryear spoiled by silly men with cameras. The Orient Express dream is all about handsome men in dinner jackets, fancy women with feather boas, a cad smoking Russian cigarettes ... not loonies with wire-bound notebooks.

Is there going to be a row? Some of us lean back, expecting free entertainment. But no, satisfied with his snaps, the culprit slams the window shut and puts his lens cap back on, blissfully unaware of spiteful stares. I'm on his side, though. The thing is, unless you actually stick your head outside and get a face full of smoke, you wouldn't even know it's a steam-hauled train. Sitting here, determinedly interior, we might just as well be on any old HST. I think the people who get the biggest thrill out of these steam trips are those who are watching the train go by. It may be a passing glimpse, but there's something exquisite about those few thunderous seconds.

It makes us feel like minor royalty, sipping tea and waving graciously to our subjects as they lean from their upstairs windows to watch us pass. The trip has been well publicised and some have been waiting for ages. Further on we see more spotters. They cling to the sides of bridges or stand amid fields of sheep, their zoom lenses peering right in at us, while their wives skulk in the warmth of family hatchbacks slowly sinking into the muddy English countryside.

In years gone by, having a meal on a train was nothing special. Nowadays only businessmen on expenses can afford the prices, so this Sunday Luncheon Special is a grand occasion. It is the kind of thing that some husbands cook up as a wedding anniversary treat, a twist on an age-old trick: hubby gets a look at some old steam trains and his wife gets the idea she's being pampered with pink napkins and Piat d'Or.

So far, all seems well with the Olde England the passengers are hoping to find – it still has its freckled-faced kids, patient wives and dotty menfolk with harmless hobbies. We unfold napkins and prepare for the great British Sunday lunch. Empires were built on such rituals. But, oh dear! This isn't the roast beef of Merrie England. With leathery slices of beef in gluey gravy, watery sprouts and seriously under-boiled spuds, this is no luncheon to recall the unhurried elegance of trips on the Cheltenham Flyer or the Pines Express. Being British (and the trip is all about being British) we suffer in silence, complaining to each other *sotto voce* but nodding politely to the waitress when she asks if everything is okay.

Nostalgia's big business these days and British Rail needs the income. But opportunists aren't the best people to trust with your dreams. Dolly birds in designer uniforms may be what marketing think the public wants (think again, chaps – the last thing an anniversary wife needs is hubby ogling the waitresses!). And they're no match for those old-time stewards who could balance spoonsful of *petits pois* at 60mph.

I hate this Orient Express snobbery, a reconstructed past with a suitable class system. The whole thing is a pose: not a love of trains, as such, more a hankering for the old upstairs/downstairs system. The yuppie years had already seen the re-emergence of shoe-shine boys, so it seemed quite fitting for people to travel first class and be served meals by stewards in red waistcoats.

The big trouble with nostalgia is that, at the end of the day, it's just a product. Not that they don't try to make it an 'experience', but they're so intent on getting it right that they'll never get it right, simply because the railways we loved were never quite right in the first place. This is nothing like the *real* past – where's Will Hay and his cack-handed crew, where's the pompous ticket inspector, the bolshy porter, and the fireman who looks like George Formby?

The stewards – the chaps who actually own the engine – travel in their own vintage coach and keep the door firmly locked against intruders. They seem to be a trifle wary of their passengers. Like old-style trainspotters, they sustain them-selves with railway gossip, fish-paste sandwiches and a flask of tea. But we passengers are not true enthusiasts, just day-trippers who have got the idea from a half-remembered Alan Whicker special.

As we near Stratford, a chap in a check jacket, one of the stewards, walks through the carriages to address us, adopting some tortured CIA-speak. 'On termination at Stratford,' he says, 'could we ask you all to de-train as quickly as possible.'

We're going to be terminated, not with extreme prejudice but with kid gloves. The reason for the hurry is – and here he coughs apologetically – 'some complicated shunting'. Shunting: now that is a robust English word, redolent of childhood nights listening to the clang of buffers in distant goods yards. But he doesn't think we'll understand 'shunting'; it's too obscure a term these days, as old-fashioned as haymaking or churning. He seems to be groping for some euphemism to make it more acceptable to non-trainspotters – the 'regrouping of passenger modules' or something like that. I want to grab him and say, 'Hey, I'm a trainspotter, there's no need to use that fancy language with me.'

But he'd just have grinned with embarrassment. And perhaps I wasn't really a trainspotter any longer. Quite the opposite: I was just another day-tripper pretending to be part of High Society, 'de-training at Stratford'.

Call me a philistine, but Stratford was crappy and boring, just another English town cashing in on its cutesy cottages and its family connections. The only thing to be thankful for is that the American tourists had gone home. We had just enough time to buy a bag of Maltesers and visit the superloo.

On our return journey, twilight turns the windows into dusty mirrors and we glimpse ourselves being served with afternoon tea. From far away, drifting back from the front of the train, we can hear the well-tempered beat of 35028's pistons. The smoke trails out for miles behind us, hanging torn and motionless in the indigo skies. Sheep stand and watch us pass. A mournful whistle scatters the dozing birds in the hedgerows.

We've almost escaped from the 1980s for a few hours – but not quite. Back at Marylebone everyone looks a bit down. They thought by coupling themselves up behind a polished-up steamer they could kid themselves they were back in 1954 again. But now, anxious to find taxis or buy Underground tickets, we are so obviously in the present. Looking for the past is a doomed enterprise: when you have to pay for it you can never escape the feeling you've been conned.

026

Almost Virtual Reality

In the mid-Eighties I 'acquired' a twelve year-old son. (The details are too personal to belong here, but readers who have paid attention will easily put two and two together.) I didn't have a clue how to begin making up for those twelve years apart. W.H. Smith had a 'parenting' section full of books – breathing exercises for mums-to-be and advice for fussing fathers – but nothing for men like me who had suddenly found themselves on the spot. Nor was there anyone I could turn to for advice. Bonding would be the first step, of course, but I was determined to avoid visits to McDonald's or the zoo.

Our first outing as father and son was to the National Railway Museum in York. The place was full of lovingly restored railway engines, every one as pretty as a carnival organ. But as we walked from exhibit to exhibit, I couldn't help feeling uneasy: not once did I hear the cracking of coal or clinker underfoot. Though imaginatively housed in the old MPD, the irony is that the museum is a strictly smoke-free zone, the slightest whiff being enough to set off alarm bells and send punters stampeding for the exits.

Old nameplates lined the walls, but they might as well have been factory-produced horse brasses for all they had to do with my experience. It was like trainspotting's trophy room, all the nice bits, snapped off from real life and somewhat mean-ingless. Everything here was too good to be true. It wasn't that Martin was bored (even children want to see the coach in which Queen Victoria did a piddle) but he didn't seem exactly fired up either. We visited the shop and returned home with the obligatory jigsaws and reproduction posters, but it hadn't been quite the triumph I'd hoped for.

I didn't want Martin to see my past as a museum exhibit – a school cap, a biro and a bottle of Tizer artfully arranged in a glass display case – I wanted him to smell it for real, the smoke, the sulphur and the sizzling grease. I wanted him to hear the rattle of wagons in the sidings and marvel at the flattened penny, still warm to the touch. Then I'd just keep my fingers crossed in the hope that he might see the fun he and I could have together, and in some small way make up for lost time. An arrogant wish really. Why should a child be stamped by his father's past? Why did it have to be on my terms? If I was that keen to bond, perhaps I should I take up skateboarding.

Severn Valley Railway, 1986. Only twenty yards separates the bare station at Kidderminster from the terminus of the Severn Valley Railway, but it's easy to feel you've stepped back forty years in time. The benches in the ticket hall are solidly wooden, polished up by a hundred years of fidgeting bottoms. Up on the walls, yesterday's poster girls beckon us to join them for fun on the beach. There's a half-oval ticket window, small enough to preserve the mystery and ritual of the ticket clerk's job. Even the act of bending to it is a lot like being in a confessional: you can't see the man clearly, only his chin and mouth, but you have to do important business with him.

'One and a half return to Bewdley, please.'

Visually the station is a treat, and it snags the other senses too. The thump of the old ticket-dating machine sounds like an echo that has taken thirty years to return to us. Even the air smells old. Warmed by sunlight, the woodwork exudes elusive half-forgotten aromas from the 1950s: lonely cigarettes, rain-damp mackintoshes, a twist of Bay Rum. It's quite spooky when the past engages all the senses simultaneously, but as you emerge from the booking hall and see a man selling Cornettos and hot dogs, reality ripples back into place. It's a relief to get your bearings again.

A train of 'rhubarb and custard' coaches stands waiting at the long and uncrowded platform, all its doors flung back, open and inviting. There is time for us to walk up and stand alongside the loco and give it the once-over. I can't resist slipping into lecturer mode.

'Well, Martin, this is a Great Western "Manor" class, it's a 4–6–0 mixed traffic loco, designed by Hawksworth and built at Swindon …'

Feeling the heat from the firebox and hearing the sizzling pent-up pressures of the boiler, Martin is intuitively respectful of the loco's power. My commentary is irrelevant. Does it matter how many wheels the Manor has or who built it? He looks disappointed by my sudden change of role, from dad to tour guide, and I make an effort to stop waffling.

After all our 1968 agonies over the end of steam, things couldn't have worked out better. Britain is choc-a-bloc with preserved railways – the Great Central, the South Devon, the Severn Valley, the Keighley and Worth Valley, the Watercress Line and dozens of others, so many that it seems as if we've created a parallel world, a country where time stopped around 1960. Most of the lines make a profit too, for which we should be grateful. Steam age purists might object to some of the marketing gimmickry – Thomas the Tank Weekends, Hot Cross Bun Specials, Santa's Winter Express – but you can't blame the managers for exploring any angle that helps keep the line alive and viable. And the kids love it. Still, it must be a shock for an old boy who turns up for communion with a fondly-remembered loco, an old friend from the past – only to find a huge Thomas face smirking at him from the smokebox door …

But none of us has a monopoly on old steamers and how they should be enjoyed, and if we can share the pleasure in different ways, so much the better for their continued survival. In any case, the Hot Cross Bun and Santa trips are one-off events. When the weekenders have returned home in their Ford Fiestas, the railways are returned to the care of their most devoted admirers, the men who love them for all their moods and not their smiley weekend faces.

Our day at Severn Valley is full of illusions. It's not just the steamers and old carriages that trick me. Sitting opposite Martin in the compartment, I feel as if it's not just him who's getting on for thirteen, but me too. We're back in the Sixties, two kids on a spotting trip. He's even trying to listen to *Sergeant Pepper* on my Walkman, while I've been making silly squeaking noises with the arm of the seat. Now, in the hope of amusing him, I bash the seat cushions with my fist, sending up mushroom clouds of ancient dust.

'Dad …' Martin looks embarrassed, in the panic-stricken way that only teenagers can, looking to the door to make sure no one's watching.

I really should remember that I'm a father now, as well as an adult. But today is proving difficult for me. This is my *Blue Remembered Hills* and the realisation that I can't return to 1965 is actually quite unsettling.

There are one or two spectators standing around on Arley station, and I deliberately avoid using the T-word here. We're not among true trainspotters at the Severn Valley. There's nothing to spot, as such, and none of these men have come in the hope of copping anything new. They've all seen 7812, 43106 and 45110 a dozen times before. The enthusiasts here today are a different species. With their Sony camcorders and Pentax SLRs they seek to capture something more elusive than mere numbers: gauzy mirages of their own childhoods, perhaps, lost lives glimpsed through gaps in the smoke. It's a paradox, this use of technology in such a spiritual quest, and I can't help thinking that a Ouija board would be more appropriate. The best thing about the SVR is that it's all pain-free and we've got all the time in the world to enjoy it. In this time bubble there is no rust, no boilers caked in limescale, no chalked-on numbers. There will be no withdrawals, no scrappings. The Manors, Halls and Blackies are as close to eternal as can be. This is locomotive heaven.

Our success in recreating this delightful semi-rural England is remarkable. Once it was possible only with the model railways in our sheds and lofts, but these people have done it for real. The stations, lovingly restored, have gas lights and Great Western fire buckets, Gold Flake adverts and penny chocolate machines.

A door creaks open and out steps an old-fashioned railwayman. He looks at the departing train, plucks a watch from his waistcoat pocket and gives a satisfied nod. These aren't real staff, of course, but trainspotters in disguise, men who give up their weekends to play at signalmen, stationmasters and porters. No role is too menial. And it's not just the uniform that looks convincing; this chap has even got the unconcerned amble off to a T. Not all them are oldies who actually remember the steam age. This one looks as if he would be more at home at a Dire Straits concert. Yet there's no denying his enthusiasm and commitment: he's even grown mutton-chop whiskers to fit in with the period flavour (though it's just possible that he bought them from a fancy dress shop).

This *trompe-l'oeil* doesn't always work. Steam locos and cute stations aren't the only things we miss. It's the whole thing, a scale of operations that even the most dedicated enthusiasts could never recreate: the round-the-clock railway activity, the sepulchral gloom of the sheds, the clang of buffers in the goods yard, the ghostly whistle in the small hours, the night train throwing panicked shadows against the slummy houses.

There are a half dozen locos on shed at Bewdley, enough to make it look busy, and with clinker crunching underfoot and oily puddles for the unwary to ruin their Hush Puppies in, it looks much like one of the smaller depots I might have bunked in the Sixties. I take a few snaps of Martin, sitting on an old boiler, standing on the footplate of a Blackie. No one bothers us. But that's part of the trouble. I wish we weren't welcome, I wish I could share with Martin the adrenalin thrill of bunking a shed. Wouldn't it be the perfect bonding experience if some old codger of a foreman was to come out of his office and chase us off?

Steam fans are chasing a past which is always receding. To stop it dwindling like the dot on a TV screen, they've had to resort to rewriting history. Not just once either, but every decade or so. Gresley's A3 *Flying Scotsman*, for instance, was originally preserved as LNER loco 4472 and painted apple green. But many of those who remember that pre-nationalisation look are now dead or senile, so to please the ones with the spending power nowadays, it has been repainted and rebadged as British Railways 60103. The old guard hate it – where has their apple green beauty gone? – but as they die off so do their opinions and values.

Having *Flying Scotsman* preserved ought to be enough, but it isn't. Everyone demands their 'rights' these days. What about the old spotters who want to see another A3 instead, *Brown Fox* say, one which was dragged off to the scrapyard well before the preservation movement got under way? They just had to lump it. Until someone said why should they? The loco was theirs, so they should be able to do what they liked. And they did, having two fibre-glass *Brown Fox* nameplates made, painting 60036 on the cabside and – hey presto! – who would know the difference?

The preserved railways have invented their own version of virtual reality, in the belief that everything can be recreated. They hold night-time events, so that photographers can recapture that special nocturnal atmosphere. They run mock freights, trainloads of empty wagons going nowhere, delivering nothing. Train numbers no longer matter. Everything is done for the benefit of the assembled photographers. It makes me a little uneasy. Nostalgia is mainly harmless, but playing around with loco names and numbers ... who knows where it will end?

Did it work? I asked myself at the end of our day at the SVR, as Martin and I headed back to Burton on our all-too-modern bog unit. Did the smell of steam and the activity of an old-fashioned railway impress him? I couldn't be sure. It had been less sterile than York, more smelly and crunchy all round. It would have been a thrill for me if Martin had taken the heavy hint and become a railway enthusiast, but I knew it wasn't that likely. This toytown steam railway, however lovingly recreated, was just another theme park.

In 1993 British steam buffs had a nasty shock. Eurocrats in Brussels noticed them. All these years they'd been happily chucking coal here and there, stoking up roaring fires, letting off high-pressure steam just inches away from passengers. The whole business was as wacky as an *It's a Knockout* game. But the nannyish rule-makers were concerned about the hot surfaces and the scalding steam. Notwithstanding the fact that most of the drivers were old hands and accepted burns and scalds (and the occasional flying coal lump) as an occupational hazard, Brussels decided that they needed protection. In future all hot surfaces had to be clearly flagged with fluorescent yellow stripes and warnings in four languages. And this would apply as much to Castles and Black 5s as it did to the school boiler and the oven in the local cafe.

When steam buffs realised that their beloved locos, so painstakingly restored in liveries of apple green or crimson lake, might have to be painted yellow, they were horrified. In the end, Britain managed to get itself a waiver, as it so often does. A victory for common sense maybe, but with overtones of old-fashioned rivalries. We'd stopped the ruddy Brussels lot messing with our sausages and our pints and, by jingo, did they really think we'd let them paint up our lovely steam engines like day-glo zebras?

THE NINETIES

027

A Day at the Speedway

Lichfield Trent Valley was always one of our favourite destinations. On our bikes we could be there in an hour or so, two or three of us taking a straight run down the A38 with the slipstreams of lorries to help us along. It would be a brave lad who made that same trip today, but back then it made a great day out in the summer holidays – and cost us next to nothing.

To kids from Burton, where the trains were mostly dependable plodders, the Trent Valley line was an exciting holiday, a silver speedway running through the flat Midlands scenery. We'd heard so much about it already, though we'd missed its heyday, just as we had in so many places. The Euston and northbound expresses were no longer hauled by Coronations, Scots or Britannias, but it was still a thrill to watch those blue electrics burning round the cambered curve at 80mph. Attention was vital: sometimes they flashed by so quickly we hardly had time to clock the small metallic numbers.

The overhead wires always held a malignant fascination. We had heard stories of boys playing with sticks, being fried as they stood. There were plenty of warnings, yet still they did it, thinking that the danger wasn't real, a lion they could safely goad by rattling a stick on its cage. But this was no lion, it was an invisible elemental force; they were playing with nature itself – and it always won. None of us would ever be that stupid … and yet we could never quite dismiss the thought that death lurked there, just a couple of feet above our heads.

Few trains deigned to stop, and the daily routine left staff with plenty of time on their hands to sweep platforms, tend flowerbeds and even construct a rockery which had LICHFIELD TRENT VALLEY spelled out in butter-coloured stones. It was easy to think you were on some sleepy country station, an impression soon dispelled by the pinched whine of the expresses and the overhead wires which seemed to fizz with trapped energy. In the afternoon, one of the stopping trains would appear in the far distance, sliding out of the heat haze and setting off a flurry of activity. A door creaked open and a porter came blinking into the light, caramel-coloured mail sacks were thrown on and off, the stationmaster cracked a joke with the train driver and – very occasionally – a passenger was seen boarding or alighting.

The station had no buffet, nothing at all to sustain spotters or passengers, apart from a solitary chocolate machine offering Needlers chocolate or the ubiquitous Paynes Poppets. There was a pub, though, at the end of the station driveway, and one of us would be deputed to go up and buy a bottle of pop and packets of cheesy biscuits from the Off Sales.

So much for memories. It's always a danger to return to places which once meant so much, but a trainspotter with any kind of track record can never really avoid it.

Trent Valley was once a dignified building of red brick, with fretworked awnings that offered shelter from the rain and shade from the sun. All that's gone now, replaced by a prefab ticket office and, on the up platform, a glorified bus shelter with squeaky tip-up seats. Time was when the British waited for their trains with a mixture of impatience and resigned languor. Now even that has been trivialised. I suspect that the architects (does a bus shelter *need* an architect?) want us to look like the matchstick citizens on their sketches – pretty and stylish and completely fictional. Law-abiding as I am, I can't help but feel some empathy for whoever has scrawled 'Baz n Sue were here' in felt-tip on the glass. Unsightly it may be, but as a protest against sterility it can scarcely be called vandalism.

31. By the 1980s the signal box at Wetmore Sidings was looking rather forlorn and vandalised, a ruined outpost of the past's 'other country'.

32. A trainspotter's love nest … the Tabac de la Gare in Fontainebleau holds some very fond memories of that August bank holiday, 1979.

33. Never mind Checkpoint Charlie – what about that right charlie who ended up in the icy wastelands of Berlin's shunting yard in a freezing January 1980?

34. Almost invisible (except to a determined spotter), a DMU lurks
in the shadows of Henley-on-Thames station, the archetypal branch
line terminus (and end of the line for yet another relationship).

35. English Electric 50043 doing a little 'hoovering'
at Paddington station in 1981.

36. The almost rural charm of Athens station in March 1982.

Nicholas Whittaker

37. 35028 *Clan Line* at Marylebone at the head of the Shakespeare Limited in 1986.

Nicholas Whittaker

Nicholas Whittaker

38. This is more fun than McDonald's! My son Martin larking about at the Severn Valley Railway in 1986.

39. The classic railway scene. An HST skirts the seawall at Dawlish in the 1990s. It's not a steamer, but it's the seaside, so stop complaining!

Derby

43090

40. HST 43090 at Derby during a day out with younger sons in the mid-1990s.

41. The nameplate of Great Western 6960 *Raveningham Hall*,
polished back to glory.

42. A Gresley A4 passing through Burton on
an enthusiasts' special in the early Noughties.

43. Ex-LNER locos A1 60129 and V2 60828 in the roundhouse at York sheds (50A) on 19 July 1965 – a building still in use today as part of the National Railway Museum.

Bill Wright

In much the same way, I'm always grateful for the presence of trainspotters. They are totally superfluous individuals, neither staff nor passengers, devoid of any revenue potential, their only function being to muck up the idealised vistas of architects and marketing men, rather like the smirking faces that always manage to get in the background when an MP or company spokesperson is being interviewed on TV, deflating any attempt at dignity or subterfuge.

Apart from the expresses, flung northwards on a cat's cradle of wires, time still ticks slowly at Trent Valley. Maybe that is why it still attracts. Trainspotting has, for many adherents, me included, a purely meditative function. While some like to sit by gurgling streams or perch atop the fells, others prefer to do their navel-gazing alongside railway lines. They're not collecting numbers, they don't take photographs, and they don't display much emotion when an express cracks through the station. A bench on a deserted platform is their retreat from the hurly-burly. What better idyll on a summer Saturday in England? Birds twitter, spiders build webs between the broken bricks, and in the short siding already disused in 1966, the rails rust with painful and immeasurable slowness.

Appreciating this tranquillity, I felt a bit guilty about introducing two boisterous children into the scene on my visit in 1994. You can't expect young boys to appreciate the meditative function of railways: for them it's pure excitement. Despite the blandishments of car culture, all that squeaky-clean bodywork doesn't do much for children. Grime and grinding is what grabs them, so what better than to sit watching a growling Class 56 stickied up with an honest patina of grease and brake dust? And no Formula One race will ever come close to the thrilling sounds and the fearsome power of an unleashed Class 90 cracking along at 100mph.

It gave me a queer feeling to return to these old haunts. Apart from the changes to the station buildings, Lichfield Trent

Valley was much the same as I remembered it. Summer holiday weather, the dusty fragrance of grass, blue skies with the needle glint of an aeroplane bound for the Americas, and the shimmering heat haze down the line, from which the trains would emerge, speed distorted by distance – until they were right on top of you, an elongated blur of paintwork, glass and faces. Standing there on the station, changed as it was, I could see myself perched on the wall by the sidings, leaning over to my saddlebag to grab my spotting book or bag of crisps. I could almost remember our stupid schoolboy jokes, the idle boasts about girls, snatches of conversation. Then I had to blink and cough loudly to wake myself from a dream – to find myself standing there with two children of my own. How could I ever have imagined this back in 1966? It was like a *Twilight Zone* episode, creepy and inexplicable, yet possessing an internal logic of its own.

The afternoon stopping trains were still running, but the greatest surprise was 017 – an EMU so antiquated that we probably saw it doing just the same job back in 1966, when we'd be V-signing the driver to get out of the way because his train was blocking our view of the fast line.

As well as the main Euston–Crewe line, Trent Valley also boasts a 'high level'. In the heyday of the railways dozens of towns had more than one station, and there were several, like Tamworth or Retford, where one line crossed over or under another. At Newark two main lines crossed each other on the same level! At Lichfield two very different cultures crossed at right angles: the clean and speedy InterCity future whizzing through below, while up above steam-hauled freights still plodded their way to Derby or Walsall.

The high-level station was shut to passengers in the Sixties and left to rot under a thin slime of moss. It has now been reopened to passengers and the platforms at Lichfield are the northern end of the West Midlands Cross-City Line. There's not so much traffic as there used to be, but it's good to see life here again after years of neglect.

Not that they call it Trent Valley High Level these days. Such old-fashioned terms would be out of place on today's railways. It was always a mouthful at the ticket office: 'Child Day Return to Lichfield Trent Valley High Level, please.' It's a shame, though, since these arcane station names added to the mystique and variety of railway life. What price now Hull Paragon, Templecombe Upper, Yeovil Pen Mill, Carlisle Citadel, or all those Victorias, Exchanges and Centrals? A reluctant hold is kept on Bristol Temple Meads, Exeter St Davids or Worcester Shrub Hill, if only to distinguish them from other stations in the same town, but given half a chance such history would be consigned to the bin. Those distinctive names are embedded in me now, even those which have been quietly dropped, and I often try to catch out the ticket office by asking for a return to Wolverhampton High Level, Derby Midland or Cheltenham Spa Lansdown.

Some towns are forever marked by the railways. My home town of Burton-on-Trent only became that to distinguish it from other stations at Burton Joyce and Burton Latimer. But no one calls it Burton-on-Trent in everyday life – we never talk of Burton-on-Trent Albion, or Burton-on-Trent ale, and none of the local firms call themselves anything other than Burton something-or-other. But there's always a reluctance to reclaim the name Burton for itself, as if this large industrial town could still be confused with Burton Joyce!

Trent Valley station may have changed, but the signal box hadn't when I visited twenty years ago.* It looked old-fashioned even in the Sixties, a steam-age structure marooned between the speeding electric trains. The windows down at track level were blackened by years of smoke and dirty water.

---

* The magnificent signal box was demolished in 2008 during an upgrading of the West Coast route.

Windolene would have been no use – you'd have needed a paint scraper and a gallon of vinegar.

Remembering the military smartness of the old station-master – polished shoes, peaked cap, clipped moustache – it was a shock to see the young signalman of the Nineties sporting a ponytail.

I've always been envious of the signalman's job and often imagined myself with a cushy posting on some lonely freight branch, with little to do except lean on the veranda on a summer's day, smoking an unhurried cigarette, retreating inside come winter to sit beside a coal stove tapping out a bestseller on a portable typewriter. No doubt a real-life signalman will tell me I'm harbouring foolish dreams and that there is some work involved.

The line was the focus of some notoriety in the late Eighties and early Nineties, when a suspiciously large number of people fell out of speeding trains. Newspapers dubbed it the 'Tamworth Triangle'. All manner of explanations were offered: the passengers were drunk or fooling about, British Rail said. The railways are falling apart, said the newspapers. Either way, I'm glad I wasn't on the station at the time, judging by some of the gruesome tales I heard about severed limbs and decapitated bodies. Railwaymen, like old sailors, love spinning yarns and the more horrible the better.

I even dreamed up a crackpot theory about an evil presence haunting the line. As well as these incidents there'd been a lot of fatal crashes along here: Lichfield in 1946, Hixon in 1968, Nuneaton in 1975, and the worst of all, further down the line at Harrow in 1952. I could picture, like a scene in a film, door locks sliding open while an unwitting passenger leans at the window to enjoy the scenery. It made me think, with a shiver, of all the years I spent leaning on doors. It never occurred to me they might be unsafe: my faith in the men at the carriage works was unquestioned.

028

Postcard from Dawlish

I've been here before, I thought, when I pitched up at Dawlish on the Western railrover of 1968. Actually, until then, I had never been further west than Bristol. But I recognised Dawlish instantly: I'd seen it a thousand times – on holiday postcards and jigsaws, on toffee-tin lids and the covers of old annuals bought at jumble sales. That picture of a Great Western 'Castle' skirting the sea wall with a holiday train, puffing benevolent cotton-wool smoke over the heads of the holiday-makers, is one of the enduring images of the Golden Age. Even today it turns up everywhere; especially, I've noticed, on birthday cards for men in the 45–60 age group.

By 1968 I'd missed the Castles and Kings by a good five years, but I did have those quirky Warships and eager-to-please little Hymeks instead. Where else but the Western Region did you get diesel-hydraulics? Where else did the locos have maroon livery? Twenty years after nationalisation, the Western Region carried on regardless, still doing its own thing. It still considered itself 'Great' – and for me it was.

Back at school, I was an insufferable show-off. At break, in between mouthfuls of Bovril crisps, I couldn't wait to tell them all about my Warship bashes, and my instant rapport with the drivers who took the Westerns from Bristol to Penzance. Some of my classmates refused to believe me: I was only fifteen, after all – my mum would never have let me stay out all night – and how had I got hold of £12 for the ticket? But I had some photographs as proof. Proof that I'd been, all right, but poor evidence of the real glories of Dawlish. These black-and-white snaps would never convince them about those distinctive terra-cotta cliffs and the maroon splendour of the diesel-hydraulics. And when I told them there were palm trees growing close to Dawlish station, they just laughed behind my back.

This is where trainspotting started, twenty years before Ian Allan, on this holiday line from Paddington to the newly-named Cornish Riviera. The Great Western, PR-wise long before PR had even been invented, milked their holidaymakers for every penny. Gimmicks and souvenirs abounded: GWR tea towels, GWR crockery, GWR guidebooks. To keep children amused on the six- or seven-hour journeys to Cornwall, there were games and jigsaws – and lists of Great Western locos to look out for along the way. Simple self-promotion it may have been, but they had hit upon a winner. The lists soon became the latest craze, one which rival railway companies were quick to copy. In 1942 the first Ian Allan *ABC*s were issued and the whole trainspotting thing took off.

Some people have never heard of Dawlish, and yet, spotters or not, they'd know it straight away. The image of steam trains skirting the sea is filed away in folk memory, a watercolour depiction of a vanished England. Steam trains, seaside, waving children – it's got all the right ingredients. Even the privatised rail companies still use it on their pamphlets, knowing that when it comes to winning hearts and minds, the best brains in advertising could never think up a better image. This is the best-loved stretch of line in Britain: few passengers remain indifferent when their train pulls away from the mudflats of the River Exe and meets the sea. There's always a rustle of excitement, some atavistic pleasure in reaching blue waters.

The line needn't have been constructed along the coast like this, but Brunel was a showman and a maverick; he always wanted to impress. And he certainly did that, but I.K. left British Rail with an awful headache in track maintenance. In winter the waves can rear up forty feet, smashing against the station walls and lashing across the tracks, where the ballast has to be securely tied with steel netting. In February 2014 the line was washed away completely, leaving all stations westward cut off from the network. It was national news, as were the ongoing repairs and the endless debates about the cost to Cornwall's economy. How had we come to be so dependent on this one stretch of track, people demanded. It was ridiculous, why wasn't there another way round? And of course there had been, until Beeching axed it.

Dawlish is the only bit of British Rail to have a station perched above the promenade in such a daring and whimsical way. What other station could set you down so directly yards from the beach? From up on the cliffs the station looks fragile and precariously poised, but closer inspection shows it to be solid, built to sound Victorian values with stiff girders and bolts as big as penny buns.

Even now, in this age of the car, a summer Saturday sees the trains come through Dawlish every ten minutes. During the Twenties and Thirties and after the war it must have been an amazing procession.

Dawlish has always been good cinema too. I've watched *The Ghost Train* countless times, but the simple humour is fresh every time: Arthur Askey pulls the communication cord as his train passes Dawlish, then goes chasing his 'titfer' along the track while the loco simmers and the guard goes mad. For a later film, not quite equal to the classic *The Ghost Train*, neighbouring Teignmouth was renamed Tinmouth when Norman Wisdom arrived there to botch up the world of journalism.

They weren't the only jokers who visited. In 1969, when I persuaded Jinx to join me on a second Western railrover, our favourite prank was to lean out of the train and strafe the strolling holidaymakers with peashooters. Harmless schoolboy fun, but looking back I do feel guilty about it, as if I abused the very thing that makes Dawlish special. We didn't do it that often, though: one time the train stopped unexpectedly, and one of our victims, a man with tattoos, sprinted towards the station bent on punishment. He didn't quite make it, fortunately, but it scared us enough to put us on our best behaviour from then on.

It's not only trainspotters who find Dawlish thrilling. This is where the trains touch everyone, and kids who've come 300 miles by road, trussed into their seats like turkeys, begin to wonder if they've been missing out. The yellow HSTs may not be an ideal image for toffee-tin lids, but they still have the power to thrill. Children look up from their sandcastles every time a train passes (even a Sprinter) and the passengers – old ladies, backpackers, even businessmen – still wave back to the paddlers and deckchair loungers and wish they could join in the fun. It's times like these, relaxed, inspired, that make you reflect on the emotional poverty of car culture versus the joyful communism of the trains.

But there are dark forces at work. Motoring and airline values continue to seep into the railways, destroying their charm. HST passengers are sealed in now, air-conditioned and sound-insulated, but they press close against the windows and look longingly out. Rail companies try hard to impress travellers with comfort, but deny them the simple pleasures: what these passengers really want to do is fling open the windows and stick their heads out, to fill their lungs with salty seaside air.

I had an emotional attachment to Dawlish, a love that was partly to do with the railways, but also so much more. It was during these late Sixties railrovers that I began to suspect there was something more to trainspotting than simply filling notebooks with numbers. Half of it was about the trains, sure enough, but the other half was about something invisible. Sitting up on Langstone Rock with Jinx during a third 1970 rover, I felt overcome by emotion, humming Beethoven's 'Ode to Joy' (Miguel Rios had a guitar version in the charts just then) as the trains headed along the coast. But songs of joy and tears of joy are not quite the ticket on a trainspotting jaunt, so I knew I'd have to keep such feelings under wraps.

Between 1976 and 1990 I never went to Dawlish at all, though I often thought of it and sometimes a maroon shadow would slide through my dreams, gone when I awoke, leaving me frustrated at not catching the number. The nearest I came to Dawlish in those years was in 1982 when I went for a job as a copywriter at a tiny advertising agency in Exmouth. It was a desperate move, since none of the posh London agencies seemed to want me, and it would mean leaving my enjoyable London life behind. Still, if I got to feeling lonely, I'd still have the railways and it would have been only a ten-minute ferry ride across the Exe to Dawlish.

Dawlish, 1994. The GWR steamers have long gone, the Warships and Westerns are as Seventies as tank tops, but the trainspotters still come here. For some it's just a couple of hours, a stopover between Exeter and Plymouth; others stay longer, booking into one of the B&Bs that cash in on their lineside locations by advertising in the railway magazines. Jinx often organises the family holiday there, so he can watch trains while his wife and children lick 99s and play pitch 'n' putt. He thinks he's being smart, but I suspect his wife cottoned on to his dodge years ago.

But maybe spotters aren't coming quite as often as they used to. The last locos to regularly haul passenger trains here were the 'Hoovers', but even they've gone now. There had been enough enthusiasts over the years for Dawlish to have its own railway bookshop, run by an enthusiast. It's a sign of the times that the premises are deserted now, though in the window pictures and book covers linger, fading in the sun but defiantly reminding townspeople and visitors of the glories of Dawlish.

At midnight Dawlish is as quiet as the grave. The pubs and the chip shop are shut, Belisha beacons blink unregarded and the only sound comes from the slap of waves against the breakwater. The station is lit up but deserted, except for one loner with a flask and a pair of binoculars. Luckily no one else sees him – the police would take him for a trespasser, a passer-by for some kind of voyeur; but watching from my holiday flat, I know he's just a harmless trainspotter.

At this time of day there are no holiday trains to record, no friendly railwayman to chat to, just solitude and discomfort. What on earth can be the attraction? Then a Railfreight Class 37 with half a dozen tanker wagons emerges from the tunnel and rattles up the coastline. It's at times like this you know that it's all worthwhile.

029

Notes from an Open Day: Worcester, 1994

From the post-war Derby Works Flower Show right up to the Severn Valley's Diesel Gala Weekends, railway open days are a long tradition. I love the atmosphere; broadened out from mere trainspotting, leavened with a colourful crowd of wives and children, it's as quaint and English as a village fete. Here are my memories of a typical open day, Worcester in 1994, with my son Robin and Mark, a friend from university.

The Yorky ice-cream van is doing a roaring trade in 99s. There's no Miss Marple at this kind of fete, of course, but there are bound to be a few clergymen wandering around the old goods yard behind Shrub Hill station.

Children, as well as vicars, love trains, and parents welcome the excuse to bring them along. They start them young, before they can even hold a biro; everywhere there are pushchairs juddering across the ballast or being lifted up over the rails as Dad homes in on a favourite engine. The locos are static, so there's no danger and the older kids can wander at will.

This isn't trainspotting as such, since no one expects to see anything fresh or out of the ordinary, but it's one of numerous events in the trainspotting 'season'. You just have to show your face, that's the main thing. No one wants to be left without a point of view when the subject of Worcester 1994 comes up over a pint, even if it's only along the lines of: 'Worcester? Our ruddy Sprinter was diverted via Lichfield because of engineering. We were forty late getting in.' Note that a true spotter, emulating railwayman's parlance, would never say *forty minutes*, just *forty*, since everyone would know he couldn't possibly mean forty hours.

One of the big attractions of an open day is the chance to climb up in the loco cabs and pull a few levers. Hauling myself up the steps into the cab of E3003 (one of the old blue-painted electrics that used to bowl through Trent Valley at 90mph) I bump into my first clergyman. He's semi-disguised in trainers and jeans, but his tweedy jacket and dog-collar are a dead giveaway. Perched in the driver's seat, he presses all the buttons like an excited child and whistles high-speed fantasies through his teeth.

The festival atmosphere is coloured by the sound of Dire Straits over the loudspeakers. They can joke about men in anoraks listening to old Kathy Kirby records or folky singalongs about navvies blasting through the Pennines, but pop music has always been important for rail fans. In the heyday of British pop, groups wrote about railways without any self-consciousness. The Beatles had 'Ticket to Ride' and 'Day Tripper', of course, but there were all kinds of oblique references elsewhere, in The Kinks' 'Waterloo Sunset' where Terry met Julie at Waterloo station; Paul Simon's 'Homeward Bound', 'sitting on the railway station with a ticket to my destination'; and The Seekers with their lovely 'train whistle blowing, makes a sleepy noise'. The Kinks also made their feelings known in 'The Last of the Steam Powered Trains'. One of my favourites was 'Euston Station' by Barbara Ruskin, a Sixties singer-songwriter who was way ahead of her time.

Privatisation has already reared its ugly head. Some of the promised exhibits have failed to turn up. Under the new rules, locomotive owners must pay Railtrack for the privilege of travelling their rails – an extra cost that's too much for some of the preservation groups. So there's no Warship or Class 52, a great disappointment to many visitors, including me. Still, their owners have managed to bring themselves and have set up a stand from where they can rattle their collecting tins and sell souvenir booklets.

The ragged parade of stalls alongside the tracks is doing good business. Or rather, it attracts lots of interest. I don't know how many of the browsers actually part with any cash. The stallholders aren't here to provide a free show, but they watch good-naturedly while a motley procession of bashers flick through old timetables and rule books and ponder whether a *Mallard* eraser is a good buy at 30p.

At the serious end of the collecting business, a stout chequebook is essential. It's hard to believe how the prices of relics have inflated. A numberplate from a steam loco – probably nicked in the first place – will now set you back at least £100, or up to £500 if it's from a Castle or a Jubilee. (If you haven't got the money, don't worry. You can always buy a realistic resin one for £9.50.) Even an uninspiring metal sign from Carshalton station circa 1966 has a price tag of £150 stuck to it. Wandering up and down, I keep an eye out for my Horninglow nameplate, though I don't know what I'd do if l saw it.

What fascinates me most is the bric-à-brac, particularly a set of buttons from a stationmaster's uniform. But what do you actually do with them? Sew them on a favourite cardigan, or keep them in a special button-collector's album? There are knives and forks from the old Great Western, seriously tarnished now, but imbued with nostalgia. You couldn't set out this cutlery for guests without making them wonder about your mental state. Perhaps it's a solitary pleasure. You eat your fish fingers and Birds Eye peas with them and, half-closing your eyes, imagine yourself in the restaurant car of the Cheltenham Flyer on a summer evening back in 1957.

At least there's something old-fashioned about the GWR cutlery. But who on earth would want a British Rail teapot from the 1970s? What fond memories could it possibly hold, apart from a buffet car full of Brummie businessmen with kipper ties? No, not even for £3, I'm sorry. And anyway, the lid doesn't close properly.

I haven't seen many anoraks today. Everything but: tracksuits, camouflage jackets, baseball caps, tweedy M&S jackets. There are one or two anoraks, but no more than in an average cross-section of British society. Who cares what people are wearing anyway? One of the best things about trainspotting is that you don't need to dress up. There's no posing involved. What count here are the unaffected and democratic principles of childhood. We're here to have fun and not bitch about each other's togs.

One of the star exhibits is *St Paddy* (back to its old pre-TOPS number of D9001). This is one of those thunderous diesels that bellowed 'get out of my goddamned way!' as it cracked through Grantham. Now, high up in the cab, it's amazing to be reminded how old-fashioned these early diesels were. The brake levers and gears are as chunky as anything from the steam age. Even the buttons and dials, certainly hi-tech in their day, look clumsy and primitive now. But it's all too easy to mock old technology from the recent past.

Worcester is crawling with photographers. And it's not only the trains that are captured for posterity; there are so many cameras clicking and camcorders whirring that you can't help but get in someone's way. I find it queer to think that some time in the future, next week or next year, a group of train buffs gathered in a front room with the curtains drawn will hiss tetchily as you stumble across the creatively framed view of Hoover 50027 and yell, just as the photographer did, 'Get out the way, you prat!'

There's one way to get round the problem. At Exeter, three weeks previously, they held a special day just for photographers. And charged them £8 for the privilege. But since every serious spotter has a camera these days, and hundreds of them turned up at Exeter, I can't see how it cures the problem of people getting in the way.

For half the afternoon I've been chasing up and down the yard, jumping up in the air as I try to see over the roofs of carriages. I'm convinced there's a steam engine here, though there was no mention of one in the programme. 'I can hear it!' I shout. 'Listen.' Robin and Mark trail patiently after me until I realise I've been pursuing a mirage — the sound is coming from a steam-age LP that one of the stallholders has been playing over his loudspeakers. I feel a right berk. Now those old recordings have been remastered and stuck on CD, a steam buff can scarcely tell the difference.

There's always been a market for sound recordings of trains, steam and diesel. Quality varies. I had *Sounds of the Great Western* crisply defined on an Argo Transacord LP, but my *Shunting in the Yard* cassette is a mish-mash of hissing and clanging, some of it recorded in a downpour. It shows admirable dedication by whoever recorded it (or did he just stick his mike out the window?) but on a hissy cassette, the sound of rain is virtually indistinguishable from billowing steam. The only joy I get from *Shunting in the Yard* is turning it up full blast and watching our neighbour scratch his head when he hears the whistle of a Jinty and the clang of wagons.

On the train home I have that lovely end-of-the-day feeling I used to get years ago, a glorious fatigue, lullabied by the rhythm of the wheels and a swaying as we rock across the points. You're out in the wild world, no more safe than a pea rattling in a cocoa tin, but this is your milieu and you know no possible harm can come to you. When I get home I'll sleep the sleep of the just.

The next day there's the paperwork to catch up with. I've bought a few souvenirs, but nothing that needs wall-brackets or regular oiling. One is an old *ABC* book. I say old, but though the staples are rusty it's never seen active service in a spotter's pocket. In that sense it lacks the authentic smell of history. With an *ABC* that's been knocked about a bit there's always a frisson, a sense of holding something once a vital part of some lad's spotting kit. I'm often disapproving too; fancy underlining without using a ruler! And how could this person have bunked all the sub-sheds of Inverness when they lived in Dorset? Sometimes there's a name and address scrawled on the inside cover and I can't help wondering where the owner might be now. David Bailey of Whaley Bridge, for instance, whose 1959 Midland book has ended up in my possession – did you know that by the Swinging Sixties your ordinary name would be world-famous?

My other souvenir of Worcester is a cabbing certificate. It cost 20p and proves that Robin and I have been up on the footplate of Class 40, D212. I know the owners have to make money somehow, but I was reluctant to fork out for this skinny bit of paper. Unless suspected of fudgery, a trainspotter's word was always his bond and we needed no certificates. We'd already cabbed half a dozen locos anyway, but I went up because Robin heard the other kids sounding the klaxon and wanted a go. The man who signed our certificates was apologetic: so many people had already had a turn that the Class 40's electrics were fagged out and there was no hoot left in its pipes. I felt sorry for Robin. A cabbing certificate was no substitute for some hands-on fun and, I must confess, I quite fancied a blast myself.

030

Indoor Trainspotting

Derby was the first place I was allowed to go on my own. As we drew into platform 1, my first cop was Jubilee 45611 Hong Kong, which was pottering about on station pilot duties. Thirty years later, in the mid-Nineties, I visited and found that Derby was still popular. What follows are my reflections on that day.

The Jubilees have long gone, as have the faithful Peaks and pea-green Bo-Bos – yet still the spotters keep coming, quite happy, it seems, with the Sprinters and HSTs which have a monopoly on passenger traffic. Will no changes ever make them give up the hobby? I suspect that with the older ones at least it's some kind of residual loyalty, a memory of the days when Derby was the epicentre of the Midland Railway and its workshops rang with hammers, unlike today when the sound is more likely to be the muffled sobs of redundant workers.

Even this cold January day with its razor-sharp winds isn't enough to put them off. I understand that too: some of my fondest memories are of brass monkey days just like this. In common with most male hobbies – fishing, football, motorbike scrambling – trainspotting demands a macho disregard for namby-pamby things like 'good weather'. In fact, the harsher the elements the better. Hence the need of an anorak – sometimes!

There's no need to overdo the masochism, though, which is why some of them – including me – have retreated to the warmth of the buffet. From here, there's a clear view across

Derby's six platforms, so there's no danger of missing anything. Sitting with my 90p pot of tea and £1.47 sandwich, I can't help wondering how much money the railways have made out of spotters over the years. Sales of sandwiches and tea must have accounted for a few million quid. And more: platform tickets, for instance, that miserly levy on people who simply wanted to see off their friends. Whatever the original purpose, it was mainly trainspotters who bought them, and however much British Rail grumbled about the hordes of boys, those twopenny tickets must have brought in more millions over the years. How long will it be, I wonder, before some number-cruncher figures out that the new railway companies are missing out? Trainspotters are loaded, he'll reason, so why should they get all that pleasure from us for free?

Cheap and cheerful – that's a good description of a day at Derby – and I think it gives us a clue about the mockery heaped on the trainspotter's head. Over the years the public has been led to believe in leisure as a *product*, and a product that must be paid for. There's a reluctance to believe that fun can be had so simply and so cheaply. There has to be a catch – and there is: being ridiculed. Some would rather pay ridiculous prices than have anything for free, believing that shelling out money makes them look good and socially successful.

It was to Derby I came when, in 1993, I had to write a piece for the *Sunday Times* in support of trainspotters. Though they ought to have known better, the newspaper's 'Culture' section wanted to do the classic demolition job – anorak and specs, etc. – but they were at least going to play fair and run a piece alongside it. The commission was a nice addition to my CV, but I felt like I had a lot of responsibility. How on earth could I put the trainspotter's case in just 800 words?

After publication the stink went up like a mushroom cloud and the railway magazines were twittering about it for weeks afterwards. I sympathised at first, but not for long. For one thing, among all the 'Disgusted of Doncaster' and 'Enraged of Enfield' letters, not one bothered to thank me for trying to stick up for the hobby.

Vanity aside, I realised what the problem was – they were all trying too hard to justify themselves. But trainspotting doesn't need justifying, any more than football or fishing or going to bingo. Once you start to defend your lifestyle it only makes things worse. The trainspotter doth protest too much, methinks. Two fingers is the only effective answer to people who make absurd demands that you justify yourself or your hobby.

The trouble is, trainspotters have begun to take the tag too literally and make claims about the multi-faceted aspects of the hobby – renovating old steamers, timing runs, making models, taking photographs. They call themselves 'rail fans' now, or 'railway enthusiasts' or 'heritage traction preservationists'. They say there's nothing wrong with trainspotting, but they do everything they can to avoid the label. It's really splitting hairs. Those who mock are going to be just as biting about a heritage traction preservationist as they are a trainspotter. I wish they could just be proud of being trainspotters and bugger the mickey-takers.

The W.H. Smith at Derby station has a fantastic display of railway books and magazines. Train magazines have come a long way since I used to buy *Railway World* in the Sixties, but even though the language has lightened up, there's still a touch too much deference and eagerness to ape railway jargon. A whole load of railway gobbledegook has sprung up, much of it swallowed wholesale by trainspotters. If railway management has decided to rename a goods train a 'freight consist', then that is what the trainspotter starts calling it. They no longer call DMUs 'bog units', for instance, but obediently adopt the official names: Sprinter, Pacer. I think this gives me a clue as to why I parted company from a lot of trainspotters – their lack of critical judgement. Without that healthy irreverence, trainspotting does risk becoming boring and nonsensical. The spotter's role should be as an observer, not as a brown-nosed flunkey.

From its literature, it's all too easy to understand why outsiders view trainspotters as self-absorbed and humourless. Some of the mockery might be deflected if spotters went back to their roots, if spotting was more tongue-in-cheek like it used to be. There's so much scope for humour, and the railways were always a good target. But it wasn't always mockery; there was a cosiness in the names of Jinties, Duck Sixes and Blackies, and even with the Tats, Bo-Bos and Baby Brush of the diesel era. But they don't seem to talk like that any more. Even the old guard are not immune: their steam-hauled specials are now 'land cruises' with 'heritage traction'. I never thought I'd hear railway enthusiasts using such pitiful pseudo-marketing lingo.

Trainspotting was all about common sense and *Beano*-style values, it was never meant to be perverted by modern life. There is humour, of course there is, but humour in railway magazines is always signalled by !!!! marks.

It seems that Derby is a good place to be baffled. Timetable-phobia has been eliminated: look even slightly bemused and a young lady in a maroon two-piece will swoop down to help you, two-way radio at the ready. Platforms, times, connections at Luton – they are able to pluck the smallest detail out of the ether. This is the smiling face of customer care. No more timidly tapping a grumpy guard and risking rebuff; these lovely ladies can answer your questions before you've even thought of them.

It's a great innovation, but one crucial point has been overlooked: even in a non-sexist PC age, many passengers instinctively place more trust in a male. They know it's in a man's blood to answer questions about railways; he'll rise to the challenge. Pretty girls, however clever and friendly, just don't command the same confidence. I watch the girl endeavouring to assist a lady passenger, who nods in all the right places as if humouring a simpleton. The lady walks away, and our platform hostess smiles to herself, happy to have helped another customer. What she doesn't see is the old lady walking straight up to a male railway worker to ask him the very same questions.

It doesn't work on trainspotters either. Especially not on trainspotters!

'Can I help you, sir?' asks the hostess, desperate to find another passenger to help. I can see trouble ahead. This is a male *and* a trainspotter and his pride is damaged. If there's anything he doesn't need it's guiding around the railway system. And worse, being taken for a member of the public. And worse still, by some slip of a lass.

'No, it's all right, thank you.'

There's your dilemma: do you brush her off like a fly, or stand with a fixed smile and suffer her do-gooding?

Yet with all the facts at their fingertips they can never tell you anything you really want to know. The platform announcer was making apologies for delays to my train because of an 'incident' at Birmingham New Street. Naturally, I tried to find out what this 'incident' was – a suicide, a bomb, a train crash? They all feigned ignorance. With absurd secrecy they insisted that it was just an incident. They'd been gagged by rules and regulations, by a topsy-turvy attitude to 'customer care' which insisted that, forty miles away from the 'incident', we might start panicking and vow never to use the railways ever again.

And I never found out until I got home and saw the New Street fire on the news. Alarming, certainly, but no one's fault and certainly nothing that we needed to be protected from.

031

The Care of Broccoli and Potato Traffic

For a while in the Nineties I tried to show my loyalty to the spotting fraternity by attending the local railway club and various railwayana fairs, though I hated those that called themselves 'fayres' and turned up wanting to find fault. This probably explains the grumpy tone of what follows, written back then.

I always make a point of going to the Burton Railway Club's annual fayre. The model railways are a big attraction for my children, but they invoke terrible envy in me. I've always wanted a layout: a large one with a dozen trains, sidings full of weathered trucks, and old-fashioned semaphore signals that flip at the touch of a button. Unfortunately, we've never really had the room. There's the loft, of course, but it would mean stripping out all that fluffy yellow insulation. I'd be fine with all the heat floating upwards to keep me warm, but the rest of the family would feel as if they were shivering in a bus shelter. I couldn't do it to them.

At one of the layouts a blonde girl sits patiently while her boyfriend explains the finer points of his layout to the reverent onlookers. At first I'm surprised that a trainspotter should have such a pretty girlfriend, then angry at myself for believing in stereotypes. Why shouldn't a girl love a man who loves small railways? It's a harmless pastime and shows feeling for old-fashioned community values, even if only in 00 gauge. It's another irrational notion: that because a man has a hobby he's useless in bed and dull company. For all we know he may have the sexual dynamism of Tom Jones and be as amusing as Tommy Cooper.

Owning a model railway gives you the chance to combine the roles of stationmaster, train driver, signalman – and the Almighty. Not that God ever took off his glasses and picked a sheep up with tweezers to give it a fresh lick of paint. These men in cardigans have worked for years on their layouts, recreating everything in 00 scale: the washing on the line, a bicycle in the station forecourt, a porter with a barrowload of newspapers. But I doubt if anyone shares my bizarre fantasy of being able to miniaturise myself and escape into the background of these imaginary market towns with names like Woodbury Junction, Rudchester or Bellfordham. What a lark it would be, to steal a newspaper from the barrow, grab the bike and pedal off furiously, flashing two fingers at the static constable with his old-fashioned helmet.

Elsewhere the stalls do a steady trade as punters flick through the neatly boxed paperwork. New books, musty books, picture books, technical books, leather-bound classics, flimsy leaflets, old timetables, Ian Allan *ABCs*, railway rule books – trainspotting has accumulated a staggering bibliography. It dates nearly two centuries now and shows no sign of tailing off. Between them, railway companies, scholars and trainspotters have produced tens of thousands of railway books. Even our local library has ten shelves of them.

With more gutsy ways of trainspotting dwindling, the hobby shows signs of reverting to its old status as a scholarly, bookish subject. Those short-trousered boys of the past are now pensioners with plenty of time for browsing, and the money to lavish on sought-after books. They aren't trainspotters – they have only disdain for the modern scene – but live firmly in the past and now have the time to rummage the railway fairs, not for simple picture books, but for learned and well-researched writing.

Personally I don't mind the picture books, but a lot of this stuff is arcane and way too specialised for me. I have absolutely no desire to own *Fifty Years of Railway Signalling*, *Nineteenth-Century Railway Carriages*, or *A Modeller's Guide to the LNER*. That said, some of these publications go so far beyond obscurity that they're too fascinating to resist. Like the Western Region's booklet instructing station staff on *The Care of Broccoli and Potato Traffic* or the LMS's *Regulations for Railway Police* which warns 'on no account must females be handcuffed'.

I love old timetables, though. They remind me of how I first began to discover the country, my joy in working out how to get from Burton to Wolverhampton and back in time for tea. I copied the times out into my notebook and kept them close throughout the journey. There was always a nagging doubt as to whether these details would really turn into solid trains. But when it all worked it gave me great confidence in my adventures.

I'm tempted by an old LMR timetable. Cynics might ask how a man can find anything to amuse him in a list of train times, and from 1960 at that. But with these details we can close our eyes and travel again on a Euston–Carlisle semi-fast, imagining ourselves at each stop. Here I am at Lancaster station, waiting for the guard's green flag, watching steam drift past the window, curling my toes in the heat from under the seats. I can live each minute of that imaginary journey, but not without the vital paperwork. The fun comes from knowing that the train did exist and that on one day, 17 January 1960 for instance, *Lovat Scout* or *Black Prince* took all those people to Carlisle. The driver and his fireman signed off and walked to the railway hostel for a bath and a meal. History comes alive through these pages.

Outside on the lawn, the local Model Engineering Society have set up a 30-yard length of track to run its loco on. The driver, who wears a real British Railways cap of course, shovels the coal in with a dessert spoon. It's so English and comforting, and I can't understand why anyone should have a downer on men who like steam trains, big or small.

After an hour or so it's time to go, but first I have to promise an old spotting pal, Darb, that I'll attend the next club night. I make the same promise every time I see him, but time and other commitments usually conspire against me. I always feel guilty, though, about going so rarely. This time I'm determined to keep my promise.

When I can get there, I usually go with Jinx, but only if there's a proper film show with some real grimy steam in it. Neither of us has much time for the slide shows — the commentaries are often slow and self-indulgent, and the presenter invariably puts some of the slides in upside down, provoking good-humoured groans from the audience.

Darb mans the door here, and after taking my money he promises to get me a pint as a reward for keeping my word. I'm pleased to see him, but it's always hard to connect the grown man with a beard with the skinny beanpole you went to Crewe with. And he probably thinks exactly the same about me. But most of the people here have never lost touch with each other. They went to junior school together, chased girls together and went to each other's weddings. The camaraderie is rock solid, and I envy them for that.

As well as being for trainspotters, the Railway Club is a reunion point for Burton's old loco men. Among their number are the very same drivers and firemen who used to nod to us at Steamer Gates all those years ago, the young married men with lunch bags and billycans. And now here they are again, in their Sunday-best ties and dentures. It's nice to know, though, that the boys at Steamer Gates got their wish in the end. Even if they were too late to be apprenticed as firemen, at least they can now buy one of the old drivers a pint and sit down with them as equals.

Trainspotting is in danger of becoming part of the

club-raffle culture, something to talk about between domino games and pints. We're not scruffs watching steamers any more, but for the price of a raffle ticket we stand a chance of winning a video of the Somerset and Dorset. When it's quiet you can hear the sipping of pints and scent the vaguely nostalgic smell of smoke from somebody's pipe.

All the same, I still have that uneasy feeling of not quite belonging. I love trains as much as the rest of them, but I know my experience is different. It starts off the same, with the impressive Britannia, then the diesels and electrics. The thrill must have been the same for all of us, whatever era we started in. But somewhere in the mid-Seventies my feelings went off at a tangent: the alienation of the China Clay Special, the weekend in Fontainebleau, the reverse rebellion of travelling first class, the unbearable sadness of returning to old haunts, the smell of wormwood — to me all of these things became as much a part of it as collecting numbers.

And then there's my mischievous wish to look underneath and gently mock. Not about anoraks or neatly packed lunchboxes, but about the funny, infuriating, and baffling aspects of it all. I know I can't explain these things to anyone else at the Railway Club. I can make funny stories out of them for the entertainment of fellow drinkers, but that's not the real truth, just a polite way of fitting in. I just have to face the obvious truth: I'm unable to enjoy my trainspotting with a clear conscience.

032

Freight's Great (Shame About the Wagons)

By the time the first edition of Platform Souls *actually hit the bookshops, my children had pretty much given up on trainspotting and moved on to easier peer-approved hobbies like Pokémon cards. But re-reading what I wrote at the time, I'd obviously seen it coming ...*

I've taken my children spotting only half a dozen times now but they're already bored with Sprinters and HSTs. I'm sorry, kids, but there's not much magic to be had in railway stations nowadays. Loco-hauled passenger trains are unlikely to come back. There'll be no more Britannias or Deltics blasting off under vaulted roofs, no more excited squeals at the noise, no running scared from the sudden belch of smoke. Those little dramas that made trainspotting such fun are increasingly hard to find.

If there's any colour left, it's probably with the freight trains. For much too long, freight was the unsung side of trainspotting. All the plaudits, and the colour plates in boys' annuals, were usually reserved for the great expresses — The Golden Arrow, the Coronation Scot, the Cornish Riviera — the named flyers that all the lads longed to see. And all the while, in the background, were the goods trains, railway's ugly ducklings, getting on with life, keeping the country supplied with coal and butter and beer.

One good thing about privatisation, from a spotter's point of view, is the return of the livery. The idea, old as history but still sound PR, has been taken up with gusto by the new freight companies Load Haul, Transrail and Mainline Freight. Some spotters were horrified when the colours were first unveiled. 'Garish! … vulgar! … inappropriate!' they yelled, and wrote to the railway magazines to say so.

It was only to be expected after so many years of British Rail uniformity. We'd got too used to drabness, so the new colours startled many. Less conservative spotters loved the new look. Freight had suddenly got big and brash, confident and colourful. The PR departments and logo-makers had, probably unwittingly, put a bit of oomph back into the hobby. It's no wonder that spotters began to flock to Bescot, Toton and Tinsley.

Never heard of any of those? Probably because they belong to 'trainspotter's Britain', a parallel country filled with many wonderful locations. The trainspotter's map has always been different to everyone else's. Names like Tinsley, Springs Branch, St Philip's Marsh and Stewarts Lane will mean nothing to most people. But these are the nodes of our railway network, the places where drivers clock on, diesels get fuelled up and spotters gather like moths round a candle.

Toton in Nottinghamshire is another one, a huge place with big zebra-striped doors and a yard full of diesels. As the only decent depot in the vicinity, it attracts plenty of spotters, even though it's in the middle of nowhere, a stiff windswept walk from Long Eaton station. On any day of the week, there's at least half a dozen of them hanging around, jotting down numbers or setting up tripods to photograph the assembled diesels.

Apart from some oil splashes and a driver's discarded *Sun*, its pages separating in the breeze, Toton, like all the other modern depots, looks remarkably pristine. From a distance the ballast looks as if it's been raked level by a lackey. The old casual chaos has been eliminated; there's no untidiness, no piles of smouldering ash, no bent rakes, no tea stains where someone has carelessly emptied out the pot. Even the engines, the Class 60s in particular, have such a clean profile they could have been drawn with the express purpose of illustrating a brochure. The bulbous noses and grilles of the old diesels have been designed away. Today's engines have no superfluous bits, nothing to puzzle or intrigue – and little to fire the imagination. Still, they do have one thing going for them: at least they are not units.

It must be fifteen years since I last bunked a depot, and I don't know if I still have the bottle. Back then it was a schoolboy escapade. But now … should I even be thinking of it? After all, I'd never dream of walking into a factory, a dairy or a fire station and taking a look around as if I owned the place, which is exactly how it had been. Mind you, unwelcome as we might have been, no one would ever have suspected us of criminal damage or industrial espionage; we were just kids being kids. Today, if anyone says anything, I have a curious child I can use as an excuse. Will that be enough?

It would be unreasonable of me to compare my Sixties bunking with this visit to Toton. We were high on the thrill of the dare, but the trainspotters here today aren't the kind of men who are going to risk tearing their trousers on a fence. They look casual and perfectly at ease. I can't help wondering if the thrill is the same it was.

In the event, Robin and I walk around unhindered. Even when I trip over a fitter's pipeline he moves it out of the way for us, not with a curse but with an apology. Am I right then in thinking that an unofficial right of access is still recognised, that anyone with a genuine interest in trains is tolerated? Or have we just been lucky? Perhaps it was always so. Meet the wrong man on the wrong day and you had your backside kicked; on another day you would meet some kindly driver who would take you for an unauthorised ride to the sidings and back.

Freight's great – dirty and noisy and gutsy – but it's thrown up an odd subculture in its wake. Wagonspotting. Railway magazines may have banned the word trainspotter (to appease those who do much more, like taking photographs and videos, chatting to railwaymen and fellow enthusiasts, soaking up the atmosphere). But a wagonspotter … what else could he be but a spotter?

A loco was never inanimate. Steam or diesel, it had a character. It could be a noisy bad-tempered bugger, often letting its drivers down, or it could be as sweet as a nut, ever eager to please, as living and loyal an entity as could ever be made of steel and electric wiring. There was a loco – and then there were carriages and wagons. You collected one and ignored the other. Wasn't that the cardinal rule that Bolt hammered into me on that very first day at Steamer Gates? You didn't write down headcodes and you didn't spot wagon numbers!

But with HSTs the lines began to get blurred. What *were* they exactly? Sleek locos of the future or just glorified bog units? Was the bit at the front a real locomotive, or just a carriage with an engine? It's still worthy of debate. But no one can deny that a wagon is an inanimate object. It is devoid of charisma. There are no heroics involved, no names of heroes or glory. Wagonspotting entails lonely visits to soulless depots, walking along long lines of identical coal trucks and mineral hoppers.

Still, every wagon has a number. And for some people that's enough.

They even have their own wagonspotters' column, wittily entitled 'Wagons Roll'. This is spotting at its worst and dullest extreme. It may be news that two men drove a diesel from A to B – it is the report of a human endeavour, no matter how mundane – but the fact that VDA van BDC210323 has gone into Doncaster Works for repair and a new grey and yellow livery is a fact of supreme uninterest. Except to wagonspotters,

I suppose. It might be tempting to mock the concerns and jargon of wagonspotters — why was an MKA, in reality a privately owned PGA hopper, disguised as a ZKAP, and what on earth is a Coalfish?

There's a wagon depot here in Burton, and I've seen these sad souls myself, walking the gullies between the wagons, jotting down the numbers of coal trucks and mineral hoppers. Some don't even jot but mumble into Dictaphones and transcribe it all later. I feel sorry for them, I do, for I can well understand it for what it is: a desperate attempt to recreate the awesome challenge that trainspotting once was. With so many carriages scattered around the country, tracking them all down will fill in a good twenty years or so.

The thing is, no spotter really, not in their hearts, wants to finish. You spot for years to finish off a class, and completing one class is all right. But once you have all of them, a frightening emptiness comes yawning up. In the Fifties there were upwards of 18,000 train numbers to collect – it was a lifetime's quest. By 1968, 16,000 of those numbers had been struck from the books. But the glee of diesel-lovers was short-lived. Ten years later their Peaks and Deltics and Warships were off to the scrapyard too.

Today's spotters, with the dosh and mobility we could only dream of, can see all of Britain's locos in three or four years. So new challenges, like wagonspotting, are imperative. But once you blur the lines, where does it stop? The answer is that it doesn't, and it exposes the lovable dottiness at the heart of the hobby. It was always OK for kids to collect steam engines, but you can't blame people for thinking the worst of a man who collects the numbers of wagons.

033

Je Suis un Trainspotter Anglais

I still potter around across the Channel from time to time, but I don't bother so much with the train numbers. It's got to a point where they are almost moving too fast – unless it's my reflexes that are slowing. It might have been amusing to write about doddery English chaps trying to decipher the numbers of 200mph TGVs, but I prefer the much lazier scene described in this 1990s piece.

The *chef de la gare* is furious. The platforms at Agde are unusually lengthy, and having walked them in the skin-sizzling sun to investigate the two bodies reported by an anxious passenger, he's flabbergasted to find two British trainspotters, one dozing, the other stretched out reading last week's *Daily Mail*. Blissfully unaware of the stir they've caused, Jim tries to engage *le chef* with a bit of schoolboy French, starting off with the obvious '*Il fait très chaud!*' and moving on to an ambitious, clumsily phrased question about whether there'll be a Class 7100 electric on the motorail train from Spain.

The stationmaster, younger than his British counterpart and quite hip in mirrored shades and crisp blue shirt, mutters a string of expletives and turns his back on them to start the long trudge back to the cool of his office. He might ring his colleagues further down the line and warn them there's some English loonies on the loose.

Trainspotters from Britain are an increasingly common sight in Europe. Self-conscious at home, ever wary for smirks and unkind remarks, they've decided to take their custom elsewhere. Many of them think that British Rail is getting too boring lately. Unwilling to take up wagonspotting (and some spotters would undoubtedly rather have a British wagon than a foreign diesel any day), they can now nip across the Channel and start again from scratch. With the Channel Tunnel, they no longer have to waste time on ferries and connecting buses. From Doncaster to Dijon, they can stay cosseted in their very own comfort zone.

Jim and Chris have stopped off at Agde after an unofficial visit to the loco works at Béziers, just down the line. They've had a good day so far and underlined a couple of dozen numbers in their spotting books – books of French locos but published in Britain. Now they're hoping to get some good shots of trains speeding up-country towards Marseille and Lyon. When the traffic eases off a bit, they might give the station a miss for a few hours and pop down to that naturist beach they've read about.

It's tempting to imagine these Eurospotters as wandering philistines, impervious to the charms of local life. Not a bit of it. Though they tend to stick to fast food (*hot dog* is the same in any language), Jim and Chris can recognise a good *salade niçoise* when they see one. They also have a grudging respect for the local beer, which looks as pale as piss, but is a great knock-out when it comes to kipping on the overnight trains. Schoolboy jokes and mild xenophobia are to be expected, but although it would have been a brilliant wind-up, neither of them dared ask Agde's *chef de la gare* if he was the man in charge of the refreshment room.

Trainspotting has always been a peculiarly British hobby, though no one has ever been able to explain exactly why. My own theory is that it was somehow tied up with patriotism and Empire. Steam locos were propaganda on wheels. Britain had an endless list of writers, admirals and victories to celebrate, hundreds of stately homes and colonies, and when steam was gone many of the names were transferred to diesels.

But an interest in railways is not unknown abroad: there are steam buffs in Canada and Australia; model railway clubs are quite popular in Denmark, Switzerland and Germany; and French mums and dads still take their children to see the Chapelon Pacifics at the railway museum in Mulhouse. But despite such widespread enthusiasm for railways, it's only the British who have had a fascination for collecting train and wagon numbers.

Browsing through the *European Loco Pocket Book* for France, it seems the various classes have little in the way of character. The B63400 class is followed by the B63500 class, the Y5100 by the Y6200s. There doesn't appear to be any equivalent to the Peaks, Warships or Deltics, though I'm sure French railwaymen will have their own nicknames. The SNCF seem to have a lot of locos named after places, but few if any named after people or chateaux, which is a shame considering all the famous French people there have been. This is in sharp contrast to Britain. Would our hobby have had the same appeal had it been purely numerical, if there'd been no Castles or Scots or Britannias, no Warships, Deltics or Peaks? The Spanish, by contrast, have a lot of locos named after virgins.

Things have changed greatly since my first jaunt to France, shivering my way to Paris on that chilly green train in November 1975. The French now have arguably the best rail network in Europe and even the most chauvinistic of trainspotters can be heard praising the SNCF.

On the 10.10 TGV from Gare de Lyon to Montpellier, Dave jabs the button of his stopwatch. 'Valence–Montélimar, 22 minutes, 12 seconds.' He does a few quick scribbles on his notepad and whistles. 'Hellfire!'

He has been won over, an instant convert to the French TGVs. His friend Pete is less sure and leaps to the defence of Britain's East Coast timetable. There follows a ping-pong match of statistics, which passes another ten minutes, until the third member of their party returns from the buffet with a can of Coke and a sandwich that looks like a small log.

'Four bloody quid!' he seethes, much to their amusement as they tuck into the Walkers crisps and lukewarm Fanta they've been carrying since they left the Midlands the day before.

The style of European trains puts bashers on their best behaviour. Back home they'd be wandering up and down the train, sticking their heads through windows to catch loco numbers in passing yards. But French trains tend to have hydraulic doors and sealed windows, a much safer practice, but one that's not appreciated by men who like to feel the wind in their hair.

Modernisation has its price. What I hate most about the TGV are the rows of seats facing the same way. It makes spontaneous friendships and inter-station flirtations sadly rare. But there's one thing Europe does have – overnight trains. Dozens of them. The whole of Europe slows right down after midnight and you can snooze the night away on dusty seats between Bordeaux and Marseille, Lisbon and Porto Campanhã or Prague and Žilina.

As yet, the trainspotter is still an enigma to the French, left to pursue his quest in peace. They come in well-mannered groups of two or three at a time, booking into modest hotels and generally keeping themselves to themselves. Isolated outbreaks of railway rowdiness have been reported in Britain, but Europe has no reason to be as wary of trainspotters as it is of football fans. But who knows …

It's not just France that attracts the Eurospotter. Germany and the Netherlands are popular destinations too, and with spotting books available for countries as far-flung as Portugal, Norway and Finland, you can be sure that wherever there's a list of locos there'll be someone who wants to tick them all off with a biro.

Few Eurospotters have more than a smattering of the local lingo. But the language of railways is an unspoken one. Just as it needs no linguistic skills to appreciate the cathedrals of Cologne and Rouen, so it takes the train buff no time to orientate himself on the railway bridges and platforms of Antwerp, Hamburg and Lyon. He has a sixth sense, honed by years of studying manuals and books. Like Superman with his X-ray vision, it takes only a brief stare at some enigmatic lineside box before he has a convincing explanation of its workings and its function in the railway system.

While many Eurospotters relish the challenges, some, like Tony from Derby, wander around looking for echoes of the past. He misses those summer days at Plymouth and Exeter, the distinctive engine throb of the Westerns and Warships. When they were scrapped in the 1970s he went off to northern Germany in pursuit of the V200s, a German loco on which the Warships were originally based. Reliving the past became easy. But when they too were withdrawn, he was disconsolate. Until he read that Deutsche Bundesbahn had sold a batch of V200s to the Greeks. Now he's planning a trip to Athens to get some last snaps for his archives.

Tony's lucky. Like many of his fellow enthusiasts he's a BR employee and, with concessionary fares, can travel the length and breadth of Europe virtually for free. For others Eurospotting can be cripplingly expensive. But Jim and Chris have got a brilliant master-plan to head off complaints about the drain on the family budgets.

They're going to break with the Paignton routine next year and bring their wives and kids down to Languedoc. It's a perfect arrangement. The family get a Mediterranean holiday, while Jim and Chris can swan off to Avignon to notch up some BB 9400s – and they can all go home with a tan to show off to the neighbours.

After Europe? Well, there's always America. They can't go

by train, of course, but the USA is the one place where they'll find anything like a trainspotting culture.

I don't know if they collect numbers there, but they certainly love their trains. And, being the Big Country, it's not surprising they do things in a big way. They've got the Casey Jones hats, of course, and replica lamps from the Rock Island Line. All quite normal, really. But where else would you get a telephone that alerts you with the sound of a steamer blowing its whistle? And would Barclays ever offer to overprint your cheques with full-colour steam locos from the Santa Fe or Illinois Central?

British enthusiasts will buy videos and books about the Illinois Central and the Rock Island Line, but the trade seems to be one-way. Americans aren't interested in books about the Somerset and Dorset or videos about the Doncaster Works open day.

The Americans have absorbed the railways into the great American adventure story, the myths and legends of the frontier. But where's *our* runaway train coming down the track? Mind you, our trains have never been chased by irritated Sioux or blasted to matchsticks by bandits with dynamite. Maybe that's why, despite the violence, the Great Train Robbery is still cherished, our one moment of Wild West adventure, misted by history, blurred through the veil of a Woolworths stocking.

The other thing is, the Americans actually sing about their trains. They revere them in a way that the British haven't yet matched. And here's the three-volume box-set to prove it, with Johnny Cash and Boxcar Willie belting out 'Night Train to Memphis', 'Freight Train Blues', 'Daddy was a Railroad Man' and 'Blow that Lonesome Whistle'. How can we match such redneck enthusiasm? Why, if trainspotting is so British, has there never been a songbook to match? Where are all the songs about the midnight sleeper to Penzance or a long, clanking train of mineral hoppers? Even when railways were mentioned in those British pop songs of the Sixties there were never any details; we were too polite to talk about rust and grease and filthy smoke. Having said that, we do have a few folk songs, mostly about poor Irish navvies who lay down their lives during the Victorian railway boom.

The Americans, though, always revelled in their traditions: even today their railways retain their associations with the old Wild West and the Depression. Hobos who hopped the box-cars are still seen as folk heroes by many, so much so that they have annual festivals to celebrate hobo history, and the tales that are told, served up with equal measures of grit and melancholy, still inspire adventurous young men (and the occasional female) to follow in their tracks.

If I could play the mouth organ, I'd go down on the platform at Burton-on-Trent and compose myself a lonely blues. It's time that trainspotting came up with some home-grown standards.

> I gone down to Burton station (ooh-wah)
> Didn't see no more Steamers up the line
> Them Jubes and Jinties is all gone now
> So I'm sittin' here a-cryin'.

> Let me tell ya it's all Sprinters now (ooh-wah)
> Ain't no romance any more
> There ain't no smoke on the 'rizon
> The whole damned scene's got such a bore.

034

Burton, 1995

This was my original Epilogue to the 1995 edition, written with one eye on my two little trainspotters and one eye on my own past. It seemed unlikely that history would repeat itself, that the wonderment of 1995 would be quite as sweet for them as it was for me in 1964. But again, I feel it worth repeating without changing too much.

Watching Robin with his first trainspotting book, I'm as excited as he is. I can feel myself clutching it, fascinated by the glossy pages, the vaporous smell and the long columns of numbers. Like me in 1964, he's not sure of the difference between one loco and another or which number you write down, but he's a quick learner. In time he'll have the jargon off pat.

An 'Egg Timer' comes blasting out from under the bridge, taking a rattling retinue of coal trucks towards Drakelow power station. At first, Robin was terrified by the screeches and booms of the railways. But now he loves it all.

How could I dream that one day I'd be standing here, within sight of where Steamer Gates once were, admiring something nicknamed an Egg Timer, aka Class 58?

When I first came to Burton station it seemed as fascinating as a medieval castle. Walking down the wide stairway onto the platforms, you found a W.H. Smith bookstall, a buffet and a comfortable waiting room with a coal fire. When we first started spotting here there was a water fountain, dated 1883, and a metal cup on a chain. It looked yucky, but we already shared the school's dispenser with 600 other boys and had built up a resistance.

The station is a piece of modernist architecture now, with windswept platforms, a waiting room like a goldfish bowl and a toilet not much bigger than a coffin.

No one took any notice of trainspotters in days gone by. They were part of railway scenery, like porters or pigeon baskets. Now, in the Nineties, they stand out and are often viewed with suspicion or wry amusement. The office girls waiting for their trains stare and giggle as a trainspotter passes. Thank God none of them has a trainspotter for a fella.

Strangely enough, they don't even notice Robin and me. There's nothing at all wrong in a man taking his young son to watch the trains.

In the Fifties and Sixties trainspotting was the Bash Street Kids versus British Rail, with grumpy porters and stationmasters kicking schoolboy ass. But the boys grew up and the relationship is a more cosy one now. Ever since British Railways took up advertising jobs in *ABC* spotting books (£350 p.a. for a boy of sixteen in 1962) the railways have been staffed by former trainspotters. Not only do they get the chance to drive trains and whistle trains off, but they welcome fellow enthusiasts with open arms.

Nose around any modest-sized station and the odds are you'll find that the chargeman's office doubles as a bashers' club, a place where shivering spotters can get warm and catch up on the gen. It doesn't matter if the station has no buffet – the chargeman will do a brew when he's finished his duties (that background crackle during his announcements isn't faulty electrics, just a basher rummaging in a packet of smoky bacon).

It's not always easy to make small talk with spotters these days, now they're all wired up to Sony Walkmans. In the old days, if you were lucky, you might have a tinny transistor; if not you just had to hum. But what are they listening to? Heavy metal is popular – Metallica, Aerosmith, Anthrax. The throb and power parallel the noise of railways and a scientist might well find identical wavelengths present in Motörhead bass guitar riffs and diesel engines.

Spotters also like the robotic sounds of Kraftwerk (their 'Trans-Europe Express' was a perfect match of lyric and rhythm), OMD and Gary Numan, all of whom are a bit uninspiring for me. At the risk of generalising, spotters don't have much time for melody and sentiment. I don't know any who are into Nanci Griffith or Sinead O'Connor. Such lady stuff is a bit too heartfelt for men who collect statistics and make small talk about engine thrusts.

Burton station is hardly the most exciting venue these days, but we don't have much choice. Most of the old spotting places have been demolished or made inaccessible – a boxing club now stands on the site of Little Burton Bridges, and the grass where we used to sprawl by Steamer Gates is now a Toyota garage.

The biggest loss of all, for me anyway, was the footbridge at Wetmore Sidings. It was in the way of 'development', so they sold off the scrap metal and burnt the rest: all those boards etched with the numbers of locos long gone and the 'tags' of Gaz, Kev and Duggy – they all went up, ironically, in a puff of smoke …

Just down the road from Wetmore, my friends Janice and Ian live in a small terrace of starter homes built across the site of Horninglow station. They don't even remember the cafe, let alone the station, yet the tracks run under their house like ley lines. I wonder whether the clack of wheels and slamming of carriage doors echo in their dreams some nights.

The old gang are still around, though none of us do any serious spotting now. Andy is News Editor on the local paper and sticks old train pictures in whenever he finds an excuse. Since a kind aunt bought him a pair of binoculars one Christmas he's been heavily into birdwatching. I wouldn't compare it with trainspotting, but it gets you out into the fresh air and, even better, unlike trainspotting, it's refreshingly free of heartbreak.

Lately, Pipsqueak – under his proper name, of course – has been a regular letter-writer to the *Burton Mail*. One letter detailed his encounter with a blind trainspotter at Steamer Gates, who could identify the trains by sounds and smell. It was a bit bizarre. Then one day I heard two biddies talking on the bus about 'that mad bloke who writes them stupid letters to the paper', and I felt insulted on Pipsqueak's behalf. I admired whatever he was trying to say about our lack of imagination, the kind of life that's available to us and our kids since the end of steam.

Nostalgia is a badly abused word these days, embracing everything from tatty horse-brasses to ploughman's lunches. Pure whimsy. Real nostalgia is a sickness. I've had it sometimes, when things weren't so good – a desperate desire to go back, to be that kid again. Not just for the trainspotting and the steam engines, but for the certainties only the past can offer: the knowledge that you can go home, that Mum will do you beans-on-toast, that there'll be a lovely fire you can sit in front of while you mark off your cops.

Smells are the surest trigger: the sulphurous whiff I often get from our coal fire, the tang of diesel perhaps, or cough sweets, and especially the dry fragrance of wormwood, that bluey-green herb that sprouts up in any old grotty patch and grew in abundance at Wetmore Sidings and Steamer Gates. A while back I actually bought some from a garden centre to plant in our garden. In summer, when the fragrance hits me, I can close my eyes and the nostalgia for the steam days hurts: the images so sharp, the pain dull and endless.

It's the past yet again. All the time, the past. That's why I don't dare look too far into the future: I'm scared it will have no smell. In the future world of electromagnetic levitation there'll be no tang of diesel fuel, no bitter whiff of brake dust, no flowers between the tracks. Even the train toilets don't smell as awful as they used to, of cheap soap and wooden seats with years of rubbed-in urine splashes.

We know it full well, but we're scared to put it into words. It's that fearful future without hobbies or humour or secret hiding places.

I can't help but wonder if I'd have started trainspotting if it hadn't been for Bolt. How easily that moment might have slipped away from me – a childish offer, so easily rebuffed. Yet I can't imagine my life without the railways in it. Would I still have travelled to all those places, and even if I had, wouldn't I have gone by aeroplane? The railways kept me down to earth and had a part to play in stopping me getting smugly private and worrying about my status. I always shared my space and willingly. Is it too fanciful to think that the railways helped make me into a democrat?

Recently I heard yet another derogatory reference to trainspotters. This time on Radio 2: a *Guardian* journalist filling in with a comic turn between pop records. Out came all the usual props and the same complaints. The joke is long past its sell-by date, yet media folk still rely on it for an easy laugh.

In fact the media claim to have science on their side now that some boffin has identified trainspotters as suffering from Asperger's Syndrome, a pathological compulsion to control and order the outside world. Is there any human being who doesn't have some urge to make sense of their world, to enjoy it in the open air and learn about its ways, and cohabit with it to the best of his or her enjoyment? Of course not. To suggest that trainspotters have taken a simple caprice and turned it into a pathological disorder is plainly nonsense.

One of the oddest things is the belief that trainspotters spend all their time trainspotting, as though it isn't just a weekend thing or a holiday thing. None of them would believe that a scuba-diver is a scuba-diver while he's at the office or that a football fan goes to a disco in his kit. So why do they believe that trainspotting is a permanent state of being?

Was it Jasper Carrott who started it all? Some trainspotters think he's got a lot to answer for, but I can forgive him (just), since in a democratic society everyone should take their turn as an Aunt Sally. It's flattering to be lampooned, and even trainspotters can laugh at themselves. What is unforgivable is the way the media have hijacked a joke and turned it into received wisdom.

And what is frightening is how they've abused the trust of their readers. People are now convinced that trainspotters, even if they don't know one, are boring, clueless and sexless.

The same old jokes. But after I'd finished yawning, I got to thinking: what the hell is it about trainspotters that they are so frightened of? What syndrome do the mickey-takers suffer from, who can worry and gnaw at the same meatless bone for years on end? It's a kind of fetishism, really. These detractors have got the anorak to get them going, but their obsession blinds them to the fact that that's all it is, a coat with a zip. Like all fetishists, just like those men who steal women's knickers from washing-lines, they desperately want the clothing to contain the object of desire. But there is no nerd with glasses or pudding-bowl haircut or four different-coloured biros. The anorak is empty.

'Get a life, get a life', is their constant admonition. But what *life* exactly are they talking about? What constitutes excitement in this leisure-based society? Watching *Match of the Day*? Shopping at B&Q? Visiting McDonald's? I'm constantly on the lookout these days for cheery faces bursting with *joie de vivre*. I want to ask them their secret of a full life. But I've yet to come across anyone who fits that description. Everyone I see seems satisfied with the video from the corner shop, the Berni-Inn meal, getting hopelessly pissed on a Friday, fighting for a parking space on Saturday, sleeping off Sunday. Where is this life? On all the evidence, trainspotting is one of the few pastimes that engages people in the general hum of society, that throws people together in a hurly-burly way to talk and watch and have a laugh and soak up a bit of history.

Back at Burton, the sun has come out, the signals are green and the 125 is off on its way to Paignton. We watch it go. I wish we were on it, but the thrill of watching other people depart is always a compensation.

This is trainspotting – the next generation. But I'm wary of setting up my children as figures of fun. It doesn't seem as if the public will ever shake the stereotyped trainspotter from their vocabulary. I'd rather see trainspotting more as a useful lesson, an introduction to a world of trains and passengers and railwaymen and women, a communal enterprise. Certainly my suspicion of cars comes into it. I don't want my boys to live the rest of their lives travelling in a metal box, seeing nothing, speeding by, tensed up over a wheel, trying to show off or becoming one of the thousands of people killed on the roads each year. Trainspotting is just the start, the first step on that InterRail journey round Europe. I'm not wishing their lives away, but I can't wait to see my sons setting off with their rucksacks and girlfriends, arm-in-arm.

As for me, I couldn't give a cuss what anyone else thinks about trainspotting. *Je ne regrette rien.* Some people might say it's been a monumental waste of thirty years, but I just can't agree.

THE NOUGHTIES

035

The Price of Fame

When *Platform Souls* came out in September 1995, I never expected fame and fortune. An invite to *The South Bank Show* would have been nice, but I didn't hold my breath.

Several magazines wanted an interview. At King's Cross I met up with Roger Tagholm, a journalist from *Publishing News*, who understood the trainspotting bug. I suppose he gave me an easy time of it. Other journalists I met had their own agenda, shaped by metropolitan prejudices and a desperate need to amuse knowing readers.

A radio gig was arranged with ABC in Australia, though it didn't seem to merit a club-class ticket to Sydney. It would all be done 'down the line', they told me, which meant I would have to go to Radio Derby's studio in Burton. Until then I didn't even know they *had* a studio in Burton.

'Just pop down to the Town Hall,' they said, 'and ask the lady on reception for the key.'

The 'studio' was high up in the rafters and I was left to make my own way, bumbling around the attic spaces until I found an arched wooden door with 'Radio Derby' on a strip of Dymotape. This couldn't be it, surely? It looked like an archway into a Tudor conspiracy. Inside were two metal school chairs and a table with an ancient BBC microphone and a laminated sheet of instructions. Reading through them, I pressed button A and waited …

I could heard a disembodied voice, thin and distant, as if from 'the other side'. It reminded me of that horror film *The Fly*, and the tiny, almost imperceptible voice desperately crying out for help. Again I heard it, this time strained and irritable. I started to panic now, unable to work out where it was coming from. I was doing something terribly wrong and thousands of Aussies were sitting by their radios cursing my stupidity.

Then, on one of the chairs, I noticed an ancient set of headphones. I picked them up. The voice got louder.

'Hello?'

'Hello,' I replied, putting them on.

'Can you get closer to the mike, please,' said the voice. 'They'll be through from Sydney in two minutes. Just sit there and wait.'

I can't remember what questions I was asked or what my replies were, but it must have played well Down Under. My publicist got in touch saying that Australian TV people wanted to make a documentary.

I bought new clothes, paid £40 to have my hair cut and coloured at Burton's top salon, and a week later I was on a train to Crewe to meet up with the, er, crew on the station. After going through what had become a routine defence of trainspotters, the producer thought we should end with a flourish. He wanted me to throw down my spotting book on the platform and say something along the lines of 'We've had enough – it's time the trainspotter came in from the cold' or some similar nonsense.

That was twenty years ago, but I have never seen the film. Unlike my old friend Kev Spiers, a long-time resident of Melbourne. Andy, Kev and I had been friends for years. A talented guitarist and natural jester, he often had us in stitches with his impromptu ditties. And there he was in Oz, eating pizza and watching TV when up I popped, ranting and raving on Crewe station! He nearly choked on his pepperoni.

Trainspotting seemed to be the hot topic. For another film-maker, I travelled up to Carlisle with my son Robin, then aged six. The irony was as bitter as the Cumbrian winds that day. I had never been able to afford Carlisle in steam days and it had always rankled with me, thinking of what I must have missed. Now here I was, getting a free ticket in return for rambling on about trains. The station wasn't quite as I'd always imagined it, and thirty years had passed since it was busy with Coronations and Britannias. But at least I had got there in the end.

The oddest experience of my fleeting fame was a TV appearance on *Good Morning with Anne and Nick*. A good morning for them, perhaps, but not for me.

Prime time television! It would lead to huge sales of the book, or so everyone thought. And so I dragged myself out of bed at 4.30am one day and caught a train to Birmingham. A limousine met me at New Street and took me off to Pebble Mill studios. The chauffeur was more used to picking up musicians, actors and politicians and didn't know what to make of me. I told him I was a writer, which had him thinking I must have written a best-selling espionage thriller – until I put him wise.

'*Platform Souls*? What's that then, fashion and stuff?'

'No, souls with a "u". It's about trains.'

'Trains?' He looked at me via his rear-view mirror. 'Nah! You one of them trainspotters then?'

Once in the studios, I soon lost my nerves and got caught up in the buzz, especially when chef Ainsley Harriott gave me a cheerful wave.

The producer's mischievous hand soon became apparent in proceedings. It would be a jolly wheeze, she thought, if I (and a couple of other rail enthusiasts they'd roped in) dressed up in anoraks and bobble hats, the very same gear that made trainspotters into a stereotype. But no, they didn't want to make fun, she assured us. After the fashion parade, we would be whisked off for an expensive makeover, reappearing in the studio reborn and kitted out in tuxedos. Then I would be invited to discuss the perceptions of the railway enthusiast in modern society. I wasn't sure about the catwalk stunt, but the other two chaps seemed game and so I went along with it.

After we had done our line-up and been suitably patronised by Anne and Nick, we were led off to have our makeover. Somewhere between the studio and make-up I got separated from the others. Trying one corridor and then another, I saw a familiar face coming towards me – the singer Petula Clark. Being a fellow guest, I thought I would say hello, but as we neared each other we got into that awful dance of neither of us knowing which way to go. I went right, she went left, and then vice versa. She looked annoyed and rather wary: my bobble hat and anorak must have made me look like someone who really did sleep in a subway. Then she exploded – 'Oh, get out of the way!' – and brushed past me. And that, dear reader, is my abiding memory of Petula, a singer I had adored since 'Downtown'.

After a hair trim and tuxedo fitting, we spotters had been transformed into James Bond clones and were led back to the studio to be patronised all over again by Anne and Nick. Little did I know – and thank God I didn't – but in the newsroom of the *Burton Mail* some of my former colleagues, including Andy, were watching and having a great laugh.

Back in make-up we were stripped of our tuxes. I hung around like a spare part wondering when I would be called back into the studio to discuss my book. But no call came. The fussing production assistants had vanished. The make-up girls stared, wondering what I was hanging around for. Slowly it dawned on me – I was now superfluous to requirements. Five minutes later I was out on the forecourt. The driver didn't even open the door for me this time and we drove back to the station in silence. Having watched my appearance he no longer felt the need to smarm.

I was furious, as were Gollancz, my publishers. Friends in the media said I had been stitched up, used to provide entertainment – and that I should demand an appearance fee. I wrote several times to the TV company to complain, but my letters went unanswered. A few months later they went bust. I can't say I cared.

Hosting a seminar at the Institute of Contemporary Arts in The Mall proved a much classier affair, even though the thought of such a high-profile event scared me. TV had an audience of millions, but at least you couldn't see or hear them – this time I would be on stage in a room full of real people. Not quite alone, though. On the platform with me would be Colin Divall, professor of railways at York University, and Stephen Dinsdale, whose recent play *Anorak of Fire* had been received with acclaim. The evening turned out much better than I expected. Descending from the stage afterwards I found myself surrounded by people telling me how much they loved the talk and asking me to sign copies of the book.

I received a lot of fan mail too – simple thank-you letters, thick envelopes full of trainspotting memoirs, appeals for help with the writer's own book (for which I would get a generous percentage). My feature in the *Daily Mail* brought more letters of gratitude for helping revive fond memories. The letters came from around the world. Admittedly, mail from North Korea and Venezuela was thin on the ground, but several people wrote from far away in Canada, Australia and South Africa, British expats delighted by my reminiscences. I exchanged several letters with a chap in Canada, Christopher Wilson, who told me he was coming to London and suggested lunch. He had a gift for me – a Warship nameplate.

We met up in a restaurant off Aldwych. Alongside the table, tightly taped up inside two extra-large Jiffy bags and looking very much like a 'suspicious package', was the nameplate from D848 *Sultan*. For some years it had been on the wall of a railway-themed restaurant in Toronto and then he had bought it at their closing down sale. Since he no longer had room for it, he wanted me to have it as a thank you for *Platform Souls*.

He had brought a couple of his old spotting books to show me. In the Fifties he had been at school near York and spent much of his free time at the lineside. The books took my breath away – page after page of Gresley A4s, A3s, A2s and A1s. He had been witness to what many would call the golden age of trainspotting.

We parted as good friends, and I thanked him for the gift. He made a point of saying that if I ever found myself short of money he would not mind at all if I sold it. I assured him that would never happen. All I had to do now was get this suspicious-looking package on to the Underground and back home.

A couple of years later, due to cash flow problems, I decided the money might come in handy after all. A friend drove me over to the Birmingham suburb of Moseley, to a rambling Victorian villa packed from floor to ceiling with railwayana – shed plates, nameplates, station signs and signal arms. The place was a health and safety nightmare. You haven't stubbed your toe until you have stubbed it on a cast-iron LBSCR No Trespassing sign! The guy seemed impressed by my *Sultan* nameplate and asked me to leave it with him. After getting a second opinion from a Western Region expert, he would get back to me.

Two weeks later I got a letter saying sorry, but after careful examination his friend had decided that the nameplate was a replica. The bolt holes, where it attached to the side of the loco, were apparently 2mm in the wrong place – evidence enough for the experts! It wasn't the Canadian man's fault, I was sure of that – he had bought it in good faith. I was welcome to come back to Moseley and pick it up. But I never did.

I was also approached by a young train driver, Tony Gregory, who wanted advice and help with knocking his memoirs into shape. I was glad to help. Tony had lived the dream, the one that all boys were supposed to have: to drive a train.

It had started back in 1974, when a driver at Burton sheds let him drive a Class 47. For just a few yards, admittedly, but it was enough to light the fire. After some crushing jobs on a farm and in a cash 'n' carry, Tony applied to be a 'traction trainee' at Leicester before being assigned to Coalville depot on the Leicester–Burton branch line, driving English Electric Type 1s and Class 47s on a variety of coal and freight workings. In between he burned up the roads around Burton as one of the 'new era' Mods inspired by the film *Quadrophenia*.

He was glad to pay for my editing skills and I, in turn, found his inside story of being a real driver quite absorbing. Maybe I had missed out after all. Jinx had had a job as a guard and then as a sort of stationmaster (with a staff of two). But Tony had been on the front line and from his memoirs it sounded like I had missed out on some great fun. Working freight trains did not carry the serious public face of passenger service, so the train crews and guards had a lot of leeway, even stopping a train in a siding so one of them could jump down to collect mushrooms for their fry-up, cooked on an electric hotplate in the cab of their diesel loco.

I was working nights in a care home at the time and needed something to occupy the long stretch between putting the laundry in at night and getting the breakfasts ready eight hours later. Watching *Countdown* at 3.30 in the morning was desperate. Tony's project was a godsend and with no distraction I was able to give it my all. I even designed a cover for him, wrote the blurb and read the proofs. Tony financed the printing from his own pocket, did his own publicity and put the word on the railway grapevine. No one was more pleased when, just a couple of years later, he told me he had no copies left – the entire print run of 2,000 had sold out. Even today, I still see desperate appeals on t'internet from people who want a copy of his *Life on the Leicester Line*! He's retired from the railways now but can take pride in adding a neat and enthusiastic biography to railway literature.

Through Tony I met one or two other drivers, including Pete who was with Midland Mainline and drove HSTs up and down between Derby and St Pancras. I had never had a cab ride before, and when he offered I jumped at the chance. I worried about getting him into trouble, but he told me to relax – as long as there were no inspectors around it would be fine.

He picked me up one afternoon and drove me over to Derby sheds, telling me to wait in his car while he booked on. He came out with a spare orange high-vis vest to put on. We climbed into the cab and I settled into the second man's seat while Pete checked over his knobs and dials. In five minutes we were pulling in to Derby station to pick up the passengers. I had stood on that platform a thousand times, but it was strange, almost dreamlike to be looking at it from the driver's point of view.

Two minutes later we were on our way. To be honest, unless you're a real geek, the cab of a modern diesel is a pretty boring place, just an office on wheels really. There isn't that much for a driver to actually do, and Pete admitted that half the reason he'd invited me was for the company. We picked up at Long Eaton, Loughborough and Leicester. Nearing Kettering I nearly had a fit when the door of the cab opened – the dreaded inspector! I turned, but instead of a railway 'Blakey' I was greeted by a smiling hostess offering me a cup of coffee. She and Pete were old hands on the Derby–London run and she stayed and chatted for a while before returning to her duties with the passengers. As soon as she'd gone, Pete spilled the beans on the 'trolley dollies', as they are known. There were a lot of beans to spill too, which passed the rest of the journey. Train drivers, it seems, have a certain sex appeal and trolley dolly-dating is common, with marriage apparently no barrier to either party. New recruits arrive at regular intervals, often replacing the ones off on maternity leave!

At St Pancras, Pete and I chilled out in the drivers' mess, eating sandwiches and reading the papers. None of the other railway staff said anything to me, apart from a cheery hello. They must have assumed I was a driver – but I didn't feel like one. An hour or so later we were off back to Derby, with coffee served by another trolley dolly and more scandals from Pete. I think I learned more about the railways in those four hours than I had in the previous forty years. I doubt that such shenanigans went on in the steam age, but who knows …

Platform Souls was read by several high-profile rail enthusiasts – Rod Stewart being one I know of for certain. A journalist friend of mine who went to interview him thought it would be a good idea to take a copy of the book as a sweetener. 'I couldn't get much out of him after that,' my friend complained, 'he was too busy reading your bloody book!'

036

The Train Now Departing ...

Toffs and tradesmen never mixed well, so railways quickly set up a caste system to keep things sweet. Even then, whichever class we found ourselves in, there was always a delicate balancing act between good manners and guarding personal space. The unease manifested itself in various ways – awkward silences, sly glances, sniffing and coughing, crossed legs and folded arms. Hiding behind a *Telegraph* or *Mail* worked for many, but rustling of said newspaper was certain to irritate someone else. The unspoken reason for having window blinds was not to block out the moon and stars, but to save passengers from catching each other's reflections in the glass.

Compartments and tables were jealously guarded, seats claimed by the placing of newspapers or hats. Some would see the marker and move on without demur, others would hover for a moment, hoping for the hat-owner's guilt to kick in; the more assertive would bridle and demand its immediate removal. It was diplomacy and warfare in miniature, on the 8.15 from Croydon.

In the 1964 film *A Hard Day's Night*, that nice Paul McCartney upset a gent in a bowler hat on the train from Marylebone. Playing loud pop on his tranny was a defiant act, meant to show that youthful spirit could not be cowed. But, to be frank, the Fab Four were acting like oiks. I wonder what Sir Paul would say about such behaviour now.

In general, though, rail travellers are a decent lot: they carry cases for old ladies, help mothers with pushchairs negotiate steps and stairs, and invariably say sorry when a fellow passenger treads on their toes. Yet these same people often seem unaware of how their habits affect others.

The railway passengers of 1890 and 1990 would probably have recognised each other easily and tried to get on. But in the 21st century our travel habits have changed, utterly and irrevocably. So deep into their shells have modern passengers retreated that it's a wonder they even see each other any more. The 4G genie is out of his bottle and shows no sign of going back.

Laptops, tablets and smartphones have given travellers an *illusion* of privacy. But that's all it is. We who bite our tongues and quietly despair at their intrusion might be more inclined to call it poor manners. And yet we rarely speak up, squirming in our seats as people air their private lives and keep us updated with Glenda's divorce and Derek's kidney transplant. This is the age of too much information. Modern mobiles will pick up a pin-drop, and yet their users persist in talking loudly. My theory is that these people know damn well what they are doing and do it deliberately: it's an 'Up yours! Look at me, I'm a tycoon/barrister/TV producer.' Yes, we are looking at you, but not because you are the most impressive person in the carriage, just the most despised! Occasionally someone will explode – 'Oh, do be bloody quiet!' – but it's a rarity. One day, inevitably, there will be fisticuffs and the media will get itself all aerated about 'carriage rage'.

The worst ones are those who are not actually holding a phone but walking through the carriage chortling as they talk to invisible friends. We used to be wary of such people.

Rail travel made us aware, opened our eyes, educated and entertained us – and sometimes bored us, it's true – but it was real life. Now we seem to have become incapable of quiet reflection, of restorative 'down-time'.

Yes, I remember Didcot—
The name, because one afternoon
Of heat, someone shouted 'I'm at Didcot Parkway'
Unwontedly. And somewhat loudly.

A door swished. A lady plugged in a laptop.
Someone crunched smelly crisps
And another farted. What I heard
Was 'Didcot – no, I'm at Didcot.

'Did you email Alison
That spreadsheet? Forward it to Ron.
Needs to go DHL Friday
To Simon.'

And for that minute an idiot babbled
Close by, and round him, louder,
As if in chorus, all the mobiles
Of first and standard class.

Now and then, of course, I still see someone reading a book. I feel as if I want to throw my arms around them and cry, 'Oh, thank God! I thought there were none of us left.'

Trainspotters still turn up at Paddington, much as they do at the other London termini. I see them only in ones or twos, so it makes me wonder just who is buying all the railway magazines on sale in W.H. Smith. There are about twenty titles on offer, nearer thirty if you count the model railway magazines. That's an impressive array and Smith's are not selling them for the fun of it. It can't be just for the trainspotters, which leads one to conclude that an awful lot of 'plain clothes' customers must be buying them. There was a time, when I was writing the original edition of this book, that men would have thought twice about being seen with a railway magazine. There was less shame in buying *Razzle* or *Men Only*. Times appear to have changed...

On my last few train trips a strange thing has happened: I've been accompanied not by a phone pest but by a ghost. After booking my ticket and reserving a seat online, I have turned up on the day to find the adjacent seat also reserved. Yes, it's true, the heart does sink a little. I sit anxiously, one eye fixed on the station clock, each tick threatening the end of my privacy. I'll just have to smile bravely and move my stuff out of the way. It's not that I'm anti-social, but today's standard class offers so little space; what we need is not privacy so much as room to spread out a little. I pray that my neighbour will turn out to be an old lady who knows nothing of technology and sits quietly reading an Agatha Christie book. Yet I know it's far more likely to be some business berk with a mobile.

And yet ... on each of the last four trips, no one has turned up. Doors are slammed, the guard blows his whistle and off we go, me and the empty seat. I'm deliriously happy! Yet I can't shake off this curious idea that the seat *is* occupied – by my guardian angel. I'm not sure what the angel's duties might be. Has he/she been sent to protect me from some awful accident? Or just save me from being irritated? It has happened to me four times now, but how the ghost manages to hack into Trainline.com to book seats is beyond me.

In the old days, reserving a seat was a major job. One had to write a letter to the local station, including the two-shilling fee (cheque or postal order) and s.a.e. for confirmation. No telephone reservations were allowed. The railways have improved in a hundred ways since then: with faster and more frequent trains, free reservations, on-board updates, free space for bikes, prams and dogs. It's no wonder more people travel by train now than at any time since the record numbers of 1914.

The London termini, and most of our major stations, have turned into shopping malls. How exciting we thought the Casey Jones burger franchise when it arrived at Euston in the Eighties. It looks rather quaint now that Waitrose, M&S, Boots, Costa Coffee et al. have moved onto the railways wholesale. But being able to buy a Marks & Spencer sandwich as opposed to a British Railways one is a vast improvement.

Yet privatisation has gone hand-in-hand with a new meanspiritedness. Things which *were* free, like loos, often cost money now. I refuse to pay to visit the toilets, however sparkling they claim to be (but never are). And why would you pay anyway when you can just wait a while and then go on the train for free? It's as if management are blind to obvious human needs. They are happy for us to wander their stations slurping coffee from Costa, but when we want to empty our bladders they make us pay for that too.

Provision of benches is another sore point. They stopped doing it, they said, to discourage vagrancy – as if that was an excuse. The ones they often provide now are awful, cold and uncomfortable metal. They provide cosier seating in magistrates' courts and prison vans. No one would choose to have one of these in their garden. For at least 150 years the railway provided solid, comfortable benches made of wood. Look up the OED definition of a bench, you railway managers! 'Typically made of wood', it says. Making passengers sit on metal benches in the middle of the winter months is not only selfish and cruel but must surely be a health and safety issue too.

Hanging baskets were removed, mainly for spurious health and/or safety reasons. But some flowerbeds would not go amiss. They used to pop up everywhere on a stationmaster's whim, but the days when staff were allowed to use their initiative are long gone. Flowerbeds? Even if management agreed, it's hardly likely that anyone would know how to go about it – they would have to be sent on a training day with Mr Fothergill.

Having said that, some stations continue to shine. The waiting room at Kingston has a nice gallery of black and white canvases by a student who was there in the Sixties – and they have a free toilet! The ticket office at Hampton also runs a mini library, where commuters bored with mobiles can lend or borrow each other's paperbacks. Initiatives like these give the railways a much needed human touch.

And imagination will be given its head, if there's money in it. Network Rail has sold off hundreds of unused parcels offices, waiting rooms and stationmasters' offices to budding entrepreneurs who have replaced the old British Rail station buffets with all kinds of smaller concerns, from simple coffee stalls to full-blown restaurants.

Most of my recent journeys have taken me west, to Bath, Chippenham and Bristol. Old territory. I miss the diesel-hydraulics of course, their colours and eccentricities. Many have survived into preservation, so it's still possible to see one if you know where to go. Apart from that, the railways around here remain enduringly familiar. At Swindon, for instance, beer is still served warm and there is always a man on the fruit machine! I feel at home here. It could be the 1980s again. The buffet has a desultory feel, but I like that. Enfolded within it, there's a friendliness you rarely come across in the big stations. Staff have time to chat, idle the time away, make a passenger's lot a happier one, which is surely as much a part of their job as selling overpriced Mexican wraps.

I suppose these days I am more of a commuter than a trainspotter. When the first edition of *Platform Souls* was published in 1995 I confessed that my devotion to the trainspotting cause had wavered. You wouldn't find me standing around taking loco numbers, nor shooting video footage on Shap Fell. And yet, the railways are still in my blood. My attention is still hooked by trains and I still strike up conversations with men I see with notebook and pen in hand, or more likely these days, dictating numbers into their mobiles. In fact, revising this book inspired me to buy the 2015 edition of *Locomotives*, no longer published by Ian Allan but by Platform 5, an innovative Sheffield-based company. This is their 57th edition, so they must be doing something right!

037

Down the Junction

Above and below, on the walkway and in the subway, Clapham Junction's crowds are on the move, hurrying to and fro between the seventeen platforms. Few have any intention of leaving the station. For most, Clapham is exactly what it says on the signs – a junction, somewhere to change trains, to sigh and pace, to while away time with posh coffee, trendy sandwiches, filled tortillas and colourful sushi.

On my first visit, half a century ago, no one had even heard of sushi. I arrived on a local from Waterloo, steam-hauled by a BR Class 4 tank loco. Clapham Junction was certainly worth seeing, but not worth *going* to see, as Dr Johnson might have put it. The only interesting thing about it happened one morning in May 1965, when the signal box fell down from its gantry and blocked off half a dozen tracks. Luckily it happened at a rare quiet moment. With all signals set immediately to Danger, trains were able to stop in time and no one was hurt. Waterloo was cut off and trains from the south-west had to terminate at Woking and Wimbledon.

My only reason for going there back then was to get to the sheds at Nine Elms, which according to the Ian Allan *Shed Directory* could be reached by taking a 77 or 77A bus from outside the station. Waiting at the stop, I looked around for signs of Nell Dunn's *Up the Junction* – her book had described an area full of 'real' Londoners whose chief leisure interests were drinking, shagging and motorbikes. Being too young for any of those things, I settled for a dusty bus seat and the long crawl towards Nine Elms.

I'd been putting off my 2015 visit, mainly because of February's chilly winds which are keenly felt in a place as exposed as Clapham. But hardier souls than I do not care for such things and in defiance of Dr Johnson they come from all over the country, considering it well worth the price of a ticket. With a train every twenty seconds or so at peak times, the pace is relentless. It's like an early Eighties computer game, with quivering metallic snakes bearing down from all directions. There are none of those dreamy *longueurs* between trains, when all there is to do is listen to the birds and watch weeds grow.

Richard's down from Doncaster, on a quest for some elusive numbers. Not that numbers *are* as elusive for his generation as they might have been for mine. In steam days we had no jungle drums or smoke signals but relied instead on chance meetings and 'gen' that often proved unreliable and out-of-date. Today's rail enthusiasts communicate by phone and text, through Facebook and Twitter, and real-time info is available at the press of a button or swipe of a touch screen.

Richard and I are not the only spotters here today: over on the next platform I spy others with notebooks and cameras. Spotting is often a solitary pleasure, yet there's also an easy and spontaneous camaraderie. A pensioner changing trains rushes up to us to ask if we got the number of the 58 unit that passed a moment before. Richard is glad to oblige and the old chap jots it down on his hand before leaping aboard his train.

To our left, scores of people hurry to and fro, glued to their mobiles, lost in a world of their own while Britain's busiest station whirls around them. The only train of interest is the one taking them to work or home. In the meantime they gabble to unseen friends, play *Candy Crush* or update their status on Facebook. Never mind 'Mind the gap' – some of these people haven't even noticed the platform. Two young women, both engrossed, collide with a bump. Serves them right, I think, wondering why only one has the courtesy to say 'Sorry', while the other just glares.

Railway stations are dangerous places in which to be distracted. A few months previously, at Goodge Street, an empty pushchair was snatched by underground draughts and blown onto the tracks. The platform was almost deserted, but there was a young chap who could easily have intervened – if he hadn't been busy with his phone and quite unaware of the drama taking place just feet away. Had there been a child in the pushchair, our man could have meant the difference between life and death and the tabloids would have hailed him a quick-thinking hero. Instead of which he was merely a useless zero.

Richard and I are of different generations and he has no memory of British steam at all. Even some of the classic diesels he has seen only in preservation. Steamers do come this way still, on specials from Victoria. Standing on Barnes station one day, a familiar whistle announced the approach of a steam engine. Joy quickly turned to anger when my own train chose that moment to arrive, blocking my view. I could hear and smell it, though, and had to be content with that brief taste of old pleasures. I looked around, expecting people to be smiling at each other in unspoken acknowledgement of something special, but no one seemed to care much.

For a station dealing with nearly half a million people a day, I wonder how Clapham makes do with one toilet. In recent years, railways have got mean with their loos and often make swingeing charges to those most in need. Seeing a turnstile I expect a demand for 20p or even 50p. I do need to go – but it's the principle. I'd rather nip out of the station and find a pub. Then I notice a square of cardboard taped to the turnstile: 'Due to a malfunction, please turn to access entry'. And so I'm able to notch up a simple but important victory – Machines 0 Passengers 1.

When I return, Richard starts telling me about the

windows on various units. This kind of trivia is often seized on as evidence of a spotter's fruitcake status. Even I, staunch defender of spotters, have been known to mock. Some units apparently have conventional metal window frames, but others have no frames at all and the glass is set flush with the side panels of the carriage. I listen more out of politeness than interest and wonder why I don't just tell him I hate Southern Region units and couldn't care less about their windows. Then I think again and stop myself.

Today, surrounded as we are by iZombies, I suddenly see things more clearly – that these things *do* matter, and matter more than ever. Spotters – of trains, planes, buses or birds – are a last redoubt for something rapidly vanishing from our lives: looking outward, seeing, observing. It dawns on me how much I have simply stopped looking at the world around me. Most people would laugh at our window conversation and say it matters not a jot. It probably doesn't. But *noticing* it – that does matter. It makes little difference to passengers whether their windows have frames or not, but to notice the difference in our increasingly unobservant society is worth remarking on. People notice things less and less these days, while watching things more and more.

But watching isn't the same as *seeing*.

Clapham may be 99 per cent units these days, but on platform 17, away from public sight, a real loco sneaks through, a Class 66 towing low wagons of girders and steel plates. Occasionally, there's a visit from a Class 73, a boxy-looking electro-diesel, unremarkable but for its staying power, having been tootling up and down around here for over half a century. Now, far from heading for the scrapyard, some are to be given a new lease of life on the Caledonian Sleeper train, replacing Class 67s which were subject to severe speed restrictions over the Highlands' bridges and viaducts. In 2015 the sleeper franchise was awarded to Serco, a company better known for transporting villains in prison vans. They unveiled a new logo too – a stylised white stag that, to be honest, looks more like a weasel emerging from a drainpipe. Serco boasts that their stag has 'a strong contemporary look' while 'its five point antlers represent the train's three Highland and two Lowland destinations'. Clever thinking, but would it occur to the average traveller? Stag is an anagram for tags, which reminds me that Serco also deploy tagging devices, which could be useful for maverick passengers who try to break their journeys in contravention of ticket conditions.

Occasionally I sense that Richard and I are the ones being watched. Terrorism has been in the background of our lives for a good twenty years now and rail staff can't be blamed for being vigilant. Even so, no one has ever been able to explain exactly what use a terrorist might make of watching trains or taking photos of them – certainly no technical or operational details that couldn't be picked up from a book or Wikipedia. Richard tells me that on one occasion a rail employee came over and asked why he was standing so far along the platform, away from everyone else, as if distance itself was just cause for suspicion.

I love Dr Johnson, but find myself disagreeing with him. Clapham Junction has been worth the effort after all. The trains may be a trifle boring, but others don't find them so. It's not all about the trains, anyway, and never has been. It's much more – time out from the hurly-burly and moments to ponder. I bid farewell to Richard and to Clapham. In years to come the junction is doomed to slip further down the table of remarkable stations, but it will always be remembered as the world's busiest, even though it isn't.

My efforts to turn my children into railway enthusiasts didn't bear much fruit, but I never held out great hopes. Fifteen years later, though, I had another go, while on pushchair duty with my three year-old grandson. I was supposed to be taking him to the park, but the nearest railway station seemed as good as any playground, so we headed in the opposite direction and ended up at Alexandra Palace station on the line out of King's Cross.

I struggled to get down the steps, but once on the platform we settled ourselves on a bench and waited for the show to begin. In the sunshine, and with Leo safely strapped in his pushchair, it was easy to be happy watching the trains belt through on their way to and from King's Cross. You can see them coming some way off, as dots of light in the blue city haze, and Leo was quick to spot them before Granddad. Every train was a thrill, and though I passed no comments, I could see that he soon made his own judgements about the sulky servility of suburban units and the can-do dynamism of East Coast and Grand Central expresses. I didn't try to bombard him with details – he was, after all, still in a pushchair, and we were there for the fun of it, nothing more.

But our visit certainly left an impression. I'd filmed some of the trains on my phone,* and back home I replayed them to amuse Leo. I ended up having to show them again and again until I felt as exhausted as my battery.

We went there several more times, but I didn't bother to buy him a trainspotting book – he was far too young to get bogged down with all that paperwork. He'd have understood the classes and numbers easily enough, but what would he make of today's loco names? I'd almost got used to *Blue Circle Cement* and *The Clothes Show*, daft as they seemed even in the Nineties, but this latest tranche of loco monikers contains some right clangers.

The 'namer' was always a high-value cop. In days of yore, loco classes *were* classes, whole sets of princesses, regiments or

---

* Yes, I did have one then, but not any more!

Grand National winners. The steam age had different values and names simply reflected the times, with locos named on the whim of paternalistic railway bigwigs. No better or worse than today – it's simply how it was.

We live in populist times and today's names are a democratic mix of traditional favourites and modern crowd-pleasers. Now, in the same class, you'll find TV personalities, fictional characters, companies and royalty all mixed up together. One can't help thinking that putting *Roy Castle* next to *Windsor Castle* is bound to confuse any child!

Pavarotti I can live with, *Isambard Kingdom Brunel*, well, of course. And naming locos in honour of old railwaymen and company bigwigs seems reasonable enough. Some of today's names are highly laudable, and it seems churlish to moan about trains named after a child cancer charity or Help for Heroes, but adding website addresses and questions ('We Save the Children – Will You?') goes beyond naming into a world of slogans and PR-speak. Locos were never intended to be mobile billboards, yet are increasingly seen as space for hire. Castles, Scots and A3s arrived already named, and no one questioned them. Modern locos are out-shopped without names, in the hope perhaps of making spare cash by renting the space. Perhaps these daft and diverse loco names simply reflect the values of our times. Much as it ever was, I suppose.

Nameplates that need further explanation – *Glofa Twr The Last Deep Mine in Wales* – seem to miss the whole point. Imagine that first Britannia of mine: 70004 *William Shakespeare Son of Warwickshire Author of Macbeth and Othello*. Or if the Western had had 7014 *Caerhays Castle Welsh Visitor Attraction 1964–1968*. Need I go on?

I get 43027 *Glorious Devon* – unashamed and cheesy, but at least slightly traditional – but what is going on with 43198 *Oxfordshire 2007*? Yes, Oxfordshire, yes, 2007, but what does it actually mean?

Some names have all the lyricism of a crossword clue: 66593 *Mersey MultiModal Gateway*, 43290 *mtu fascination of power*, or the highly dubious 66185 *DP World London Gateway*. The worst one of all is 43025 *IRO. The Institute of Railway Operators 2000–2010. Ten Years of Promoting Operational Excellence*. No, guys, have some humility – It's Really 'Orrible.

As Cole Porter might have put it, had he been a spotter:

> In olden days a Coronation
> Was looked on with admiration
> But now, Heaven knows,
> Anything goes.

There's a dumpy diesel shunter (max. 15mph) that labours under the (presumably ironic) name of *Concorde*. But what about 66527 *Don Raider* and 43049 *Neville Hill*? Who are these guys? Raider and Hill sound like they belong in a Seventies cop show. Oh, I see now – one is a Class 66 named after a Yorkshire river and the other an HST named after a railway depot. I prefer my interpretation, though, and I feel it's high time we did have a Cop Show class, with locos called *The Sweeney, Callan, Kojak*, and *Juliet Bravo*. Do railway bosses have no imagination?

In 2011 someone set up a Facebook page to campaign for an East Coast train to be named after Jimmy 'age of the train' Savile, who had just died and was (at the time) mourned by many. The Facebooker had already won the support of East Coast Trains and thought if more signed up the idea would definitely come to fruition. Not long afterwards this group fizzled out, the last comment being: 'Ha ha Whoops. Didn't see this train coming ...'

One wonders what might have happened if the *Jimmy Savile* loco had already existed. No doubt it would have been splattered with paint and had its windows smashed. Drivers would have refused to work on it. Perhaps there would have been a highly-publicised de-naming ceremony, to show that East Coast had no truck with sex monsters. The nameplates would have then disappeared, probably turning up on eBay, for sale by the same people who deal in Nazi souvenirs.

In this age of PC and revisionary history, a similar fate might have befallen old steam engines named after contentious First World War generals, or Britannia 70013, named after the man who sanctioned the execution of King Charles I, or 70040 which glorified Clive of India.

The nearest thing to consistency could be the Class 92s running between London and Paris, proudly bearing the names of Europe's best. They're all there – *Goethe*, *Jane Austen* and *Bertolt Brecht*, *Vaughan Williams*, *Debussy* and *Wagner* – enough Anglo-French-German talent to get the Muswell Hill set trainspotting, postmodernly of course. What better way to keep Hugo and Benedict occupied as they head off to the Dordogne? Even before they get to Stratford they've copped *Stendhal* and *Molière* and *Berlioz*. Then one of them spots 92032 *ImechE*. 'Daddy,' says young Hugo, 'wasn't Imeche one of the mid-period Baroque composers?' Daddy sighs heavily, thinking that his wheeze is backfiring big-time. 'No,' he says patiently, 'that one is the Institute of Mechanical Engineers.' The boys look puzzled, but before long they spot 92017, which is called *Bart the Engine*. Time to head to the buffet car for a bottle of Pinot Noir …

038

Museum Pieces

A visit to the London Transport Museum seemed like great fun, but things started badly when I arrived at Covent Garden station to find a heaving multilingual crush for the lifts. I made for the stairs instead, coming face-to-face with some teenagers who had just reached the bottom.

'Please don't,' one of the girls begged me, 'you'll regret it.'

She was only concerned for my welfare, I suppose, but what a cheek. Me, who once regularly took the stairs at Belsize Park, the second-deepest Tube in London. Me, who had breezed up the 700 steps of the Eiffel Tower and the 311 of the Monument. They were *real* staircases, so piddly Covent Garden would hold no fears for me, despite the warning notice: 'For Emergency Use Only. This staircase has 193 steps.' They have to put that for health and safety reasons, but really, anyone would think it was a ladder up The Shard!

I'd be slower than the old days, I knew that, but I resolved to do it in one go, without stopping. I'd just booked to see The Who in concert and I thought: Roger Daltrey's 71 and still belting out 'My Generation'. Jagger carries on prancing and Madonna insists on dancing, so I'd be letting the side down if I let a staircase beat me.

I'd like to say I forged ahead, but I thought it wiser to pace myself. I heard some young chaps coming up behind but had no fears about holding them up. All too soon I felt them breathing down my neck and imagined their exasperated faces. In the end I stopped and waved them by. 'Time for a fag break,' I joked, wondering if they would get it or turn to give me pitying looks as they strode effortlessly onwards and upwards.

The London Transport Museum is a metropolitan must-see – and must-do, with buttons, levers and switches galore. Panoramic sepia photos are a sobering reminder of the upheaval railways brought, especially to London, where the deep, wide cuttings of Euston and Camden were excavated by bucket and spade. Children will look at the photos when they're pointed out, but the nameless, faceless multitudes of Irish navvies are of little interest compared to the clambering fun of horse-drawn buses, trams and a full-size Metropolitan Railway steam loco.

For the kids, everything here is amusingly quaint, but we oldies see things slightly differently. Some of these buses and Tube trains are the same ones I travelled on in my Belsize Park heydays. Does that mean my age group now qualify as museum pieces? Judging by my performance on the spiral staircase you'd be forgiven for thinking so. Perhaps it's time to consider donating my body, not to science, but to the Transport Museum. They could make a wax dummy of me and sit it on the Tube train, with a caption: 'Author Nicholas Whittaker travelling on the Northern Line in the 1980s'. Kids could tap my head to see if I'm real or not.

Exciting as it is here, everything is very safe and above-board, and it brings home to me just how privileged we spotters of the 20th century were. We had no time for museums or visitor attractions. We made our own rules and went where we liked, climbing up on the footplate of *real* locos, with no Perspex dividers to keep us at a distance from the controls. Railwaymen were not made of wax with moustaches of horse-hair, but breathed Woodbine smoke and read the *Daily Mirror* – and occasionally sprang to life to yell 'Bugger off, you little buggers'. Despite that, we still did pretty much as we pleased. We could easily have driven a 70-ton loco off shed if we'd had a mind – a lark that would make today's joyriders look like sad amateurs. But we knew our limits.

In hindsight, with all those grown-ups turning a blind eye to our habitual trespass, it all looks rather incredible and no doubt do-gooders would classify it as a form of child neglect.

The London Transport Museum is a godsend for parents desperate for school holiday distraction. Children willingly string along, not just to look at the trains, but knowing that the day is bound to include burgers, ice creams, and something from the gift shop. It makes me wonder if any of these children would ever take it upon themselves to come here? I suspect that, given a choice, today's nine to twelve year-olds would rather go shopping for 'stuff'. Anyway, entry is forbidden to unaccompanied children under twelve, which probably makes sense, though we often went to Burton's museum aged only nine or ten. They were glad of the custom and the curator rarely stirred from his office to check on us. There were no interactive displays, though, and we were eventually banned after having a go on the spinning wheel in the lobby and reducing it to a pile of sticks.

The London Transport Museum is a business as much as it is a museum and it's hard to get out without passing through the gift shop. Railways and buses are the theme, of course, and I rather like the idea of designing your own mugs, mouse mats and T-shirts with favourite segments from the Underground map.

They push it a bit, though. London's bus and Tube upholstery is a jealously protected brand. 'You can be the proud owner of a cushion in one of our original designs', they declare. And it doesn't stop at cushions. 'Whether it's a single statement piece or an entire collection, your décor as well as your hospitality are guaranteed to be memorable!' What kind of person wants a foot stool, floor cushion or even a whole sofa upholstered in Northern Line moquette? And it would be an odd couple who wanted a headboard padded like London bus seats. We spend long, dreary hours staring at these patterns on tiresome commuter journeys – would anyone want to see them in their dreams or, worse, while making love?

As for dog coats in District Line moquette, that veers towards animal cruelty and I wouldn't want to try coaxing a Rottweiler into one. With a £45 price tag there's a bit of people cruelty too. But heck, when you have a Routemaster wallet to show off, paying out becomes a pleasure. Hip thirty-somethings can also have moquette covers for iPhones, iPads and Kindles, which they use ironically of course.

Britain's transport museums have had a chequered history. In 1948, the British Transport Commission (BTC) called for a coordinated approach to Britain's haphazard collection of railway memorabilia. A museum should be established in London, they said, suggesting the disused Nine Elms railway station in Vauxhall. British Railways wanted it for a goods depot, though, so our Museum of British Transport eventually found a home in an old bus garage in Clapham. We had other railway museums scattered around – in York, Glasgow and Swindon, for instance – which Dr Beeching recommended should be closed, forcing the new British Rail to team up with London's Science Museum to develop what would become York's National Railway Museum (NRM), which opened in 1975 to coincide with the 150th anniversary of mainline railways.

The 1968 Ian Allan *Combine* had two pages of preserved locos, for anyone who felt like underlining them. They ranged from a numberless 0–4–0 from Hetton Colliery to a 1947 pannier tank, preserved at Swindon when barely twenty years old. These locos were worth underlining, but it seemed rather pointless, since no one would ever get the rest of the class. Our favourite was Furness Railway's *Coppernob*, followed closely by the LNWR's *Hardwicke*, both of which we found highly amusing for some reason.

One of the UK's top visitor attractions, today's NRM welcomes you with open arms and quality refreshments. Each year there are fewer and fewer of us who remember the place as it once was – a working steam shed. Back then we were part of the scenery, the sparrows perched on the hippo's back; not much you could do about us. The grumpy old beast flicked us off again and again, but we just kept coming back.

No one has any memories of *Coppernob* and *Hardwicke*, so quibbles about authenticity are rare. Curating more recent locos, though, can often prove a thankless task. Different people have different memories, which is often the cause of unseemly spats between the senior citizens of Trainspotterland.

In 1973, five years after the end of steam, Andy Parker and I met up at a crossing in Burton to see *Flying Scotsman*, back in Britain after a long tour of the USA. After saving it from scrap, businessman Alan Pegler had restored the loco's LNER appearance, with 'apple green' livery and number 4472. Shortly afterwards he took it on a tour of America, where the authentic look was spoiled by US laws requiring the fitting of a bell and cow-catcher. The tour ended with Pegler £132,000 in debt and having to work his passage home, leaving *Flying Scotsman* impounded in Boston, until eventually rescued by Sir William McAlpine.

So there we stood, with scores of others who had come out to cheer. *Flying Scotsman* was a celebrity, with fame that spread well beyond the trainspotting fraternity. Part of British heritage, it had been spoken of for generations. Even today it is probably the world's best-known loco, though it's hard to say exactly why. Was it the 100mph speed record set in 1934, or just the daft name which appealed to us? Whatever the reasons, many have relived their boyhoods through it. And therein lies the trouble. *Scotsman* has taken on so many forms during its 90-year lifespan that it is now impossible to present it in a way that pleases everyone. It has been numbered 1472, 4472, 502, 103 and finally 60103. Smartly turned out in apple green during LNER days, it was painted black during the war years and finally ended up in British Railways 'Brunswick green'. For the majority of its life it ran without smoke deflectors, but boys who started spotting in the post-war years remember it only with 'blinkers' – an abomination to those who recalled its original appearance.

Put bluntly, *Flying Scotsman* has spent half its life as a Frankenstein's monster – which would not have been so bad with only one mad doctor, instead of half a dozen agencies who all had their own ideas of what the loco should look like.

Andy and I saw it in LNER apple green without smoke deflectors, which was pretty much its original appearance, except for its two tenders, the extra one necessary because the railways no longer had any watering and coaling facilities. Later on the loco was to be seen in apple green *with* smoke deflectors, an anomaly that enraged many. Traditionalists still call for the blinkers to be removed and the original appearance restored, while others insist that authenticity is all and the loco should now stay in BR livery and blinkers, since that is how the majority of spotters remember it. The arguments will go on, though, with people now pointing out that the loco is fine in BR green, but it never ran with two tenders then. The ethics of three-parent babies are straightforward by comparison and I stay well clear.

I prefer to stay in with a cup of tea and a book. My library includes old railway magazines, Ian Allan spotting books and a couple of original notebooks, still marked by sooty fingerprints and smudges of diesel. My current favourite is the 1964–65 London Midland timetable. It's like a 'Remembrance of Things Past', though my trigger would be Heinz Sandwich Spread rather than Proust's madeleines.

I started young with timetables and (to my cost) spent more time on them than school textbooks. But timetables *were* an education, a mix of maths and geography, with theory backed up by exciting field trips, my first being 1965's jaunt from Burton to Wolverhampton. It was real-world orienteering, but without the fear of a teacher lurking in the bushes to catch any skivers. Timetables worked, and they gave boys like me the confidence to venture far and wide. We put our trust in them and learned to mesh with all the complex comings and goings of our busy little country.

Everything is on the internet and mobile apps now, which provide all the info people need – and none that they don't. So much snappier, of course, yet we learned much more by doing things ourselves. The old timetables let you check up on mileages as well, see which stations lay along the way and whether they had a buffet or not. And most importantly, work out a train to get you home.

A decision by the Western Region in the mid-Sixties to remove mileages from their timetables caused great irritation. Railway professionals may have considered distances an irrelevance to the public – but they were wrong. Mileages were exactly the kind of details that appealed to schoolboys and chaps with pipes and pullovers. The Western Region bosses were forced to apologise and put them back.

For those who knew what they were doing, a paper timetable was ten times faster than the internet will ever be.

It's nice to see Burton in the 1964–65 list of refreshment rooms. I remember going there on the morning of the Wolverhampton trip and having chicken soup, served in a thick earthenware bowl with a British Railways spoon. Chicken soup for breakfast! Mum would not have approved, but I was on my own and could do as I liked.

Refreshment rooms did not limit their services to people dining in, and I liked the sound of their packed meals. For half a crown you could get a cheese sandwich, sausage roll, biscuits and fruit. An extra shilling upgraded you to pork pie, egg roll, cheese and biscuits, fruit cake – and chocolate wafer. Sadly I could afford neither. They also sold cake by the slice, wrapped in cellophane, so I bought a 'cherry farmhouse' to sustain me on the journey.

My timetables are fifty years out of date now, of course, but they encompass a fascinating social history, a travel guide to a long-lost land where trains were slow and the sandwiches defiantly unwrapped.

Not long after meeting Richard at Clapham Junction, I embarked on a long-held ambition to take up watercolours. The word had always appealed to me, associated as it is with old scenes and nostalgia in a way that other mediums never are – oils and charcoals hold no old-time charms for me, but watercolour memories seemed to make perfect sense.

My first project, predictably, was based on one of the photos in this book, the Blackie crossing the bridge near Wetmore Sidings. I'd set myself a mighty challenge – not only to learn brush techniques and colour theory, but to bring to life a black-and-white scene from nearly fifty years ago. Who remembers the colour of paving slabs, the painting of house doors, or the clothes we wore? Trees, bricks and skies must have always been the same colour, we imagine – but what exactly? One thing you soon learn is that trees are rarely brown, and skies sporadically blue. We'd all paint the Blackie an appropriate black, of course, but can we be sure it wasn't more of a very dark and smoky blue? Were the coal wagons white or grey? The bridge I remember clearly enough, the steel girder painted a cheerful light blue with streaks of rusted orange.

The spot has totally changed, of course, the bridge and embankments long gone, the road much busier, and the skyline dominated by Burton Albion's Pirelli Stadium. I've now looked for longer at this one railway photo than any other, staring and squinting for tell-tale details, pondering the unanswerable. What happened to the two locomen, I wonder, and the man on the bike? Why did someone feel a need to take that photo, and why fifty years later am I getting so involved in it? The two events, fifty years apart, must surely have a connection, but only an Eastern mystic could unravel it.

Fifty years and thirty miles of railway line separate this steam world photo from today's Birmingham New Street, a subject to which I promised myself I would return. The shadows have been vanquished – but shadows are not always to be despised and may be there for a purpose. Bring them back, I say. Re-reading my 1995 prologue, I feel I may have been a little unfair. The old New Street was pretty grim, admittedly, but did it really matter? I had passed through plenty of other gloomy stations, Montpellier for one, and to deny passengers the sunlight of France is surely a much greater crime. Birmingham has almost too much light now. Once merely a godsend, it is now hailed as a premium experience for which we should thank the clever architects who factored it into their vision.

'Station' is too old-fashioned a word for this 'transport and retail development'. Doubtless beautiful to some, for me it is as stark and soulless as anything ever built, a nightmare from a sci-fi film. We had seen many – *Modern Times* and *Metropolis*, *Logan's Run* and *Westworld* – in which humans became subordinate to the built world, but few of us dreamed such a world would really come to pass. New Street will be dominated by giant 'media eyes'. The human eye is a beautiful thing, but its artificial non-human equivalent is scary. Have these people never read *Nineteen Eighty-four*? The concept of the ever-present eye is disturbing – and it's no wonder that HMRC used the idea in their anti-tax-dodging posters.

One thing is sure, there will be no loving watercolours of

this place. If this is the future of railways, then thank heaven I'm not part of it. But perhaps one day, in the shadowless smell-free future that awaits, people will again ask awkward questions about what railways used to be like, and an old white-beard who runs a *Twilight Zone* antique shop will show them some old photos and books. This is just one of those books, but it may give tomorrow's people an idea of how things used to be.

EPILOGUE:
BEFORE TRAINSPOTTING

1957. It didn't really start in 1964, but many years before that, perhaps in those infant days when I climbed up on the kitchen table to look at the trains running behind our flats, at the bottom of the garden and across the muddy brook. One day, all of a sudden it seemed, a passenger train appeared, with maroon carriages as packed and rowdy as carnival floats. People leaned out at the end doors, hair blowing, some smoking, others taking photographs. Seeing me at the window, they grinned and waved. I returned their waves, time after time after time, until every grinning face had passed and the train disappeared up the track, leaving grey wisps of smoke settling over the allotment cabbages.

For many years, for much of my life in fact, I thought this event had been a dream, an infant fever perhaps, for I soon learned that it was a freight-only branch, worked by dusty tank engines with wooden wagons. When I told people about the passengers they laughed. It was normal to have an imaginary friend – but a whole trainload?

Investigation brought the truth: it *had* happened, but only that once, on a sleepy Sunday afternoon in June 1957, when the urgent beating of loco pistons intermingled with rolling church bells. The friendly folk had been on a trainspotters' excursion, squeezing itself along secret branch lines like a badger forcing its way through a cat flap.

1961. On the railway sidings near Horninglow station were two rows of maroon carriages, forsaken and derelict. Most of the windows had been shattered by stones, but they still provided dens of a superior class – quite literally for boys like Jonah, who staked a claim on one of the first-class compartments. It had a mirror, still intact, a framed picture of a stately home, and springy seats that still had antimacassars, very handy if you had a runny nose. You'd often see Jonah at the door, leaning out through the glassless window and smoking a cigarette, for all the world like some toff on a first-class excursion to nowhere. The facilities were a disgrace, though. With no water for flushing, the toilets were permanently clogged with shit and torn newspaper.

Jonah was always calling me over to join him, but I was too scared. Railway trespassing was a deadly sin – Mum often read out court reports of what befell those who got caught. But it wasn't the law that made me hesitate – it was a fear of being trapped. Friendships were volatile – if Jonah turned on me, I'd be at his mercy, too far from the houses to call for help …

Every now and then we'd catch a whiff of smoke and run over to the tracks to see flames licking along the embankment, blackening the yellow grass, crackling and sizzling through the brambles. Enmities put aside, we all set to, jumping over the wooden fence to do our bit, stamping and trampling on the flames as we coughed and spluttered in the blackberry-flavoured smoke.

Nicholas Whittaker

Buffers (no comment).

A GLOSSARY OF RAILWAY NICKNAMES

This list is by no means exhaustive and there were always many regional variations. It refers mainly to locos from my own spotting days, some of which are mentioned in the book, but I expect there are lots of modern slang terms I have not yet come across.

Baby Deltic
Exactly what its name suggests, BR's Class 23 (numbered D5900–5909) was a smaller version of the mighty Deltic, with a half-size engine and a very similar profile.

Basher
A diesel-age term for a spotter who tends to focus on one particular loco or activity, e.g. Peak or Brush bashers. Also 'shed-bashing', which is the same as bunking (see below).

Bunking
Getting into railway depots by fair means or foul to take down loco numbers, keeping a low profile and avoiding railway staff.

Blackie or Black 5
The LMS Class 5 4–6–0 designed by Sir William Stanier was widely called the Blackie or Black 5. I never quite understood why, as most steam locos were black anyway. But 842 of them were built and for thirty-odd years operated in every part of the country, lasting right until the very last day of steam. Even today, eighteen of them are still puffing strong.

Bo-Bo

A wheel arrangement on diesel and electric locos, referring to four axles on two individual bogies, all driven by their own motors. Similar to Co-Co, not a clown after all, but six axles on two bogies.

Bone

A Class 58 diesel – see Egg Timer.

Brit

British Railways Britannia Pacific loco.

Brush

Brush Traction is a manufacturer of diesel locos based in Loughborough in the East Midlands. In my day the name was used to refer to what eventually became known as the Class 47, a Type 4 diesel built in the early 1960s and found all over mainland Britain on freight and passenger duties for nearly half a century. There are still a couple of dozen in operation even today. The smaller version was inevitably called the Baby Brush and at the time of writing there are still a few of those around too.

Chopper

British Railways Class 20 diesel.

Crab

An LMS 2–6–0 loco built in the early 1930s whose large, high-angled cylinders and link motion were likened by some to a crab's pincers. Others have said the nickname comes from the scuttling motion felt when standing on the footplate.

Deltic

The British Railways class of diesel loco built in 1961/2 by English Electric for use on the high-speed express passenger services between London King's Cross and Leeds, Newcastle and Edinburgh. The loco's name derives from its Napier Deltic engine, whose cylinders were divided in three blocks in a triangular arrangement – hence the adjective 'deltic' from the Greek letter delta (Δ).

DMU

The diesel multiple unit, unloved and despised by so many, referred to as 'bog units'. Who would have thought that, like the cockroach, they would not only survive the abuse but make their home in every available railway patch?

Duck Six

An ancient Midland Railway freight loco, built between 1875 and 1908, scores of which were still around when I started spotting in 1964. The nickname comes from the wheel arrangement (0–6–0). At least one person disputed this and told me if that were the case it should be Duck Six Duck – but he was an idiot and is now on medication.

Dusty Bin

British Rail EMU (see below) built in the late 1980s, intended for city/suburban routes and replacing many of the older 'slam door' units.

Dyson

Class 92 diesels, so called because of the sound they make as they go past.

Egg Timer

A Class 58 diesel – see Bone.

8-Freight

Ubiquitous Stanier-designed 2–8–0 freight loco, of which there were nearly 800. Pretty much the workhorse of the railways, at least in the steam days I was lucky enough to know.

EMU

See DMU, but add some electricity. The EMUs now outnumber the DMUs; Rod Hull would be proud.

Fag Packet

Applied to HSTs of First Great Western whose original livery was green with a gold stripe below the windows, similar to a well known cigarette pack.

Ferret and Dartboard

Applied to the old British Railways logo, used between 1956 and 1965, which was actually a lion with a locomotive wheel.

Flying Banana

Description of the first generation of HSTs in their largely yellow livery.

Fudger

A trainspotting fraud.

Goyle

Short for 'gargoyle', British Railways Class 31 diesels which had a rather ungainly design.

Gricer

Simply a trainspotter. A comparatively recent usage which supposedly comes from a humorous pronunciation of 'grouse', and a dodgy resemblance of trainspotting to grouse-shooting.

Gronk

The Class 08 diesel-shunter, once found everywhere from Wick to Penzance.

Growlers

Class 37 diesels, from the sound of their engines.

Gurglers

Class 31 diesels, again from their sound.

Happy Train

British Rail Class 365 units – 'happy' not because of a free bar, but because their front ends rather resemble a happy face.

Hoover

A British Rail Class 50 diesel-electric locomotive – from the sound of its cooling fans being similar to a vacuum cleaner.

Hymek

A Western Region D7000 class. The 'Hy' comes from its hydraulic transmission, but it's unclear how the 'mek' came about.

Jinty

A Fowler-designed 0–6–0 tank loco, originally employed by the Midland Railway and later the LMS. As to where this particular nickname arose, no one is quite sure.

Jube

Short for 'Jubilee', a class of LMS 4–6–0 locos, the majority of which were named after British Commonwealth places and various British heroes. Often we would shout out 'Jube!' – causing other spotters to swivel in expectation of a cop – then innocently continue with '… believe in ghosts?'

Lekky

Slang for electric loco.

Metrovicks

Diesel locos constructed by Metropolitan-Vickers, especially D5700 class Co-Bos, the mutant offspring of a Co-Co and a Bo-Bo (see Bo-Bo).

Mickey Mouse

An Ivatt-designed 2MT class 2–6–0 freight loco.

Nodding Donkey

British Rail's Pacer units, because of their bouncing up and down and the awful noise they tend to make on tight corners.

Ozzie

Short for 'Austerity' – a class of 2–8–0s, unloved by most spotters and based on the 8-Freight. They were introduced in 1943 for use during the Second World War. A total of 935 were built, a fair number of which were used overseas and never came back.

Pacific

A name based on the Whyte Notation for classifying steam loco-motives according to their wheel arrangement. A Pacific was a 4–6–2 – these being the leading wheels, driving wheels and trail-ing wheels. Others are the Mogul (2–6–0), Prairie (2–6–2), Atlantic (4–4–2), Mikado (2–8–2) and various others right up to the massive Centipede (2–10–0). The logic behind the naming isn't entirely con-sistent, but many simply took the name of the first locomotive to use that particular arrangement. Sadly, the Duck Six (0–6–0) was officially the more prosaic 'Six-coupled', but I'm sure you'll agree our nickname was more fun.

Peak

Class 44 diesels built at Derby between 1959 to 1960, named after British mountains. However, most spotters used the name to refer to the almost identical Classes 45 and 46, of which there were 150-odd.

Pegs
Semaphore signals.

Rat
The ubiquitous Class 25 diesel, which were 'as common as rats'.

Semi
The LMS Coronation class loco after the streamlining had been removed in the late 1940s, having been of questionable value. This originally left the smokebox with a slightly sloping top, leading spotters to refer to it as 'semi-streamlined'.

Skip
A Class 67 diesel-electric locomotive, whose shape resembles an upside-down skip.

Spam Can
Nickname applied to some of the Southern Railway's Bulleid Pacifics because of their squared streamlining, thought to resemble tins of Spam – see the photo of my first Bulleid 34057 *Biggin Hill* at Oxford sheds.

Splut
Another name for the British Rail Class 25 diesel, whose engines had a habit of spluttering and dying.

Streaks
Sir Nigel Gresley's celebrated streamlined A4 Pacifics, one of which broke the world speed record.

Tat
The Class 40 English Electric Type 4 diesel, used on heavy passenger trains.

Teddy Bear

British Rail Class 14 diesel-hydraulic locos for shunting and trip working. Allegedly from workers at Swindon Works who had built the famous *Great Bear* steam loco and were now going to build a much smaller 'Teddy Bear'.

Terrier

Southern Region 0–6–0 steam loco which had a distinctive 'bark'.

Thousands

The Class 52 'Western' diesel-hydraulics, due to their numbers D1000–D1073.

Whistler

A Class 40 English Electric Type 4 diesel (see Tat).

Wizzo

The Class 52 'Western' diesel-hydraulic.